Globalisation, State and Labour

The world is undergoing enormous change involving politics, the economy and society; however, the position and place of the state and the significance of state policy in this process are heavily contested. *Globalisation, State and Labour* presents a timely opportunity to review and re-assess the modern state in regard to labour.

Using major studies from four countries (the UK, Denmark, Australia and New Zealand) the contributors to this volume challenge many preconceptions regarding globalisation and labour organisation including the notions that the state is being marginalised by the processes of globalisation and trade unions are becoming irrelevant. The essays, written by leading researchers in the area, develop an approach that puts state work, workers and their organisations at the heart of analysing state restructuring.

This book is an important corrective to much recent work on work, employment and restructuring and the role of organised labour. Combining a distinctive approach with comparative analysis, this book will be of vital interest to anyone concerned with globalisation debates, the future of the state and organised labour.

Peter Fairbrother is Professor of Sociology, Cardiff School of Social Sciences, Cardiff University, United Kingdom.

Al Rainnie is Director of the Institute for Regional Studies and Professor, Department of Management, Monash University, Victoria, Australia.

Routledge Studies in Employment and Work Relations in Context

Edited by Tony Elger
Department of Sociology, University of Warwick

Peter Fairbrother
Cardiff School of Social Sciences, Cardiff University

The aim of the *Employment and Work Relations in Context* series is to address questions relating to the evolving patterns and politics of work, employment, management and industrial relations. There is a concern to trace out the ways in which wider policy-making, especially by national governments and transnational corporations, impinges upon specific workplaces, occupations, labour markets, localities and regions. This invites attention to developments at an international level, marking out patterns of globalisation, state policy and practices in the context of globalisation and the impact of these processes on labour. A particular feature of the series is the consideration of forms of worker and citizen organisation and mobilisation. The studies address major analytical and policy issues through case study and comparative research.

1. **Employment Relations in the Health Service**
   The management of reforms
   Stephen Bach

2. **Globalisation, State and Labour**
   Edited by Peter Fairbrother and Al Rainnie

Previous titles to appear in Routledge Studies in Employment and Work Relations in Context include:

Work, Locality and the Rhythms of Capital
The labour process reconsidered
Jamie Gough

Work and Employment in the High Performance Workplace
Edited by Gregor Murray, Jacques Belanger, Anthony Giles and Paul-Andre Lapointe

Trade Unions in Renewal
A comparative study
Edited by Peter Fairbrother and Charlotte Yates

Trade Unions and Global Governance
The debate on a social clause
Gerda van Roozendaal

Reshaping the North American Automobile Industry
Restructuring, corporatism and union democracy in Mexico
John P. Tuman

Changing Prospects for Trade Unionism
Comparisons between six countries
Edited by Peter Fairbrother and Gerard Griffin

Globalisation, State and Labour

Edited by
Peter Fairbrother and Al Rainnie

WITHDRAWN
UTSA LIBRARIES

Routledge
Taylor & Francis Group

LONDON AND NEW YORK

First published 2006
by Routledge
2 Park Square, Milton Park, Abingdon, Oxon OX14 4RN

Simultaneously published in the USA and Canada
by Routledge
270 Madison Ave, New York, NY 10016

Transferred to Digital Printing 2006

Routledge is an imprint of the Taylor & Francis Group

© 2006 Peter Fairbrother and Al Rainnie, selection and
editorial matter; the contributors, their own chapters

Typeset in Garamond by
Newgen Imaging Systems (P) Ltd, Chennai, India
Printed and bound in Great Britain by
Biddles Ltd, King's Lynn

All rights reserved. No part of this book may be reprinted or
reproduced or utilised in any form or by any electronic,
mechanical, or other means, now known or hereafter
invented, including photocopying and recording, or in any
information storage or retrieval system, without permission in
writing from the publishers.

British Library Cataloguing in Publication Data
A catalogue record for this book is available from the British Library

Library of Congress Cataloging in Publication Data
A catalog record for this book has been requested

ISBN 0–415–37551–7

**Library
University of Texas
at San Antonio**

Contents

Contributors

Søren Kaj Andersen is Associate Professor at FAOS (Employment Relations Research Centre), Department of Sociology, University of Copenhagen, Denmark. His main research areas are public sector employment relations, developments in collective bargaining systems and social partnership strategies.

Peter Burnham is Professor of Politics, University of Warwick, United Kingdom. He has researched and written extensively on political economy and the British state.

Bob Carter is Reader, Department of Sociology, University of Leicester, United Kingdom. He has worked extensively on state theory and implications for labour, as well as researching on public sector trade unionism.

Peter Fairbrother is Professor of Sociology, Cardiff School of Social Sciences, Cardiff University, United Kingdom. He has researched and published widely on political economy, labour and the modern state, and trade unionism.

Nikolaj Lubanski is Director at the Danish School of Public Administration, Denmark. His main research areas are international employment relations, organisational theory and educational policy.

John O'Brien is Associate Professor of Industrial Relations, School of Organisation and Management, University of New South Wales, New South Wales, Australia. He is a leading expert on public sector industrial relations in Australia.

Sarah Oxenbridge is Senior Research Officer at the Advisory, Conciliation and Arbitration Service (Acas) of Great Britain. She researches on trade unions and employment relations in the United Kingdom and New Zealand.

Al Rainnie is Professor and Director of the Institute for Regional Studies, Monash University, Victoria, Australia. He has conducted extensive research on employment and work, trade unionism and politics and has published widely on state and regionalism.

Pat Walsh is now the Vice-Chancellor of Victoria University of Wellington, New Zealand. In a former life he was Professor of Industrial Relations and Human Resource Management in the Victoria Management School. He has published widely on public sector employment relations, union and employer strategies and restructuring.

Kurt Wetzel is Professor of Industrial Relations and Organizational Behaviour, College of Commerce, University of Saskatchewan, Canada. He researches widely on employment, management and trade unions, with specific reference to the public sector.

Preface

This book is written at a time of enormous change involving politics, the economy and social life. In this process the modern state is central, with changes taking place under the general rubric of globalisation. However, the interpretation of the significance of state policy and the position and place of the state in this process is heavily contested. In this sense the book presents a timely opportunity to review and re-assess the modern state.

The origins of the book lie in a conference at the University of Warwick, United Kingdom, in March 1998. A group of researchers came together to discuss the contested restructuring of the modern state and the implications that such developments had for labour. These researchers had expertise on Australia, Britain, Denmark, Hungary, New Zealand, Poland and Russia.

As the discussions proceeded it became apparent that it was important to understand the actual changes that had occurred in each country, and in particular the role of different governments in this process irrespective of their political complexion. After all, four of these countries had long established liberal democratic regimes and, irrespective of particular emphasis, all appeared to be reassessing the place and position of state rule and provision. The other countries, all members of the former Soviet bloc, were also undergoing dramatic change, and while there is much merit in exploring the variation between these two groups of states, there are distinctive features to each. There was a danger in these early discussions that the authors of the various papers presented at the conference would be overwhelmed by the differences between these state regimes or that superficial comparisons would be drawn. In the end, we decided to work on a book that addressed a focused set of issues relating to state and labour in four liberal democratic states, Australia, Britain, Denmark and New Zealand.

It has taken some time to assemble and present this book. First, three states had undergone a change of government towards the end of the 1990s, Australia (1996), Britain (1997) and New Zealand (1999). The importance of these events lay not so much in any shifts in policy but because it took time to assess the importance of these changes in government. Second, as authors we were all concerned to explore some of the more recent theoretical developments in state analysis, as they bore upon the understandings of public sector change. For this reason, we have taken our time in finalising the book.

The book is the first step in an ongoing analysis of state and labour, involving the contributors and others. The developments presented are major, pointing to a repositioned state in a globalised world. While the contributors are not all agreed on the direction and thrust of change, there is a common recognition that any adequate understanding of globalisation requires a thorough engagement with state policy and practice and the way a *leitmotif* of change has been 'new public management'. More than this, there is an acknowledgement that one of the keys to understanding recent changes is to consider the position and place of labour in this process.

The editors would like to thank all the contributors for their patience with the production of this book. It is our hope that this book will spark debate and controversy about our interpretation of the modern state and the role and place of labour in the changes that are now under way. For us this is a step towards an understanding of the complex process of economic and social change of the modern state in the current era.

Peter Fairbrother and Al Rainnie

January 2004

Abbreviations

ACTU	Australian Council of Trade Unions
APEC	Asia-Pacific Economic Cooperation
APS	Australian Public Service
ARF	Danish Federation of County Councils
ASMS	Association of Salaried Medical Specialists
AWA	Australian Workplace Agreement
CCT	Compulsory Competitive Tendering
CES	Commonwealth Employment Service
CPSU	Community and Public Sector Union
CSE	Conference of Socialist Economists
DEETYA	Department of Employment, Education, Training and Youth Affairs
DFAT	Department of Foreign Affairs and Trade
DoFA	Department of Finance and Administration
DSB	Danish State Railways
DUA	Det Udviklende Arbejde
ECA	Employment Contracts Act, 1991
ECNZ	Electricity Corporation of New Zealand
EEO	Equal Employment Opportunity
EMS	European Monetary System
EMU	European Monetary Union
EN	Employment National
ERM	Exchange Rate Mechanism
EU	European Union
FDI	Foreign Direct Investment
G7	Group of Seven
GATS	General Agreement on Trades and Services
GDP	Gross Domestic Product
HRM	Human Resource Management
IMF	International Monetary Fund
IPE	International Political Economy
KL	National Association of Local Authorities
LEA	Local Education Authority

LO	Danish Confederation of Trade Unions
MAI	MedArbejderIndflydelse
MIO	MedarbejderIndflydelsesOrgan
NAFTA	North American Free Trade Agreement
NGO	Non-Government Organisation
NHS	National Health Service
NIC	Newly Industrialised Countries
NIS	New Institutionalist School
NPM	New Public Management
NZ	New Zealand
NZNO	New Zealand Nurses Organisation
OECD	Organisation for Economic Co-operation and Development
PFI	Private Finance Initiative
PPP	Public–Private Partnership
PSA	Public Services Association
PUMA	OECD Public Management Programme
SOE	State-Owned Enterprise
SSC	State Services Commission
SWU	Service Workers Union
TNC	Transnational Corporation
TUC	Trades Union Congress
WTO	World Trade Organisation

1   The enduring question of the state

Peter Fairbrother and Al Rainnie

The modern liberal democratic state has been transformed again in the past twenty-five years. Prior to that, and involving a long and contested history, this particular state form had emerged as an electorally accountable set of representative arrangements, supplemented by institutions which administered and implemented policy. During the twentieth century, many of these states developed interventionist policies, supporting a comprehensive range of Keynesian-type economic policies and welfare measures. This was also a state committed to a substantial military presence, particularly in the context of the forty-year cold war. However, towards the end of the twentieth century, the modern state became a focus of attention for governments and a process of transformation was set in process. It is this patterning of change that is the subject of this book.

The emergent liberal democratic state

Until well into the twentieth century, the state apparatus was relatively small. Three events provided turning points for a dramatic increase in the scale and scope of the state. First, the Russian Revolution, establishing the Soviet Union, became an important point of reference for the articulation of liberal democratic capitalist economies. Soviet political and economic arrangements were marked by the abolition of private property and complex patterns of state control over all economic activity. Second, the Great Depression of the 1930s was a focal moment for the reassessment of government approaches to state intervention in capitalist economies. This was a period of momentous economic devastation and social misery. Third, the Second World War marked a major challenge to liberal democratic systems of government and resulted in the comprehensive defeat of fascist forms of governance. These two latter events provided the stimulus for liberal democratic governments to experiment with policies of state intervention, in welfare as well as economic activity. Following the Second World War, there began a period of activist government in the liberal democratic states, which lasted until the 1980s.

There was a (Keynesian) consensus in liberal democratic states about the post-war approach. First, there was a commitment to create the infrastructure for welfare provision for the most needy in society. Second, these economies were based on a mix of private and public economic relations, in some cases involving nationalisation of major utilities and other sectors of the economy. Third, there was the development of co-ordinated macro-economic policies, covering such goals as full employment, price stability and balance of payments equilibrium. There was an expansion of state activity as well as the involvement of the state in new areas of the economy. This was a period of economic growth, a stabilisation of the liberal democratic form of governance, with the emergence of a relatively confident working class that was part of the political settlement of this period.

In the 1970s, these strategies of state intervention were challenged. During this period, there was growing economic instability, marked by external economic events, such as the oil price shocks of the early 1970s, increasing public debt and economies beset by inflationary problems (Brenner, 1998). There was also increased evidence of growing dissatisfaction with the so-called welfare state. Keynesianism appeared to fail both analytically and as a policy driver. This began a period when governments in the liberal democracies, particularly the Anglo-American states, began to reassess the scope and scale of state intervention in the economy. One critical dimension in this reassessment was the consideration of the role of the state in increasingly internationalised markets. It appeared that during the 1970s there was a loss of control over the global economy by nation states.

The globalised state?

Over the past two decades there has been a widespread debate questioning the way in which the modern state is changing and the form that is emerging in the context of a globalised economy (Pusey, 1991; Osborne and Gaebler, 1992; Whitfield, 1992). One theme that gained a particular prominence in a number of economies is that the public sector should be restructured and reorganised, so as to redefine the boundaries of the state, via privatisation, and to recompose the state, with the embrace of managerial practices and organisation (OECD, 1994; Kelsey, 1995). These initiatives were promoted worldwide, through structural adjustment programmes, by governments, international agencies and private consultancies (Williams *et al.*, 1995). In effect, the debate over state reform and restructuring in the context of globalisation has been between social democratic models of governance and liberal market models, with the latter very much in the ascendancy in the Anglo-American world (United Kingdom, United States of America, New Zealand and Australia).

The major divisions which have emerged are between deregulating states and those maintaining forms of governance and interaction with the social relations of production characteristic of the various post-war settlements (Jessop, 1994; Williams *et al.*, 1995). Within the deregulating states there is an important assumption of the necessity of increased marketisation and commercialisation of state formations, but this can take a number of different forms, including privatisation, compulsory competitive tendering (CCT) and purchaser/provider splits within the state (Cutler and Waine, 1994). In practice, there has been much examination and transfer of models of state reorganisation and restructuring, particularly as developed in the United States and the United Kingdom (Pollitt, 1990; Ferlie *et al.*, 1996). However, the precise linkages between the origins of these models and their implementation in different parts of the world remain unclear.

One of the key responses to the perceived difficulties faced by liberal democratic states has been to initiate a process of depoliticisation, whereby governments took steps to distance themselves from the formulation and implementation of economic policy (for earlier versions of the argument advanced here, see Fairbrother and Macdonald, 1999; Fairbrother and O'Brien, 2000). By depoliticisation is meant the process of disengagement by the state apparatus from direct management of aspects of the economy, for example, defining the problem of inflation as a technical economic question, rather than as a set of class-based relations (Bonefeld *et al.*, 1995: 3–4; Burnham, 1999a,b). The most frequently cited example of this process for the UK is the 1997 transfer of direct responsibility for interest rate settlement from the treasury to the semi-autonomous reserve bank (Burnham, 1999a,b; see also Chapter 3 in this book).

If this specific argument is accepted, then the depoliticisation thesis could be viewed as one of the defining features of the development of a managerial state, whereby the hierarchies of the public sector are redefined and recomposed away from the layered and rule-bound organisations of the past. The claim would be that as part of the process of recomposing relations between state managers and labour, the responsibility for the operational activity of state bodies was increasingly removed from politicians and placed in the hands of state managers. Such reforms are only possible with the creation of managerial grades and a reconstitution of relations between managers *qua* management and workers *qua* labour in the state sector and related agencies. A further aspect of these developments is that market relations begin to define the organisation and operation of the public services, giving rise to notions of customer and client (for an elaboration of this argument, see Fairbrother and Poynter, 2001). These processes, in effect, replace direct state direction and control with a more distanced and disembodied form of central regulation, via financial control and restriction (Pollitt, 1990). The result is the curious paradox of decentralisation of operational organisation and practice, on the one hand, and continuing centralised control and regulation, on the other.

However, while these analyses have a persuasiveness to them, the debate about state management and labour relations has been cast in terms of the reorganisation of the public sector under the new public management (NPM). Three key arguments can be identified. First, there is the argument that NPM is derived from the importation of models of private sector management into the public sector. This process of reconstruction of the public sector involves financial responsibilities, managerial control and hierarchy, deregulation of the public sector labour market and the advent of new forms of corporate governance. The weakness of this account is that it fails to recognise the distinctive features of public sector organisation and the diverse practices of public service provision (Ferlie *et al.*, 1996: 10–12). There is a second argument, which begins with the claim that the public sector in major Organisation for Economic Co-operation and Development (OECD) countries had become a type of Fordist organisation. The indication of this form of rule is hierarchy, impersonal rules and regulations and thus a bureaucratised enterprise (Hoggett, 1994). In this context the public sector and the provision of public services were reformed via quasi-market relations, flatter organisational structures, contract management and a fragmentation of organisation. Third, a further argument focuses on the theme that there has been a major break with past forms of 'public administration' (Dunleavy and Hood, 1994; Ferlie *et al.*, 1996). The thesis is that a distinct public service model remains in existence, but it is one that incorporates private sector practices *and* distinctive public sector routines and values, although adapted to meet the new circumstances of public service provision (Osborne and Gaebler, 1992).

The NPM debate is, however, a flawed one in that it is decontextualised in two respects. First, examinations of NPM have usually taken place within a public sector organisational framework and not as a feature and focus of state restructuring. The importance of this observation is that the key to public sector restructuring is the recomposition of managerial hierarchies as the definitive feature of these changes (Carter and Fairbrother, 1999). Thus, as the depoliticisation of the state on economic policy has proceeded, the state apparatus has been reorganised and recomposed as part of this process of change. Second, and related, the reorganisation of the state apparatus is a complicated process involving diverse and distinctive management–labour relations. A limitation of the NPM debates is that while management, as a reconstituted stratum of the state apparatus, has been centre stage of enquiry, little attention has been given to labour and the ways in which labour–management relations define the processes of change taking place. The outcomes are a variety of disparate and often contradictory trends and traits, prompting the identification of different models of change (Ferlie *et al.*, 1996). However, what is striking about this literature is the almost total absence of labour, with almost no discussion of what such developments might mean for the social relations of public sector production and provision.

The question of labour

In the many debates about globalisation, there has been much comment on the role and function of the state, ranging from a view that the capacity of the state to function as a sovereign body is diminishing (Ohmae, 1990, 1995) to another view that while the state retains a capability as a manager of national economies, it is becoming more complex (Boyer and Drache, 1996; Hirst and Thomspon, 1999). While this is an important debate, what is not addressed in such accounts is a consideration of the implications of the changes taking place in the form of the state. Even in those studies where the state as such has been the focus of attention, the implications of radical state restructuring for its own employment, labour organisation and employee acquiescence or resistance have received little detailed consideration.

The neglect of labour both as an agent and victim of changing global state relations has a two-fold nature. The social relations of labour, it is argued, are no longer bound by or defined by the nation state. Responses range from a celebration of the importance of globalisation, on the one hand (Ohmae, 1990, 1995), to a focus on its invidious effect on workers and the uncertainty and unevenness of their response and resistance, on the other (Elger and Smith, 1994). What is more to the point is that state workers remain one of the most highly unionised workforces in many countries, pursuing their interests in a variety of ways in both metropolitan and non-metropolitan states.

It can be argued that the complicated processes of state restructuring confront trade unions with new challenges and uncertain futures, where long established forms of union organisation and approaches may no longer suffice. Faced with the comprehensive restructuring of state employment in many countries, trade unions found themselves ill prepared for change, with relatively unstable bases for collective organisation (International Labour Organisation, 1997). Overall, public service workers have responded to these developments in quite active ways. Going back to the early 1970s, it can be argued that in many OECD countries, the trade unions that organised in the public services actively responded to government policies on work and employment conditions, as well as the early steps in public sector restructuring. Throughout the 1980s and 1990s, public service unions campaigned to defend themselves in relatively hostile work and employment environments. While in many countries this action was largely defensive in its focus, during the 1990s, there was evidence that unions were beginning to rediscover a confidence and assertiveness in their activities that had not been evident previously (for an elaboration of these themes, see Fairbrother and Yates, 2003).

These patterns of restructuring present new challenges and new opportunities for unions (developed further in Fairbrother and Poynter, 2001). First, at a local level, the restructuring and reorganisation of public sectors in many countries provides an opportunity for organisation and mobilisation. Second, at a national and an international level, the redrawing of the boundaries of the public sector, particularly via the privatisation of major utilities, signifies a shifting terrain of organisation and ownership. Not only may unions begin to look at the potential for strengthening localised forms of representation, but increasingly they face the prospect of internationalised forms of negotiation and bargaining (Fairbrother, 2000a). An added dimension is that many states have opened up their public service provision to external and often international bodies, as part of the competition strategies now being pursued. Such developments add further dimensions of complexity to national-based trade unions.

This constellation of developments has stimulated debate about the form of unionism that may be emerging in these areas of employment. One theme has focused on the possibility and importance of union renewal in these sectors, with particular emphasis on the possibility of revitalised membership involvement and activism (Fairbrother, 2000b: 167–308; Fairbrother and Yates, 2003). With the internationalisation of work and employment, in the state sector as well as elsewhere, the relevance and salience of international awareness, the necessity of links and concerted action is reinforced. Increasingly, questions to do with employment and unemployment, poverty and inequality, environment and health, land and water (to name but a few) are becoming connected with the anti-social activities of the state and supra-state organisations (e.g. transnational corporations (TNCs) and the International Monetary Fund (IMF)). At the same time the dominant political orthodoxy increasingly attempts to lay the blame for political and social problems on the individual 'failings' of the poor and oppressed (Bauman, 1998). These developments place politics at the heart of public sector restructuring and place labour within this equation (for one version of such politics, see Waterman, 1998).

Increasingly, the thrust of reform in the public sector and privatised services is driven and qualified by the complex relations between governments, international agencies and international enterprises and by complex financial arrangements. The question is whether and under what circumstances these relationships can be focused in the form of solidaristic action, both within and between states (for an example of a campaign combining local and international solidarity, see Russo, 1998). This is likely to require a re-examination of the traditional principles of solidarity and unity, with a close consideration of the way these principles are expressed in practice. In particular, it draws attention to questions relating to equity, participation and human rights. Policy that is not informed by these concerns is bereft of the principles that allow workers to combine, within sectors, between sectors and between states.

From centre to periphery and back again

These developments point to the emergence of the internationalised state. State policies are no longer confined to nation-state boundaries. The internationalisation of economies has redefined the parameters of state involvement and activity. State structures and apparatuses have been reconfigured in distinctive ways. Thus, the question is how are these developments to be interpreted and explained.

Writing at the turn of the century, Ulrich Beck summed up the concern and anxiety that globalisation then raised:

> With the peaceful fall of the Berlin Wall and the collapse of the Soviet empire, many thought that the end of politics was nigh as we entered an age beyond social-ism and capitalism, utopia and emancipation. In the years since then, however, the ceremonial farewells to politics have become rather more subdued. The current scare-word 'globalization', seemingly unavoidable in any public statements, points not to an end of politics but to its *escape* from the categories of the national state, and even from the schema defining what is 'political' and 'non-political' action. For whatever the referent of the new globalization rhetoric (economy, markets, job competition, production, goods and services, financial flows, information, lifestyles), the political consequences of the stage-managed *economic* globalization of risk stand out in sharp relief. Institutions of industrial society which seemed shut tight can be 'cracked' and opened up to political intervention. The premises of the welfare state and pension system, of income support, local government and infra-structural policies, the power of organized labour, industry-wide free collective bargaining, state expenditure, the fiscal system and 'fair taxation' – all this melts under the withering sun of globalization and becomes susceptible to (demands for) political moulding. Every social actor must respond in one way or another; and the typical responses do *not* fit into the old left–right schema of political action.
>
> (1999: 1, emphasis in original)

This assessment was challenged by the events of 2001. In the wake of the September 11 attack on the World Trade Center, there has been a repositioning of the liberal democratic state. For Beck, a re-reading of his earlier prognosis suggested the emergence of more powerful, intrusive and active states (*Australian Financial Review*, 9 November 2001). Crucially, states would act now in a more transnational form and, in the surveillance state form, build military complexes and increasingly undermine democracy and freedom. Attacks around the world on civil liberties in the name of the 'war on terrorism' would seem to support Beck's thesis. Furthermore, President George W. Bush has used the war on terrorism and national security as justification for action against organised labour (Davies, 2002). Complementing these developments, there has also been a partial rediscovery of Keynesian economic practices. President George W. Bush, confronted by a struggling US economy, not only resurrected military Keynesianism with a $US40 billion budget for the war on terrorism, but also introduced a $US51 billion reflationary package for the US economy which included extending benefits for unemployed workers. It would appear that the state will remain a site of contest and confrontation for the foreseeable future.

The book

The focus of the book is on the relationship between the processes of globalisation, the changing form and focus of the liberal democratic state in this context and the position and place of state labour. These themes are addressed through a set of related commissioned contributions. The choice of contributors is deliberate, each providing an insight into the core organising themes that make up the book.

The argument of the book is opened up by Peter Burnham (University of Warwick), in Chapter 2, with an elaboration of the thesis of depoliticisation. He presents a theoretically focused account of the restructuring of the relationship between the polity and the economy over the past thirty years. Through the elaboration of the concept of depoliticisation he shows how the British state has been transformed, focusing on the changing and uneven relationship between economic theory and political practice. The central argument is that the British government has restructured such relations since the mid-1990s. Aspects of traditional economic management were combined with new initiatives to create a powerful tool of governing organised on the basis of the principle of depoliticisation. As defined by Burnham, depoliticisation refers to 'the process of placing at one remove the political character of decision making' (Chapter 2, pp. 12, 13). He claims that successive governments have used this relationship as a powerful ideological device in restructuring political relationships and practices so that they are in alignment with the changes taking place in the wider international political economy.

This analysis is complemented, in Chapter 3, by a critical assessment of the account presented by Peter Burnham, where Al Rainnie (Monash University) and Peter Fairbrother (Cardiff University) argue that this analysis must be developed with reference to those advanced about the processes and direction of globalisation. First, they show how the restructuring of the modern liberal democratic state in the 1980s and 1990s came after nearly fifty years where the state was structured in an interventionist way, to secure a Keynesian economic and political settlement between labour and capital. The second point that they make is that the prevailing analyses of state restructuring emphasise the hollowed out character of the state, with a neglect of the complex processes of change that are occurring, involving debates about NPM and structural adjustment programmes. Third, the authors argue that the state is a site of contested politics in a way that is often unrecognised and unacknowledged. Thus, they argue that the modern liberal democratic state continues to be defined by a complex set of class relations, characterised by exploitation and resistance.

In the following four chapters, the aim is to detail the patterns and processes of change in four contrasting states: the United Kingdom, which arguably has been an influential model for the restructuring of liberal democratic states; Denmark, which retains a social democratic ethos, while undergoing a slow process of state restructuring; Australia, which has embraced much of the neo-liberal reform agenda, initially under a social democratic regime and then a conservative one; and finally New Zealand, which followed the initial trajectory of Australia and the United Kingdom, but which rapidly went far beyond the measures embraced by these governments. An implicit argument is that there has been a process of modelling and an exchange of ideas about these processes of restructuring, either positively or negatively between these governments and the United States. The outcome is a contested pattern of state restructuring.

The first of these chapters, Chapter 4 by Peter Fairbrother (Cardiff University), develops a political–historical account of the restructuring and recomposition of the British state over the past thirty years. There are two parts to the argument. First, the British state was restructured in two decisive ways, with a redrawing of the boundaries of the state, via privatisation, and through the recomposition of the state apparatus, via a decentralisation and devolution of managerial structures. One result was a distancing of state responsibility for the direct management of labour while at the same time it maintained control over the provision of public services via budgetary mechanisms. Second, the implications of these developments are explored with specific reference to workers and their trade unions in the provision of public services. The argument is that the restructuring of the state apparatus resulted in a remaking of the state labour force, providing the basis for an uneven revitalisation of unions in this sector.

The next contribution, Chapter 5 by Nikolaj Lubanski (Danish School of Public Administration) and Søren Kaj Andersen (University of Copenhagen), examines a long established social democratic state, namely Denmark. The argument presented by these two authors is that the Danish public sector labour market is an integral part of the Danish welfare state, in the sense that the public sector labour market is a politically organised system rather than a market for public goods. Nonetheless, a process of public sector restructuring has taken place in Denmark over the past two decades, including NPM-type initiatives. The focus shifted from an emphasis on improving efficiency during the 1980s to fragmenting public structures and developing managerially based practices. Trade unions have been part of these developments and there has been a process of changed relations, whereby industrial issues, particularly pay, have become an integral feature of the way the public sector is organised.

Chapter 6, by John O'Brien (University of New South Wales), addresses these themes with reference to the Australian federal state, focusing on the relationship between the roles of the federal government as an employer, as a prime generator of policy, as regulator and as a financial controller. Through an examination of the Australian state over the past twenty-five years, O'Brien traces out the way the political basis of the state has shifted from a social democratic-type settlement to one where the emphasis is on neo-liberal policies and practices. The chapter argues that there are significant limits to the decentralisation of public sector industrial relations given the overall fiscal, policy, regulatory and employer responsibilities of government, even if there is a strong policy to decentralise industrial relations processes generally. The chapter considers how workers and their trade unions have responded to the attempts by government to restructure the public sector in devolved and re-regulated ways.

In Chapter 7, Pat Walsh (Victoria University, Wellington), Sarah Oxenbridge (Acas) and Kurt Wetzel (University of Saskatchewan), present a parallel picture of the New Zealand state. Beginning in 1984, the New Zealand state has been comprehensively restructured, thereby repositioning the state in relation to civil society and the economy. This programme signified the move from a well-developed welfare state, with a high degree of regulated economic activity, to a marketised economy, with a massively restructured state sector. In conventional terms, the outcome was a highly de-regulated economy. The result was a radical repositioning of the New Zealand state and its withdrawal from areas of activity for which it had historically accepted responsibility. For state labour and their trade unions these developments resulted in substantial job loss, a recomposition of the state sector workforce and the threatened demobilisation of state trade unions. In the process of developing this analysis, the authors draw attention to the importance of state policies in laying the foundation for a political settlement that rests on the formal recognition of trade unions and a regulated industrial relations process.

These themes are reassessed in Chapter 8, by Bob Carter (University of Leicester), who develops an argument that states are and remain the site of class relations. He elaborates his case by exploring in detail the class character of the modern state, presenting a critical assessment of the depoliticisation thesis presented by a number of authors, but particularly Burnham. In doing this he identifies the limitations of many of the contributions in the book, pointing to the increasing complexity of class relations, the complicated processes of centralisation and decentralisation of state relations and the emergence of the managerial state. This focus is complemented by a critical account of the union form of resistance to these processes of transformation and the prospects of union revival and revitalisation. The result is a critical and thoughtful assessment of the contributions to this book, hopefully laying the foundation for further debate and discussion about these complex processes.

The analysis developed in this book points to the way the modern liberal democratic state is being repositioned in a globalised world. One lesson that arises from this account is that an adequate examination of the complex processes of globalisation requires a detailed consideration of the relationship between state and labour. Another is that, as with all complex processes of change in a capitalist society, the position and place of labour is critical. While there are particular processes of labour revitalisation taking place, each specific to the form of state restructuring that is in process, it is also the case that the foundations for resistance and the articulation of alternatives remain a possibility in ways that hitherto have been seldom acknowledged.

Bibliography

Australian Financial Review, 9 November 2001.

Baumann, Z. (1998) *Work, Consumption and the New Poor*, Milton Keynes: Open University Press.

Beck, U. (1999) *What Is Globalization?*, Cambridge: Polity Press.

Bonefeld, W., Brown, A. and Burnham, P. (1995) *A Major Crisis? The Politics of Economic Policy in Britain in the 1990s*, Aldershot: Dartmouth.

Boyer, R. and Drache, M. (1996) *State against Markets: The Limits of Globalisation*, London: Routledge.

Brenner, R. (1998) 'The Economics of Global Turbulence: A Special Report on the World Economy, 1950–98', *New Left Review*, 229(May/June): 1–265.

Burnham, P. (1999a) 'The Politics of Economic Management in the 1990s', *New Political Economy*, 4(1): 37–54.

Burnham, P. (1999b) 'The Recomposition of National States in the Global Economy: From Politicised to Depoliticised Forms of Labour Regulation', in P. Edwards and T. Elger (eds), *The Global Economy, National States and the Regulation of Labour*, London: Mansell, pp. 42–63.

Carter, B. (1997) 'Restructuring State Employment: Labour and Non-Labour in the Capitalist State', *Capital & Class*, 63: 65–84.

Carter, B. and Fairbrother, P. (1999) 'The Transformation of British Public-Sector Industrial Relations: From "Model Employer" to Marketized Relations', *Historical Studies in Industrial Relations*, 7(Spring): 119–146.

Cutler, T. and Waine, B. (1994) *Managing the Welfare State: The Politics of Public Sector Management*, Oxford: Berg.

Davies, S. (2002) 'Under Cover of the Fright', *Red Pepper*, December, http://www.redpepper.org.uk

Dunleavy, P. and Hood, C. (1994) 'From Old Public Administration to New Public Management', *Public Money and Management*, 14(3): 9–16.

Elger, T. and Smith, C. (eds) (1994) *Global Japanisation: The Transnational Transformation of the Labour Process*, London: Routledge.

Fairbrother, P. (2000a) *Trade Unions at the Crossroads*, London: Mansell.

Fairbrother, P. (2000b) 'British Trade Unions Facing the Future', *Capital & Class*, 71: 47–78.

Fairbrother, P. and Macdonald, D. (1999) 'The Role of the State and Australian Public Sector Industrial Relations: Depoliticisation and Direct Intervention', *New Zealand Journal of Industrial Relations*, 24(3): 343–363.

Fairbrother, P. and O'Brien, J. (2000) 'Introduction: Changing Public Sector Industrial Relations in the Australian State', *Australian Journal of Public Administration*, 59(4): 54–59.

Fairbrother, P. and Poynter, G. (2001) 'State Restructuring: Managerialism, Marketisation and the Implications for Labour', *Competition & Change*, 5(3): 311–333.

Fairbrother, P. and Yates, C. (eds) (2003) *Trade Unions in Renewal: A Comparative Study of Trade Union Movements in Five Countries*, London: Continuum.

Ferlie, E., Ashburner, L., Fitzgerald, L. and Pettigrew, A. (1996) *The New Public Management in Action*, Oxford: Oxford University Press.

Hirst, P. and Thompson, G. (1999) *Globalisation in Question: The International Economy and the Possibilities of Governance*, Second edition, Cambridge: Polity Press.

Hoggett, P. (1994) 'The Politics of the Modernisation of the UK Welfare State', in R. Burrows and B. Loader (eds), *Towards a Post-Fordist Welfare State*, London: Routledge, pp. 38–48.

International Labour Organisation (1997) *World Labour Report: Industrial Relations, Democracy and Social Stability*, Geneva: International Labour Organisation.

Jessop, R. (1994) 'Post-Fordism and the State', in A. Amin (ed.), *Post-Fordism: A Reader*, Oxford: Blackwell Publishers, pp. 251–279.

Kelly, J. (1996) 'Union Militancy and Social Partnership', in P. Ackers, C. Smith and P. Smith (eds), *The New Workplace and Trade Unionism*, London: Routledge, pp. 77–109.

Kelsey, J. (1995) *The New Zealand Experiment: A World Model for Structural Adjustment*, Auckland: Auckland University Press with Bridget Williams Books.

McIlroy, J. (1997) 'Still under Siege: British Trade Unions at the Turn of the Century', *Historical Studies in Industrial Relations*, 3(March): 93–122.

O'Brien, J. and Fairbrother, P. (2000) 'A Changing Public Sector: Developments at the Commonwealth Level', *Australian Journal of Public Administration*, 59(4): 59–66.

OECD (1994) *Industrial Policy in OECD Countries: Annual Review*, Paris: OECD.

Ohmae, K. (1990) *The Borderless World: Power and Strategy in the Interlinked Economy*, London: Harper Collins.

Ohmae, K. (1995) *The End of the Nation State*, New York: Harper Collins.

Osborne, D. and Gaebler, T. (eds) (1992) *Reinventing Government: How the Entrepreneurial Spirit is Transforming the Public Sector*, Reading, MA: Addison-Wesley.

Pollitt, C. (1990) *Managerialism and the Public Services*, Oxford: Blackwell.

Pusey, M. (1991) *Economic Rationalism in Canberra: A Nation Building State Changes Its Mind*, Melbourne: Cambridge University Press.

Russo, J. (1998) 'Strategic Campaigns and International Collective Bargaining: The Case of the IBT, FIET, and Royal Ahold NV', paper presented at 11th World Congress, *Developing Competitiveness and Social Justice: The Interplay between Institutions and Social Partners*, International Industrial Relations Research Association, Bologna, Italy, 25 September.

Sabel, C. (1994) 'Flexible Specialisation and the Re-emergence of the Regional Economies', in A. Amin (ed.), *Post-Fordism: A Reader*, Oxford: Basil Blackwell.

Sklair, L. (1995) *Sociology of the Global System*, Second edition, London: Prentice Hall.

The Age, 6 February 2002.

Waterman, P. (1998) *Globalisation, Social Movements and the New Internationalisms*, London: Mansell.

Whitfield, D. (1992) *The Welfare State: Privatisation, Deregulation, Commercialisation of Public Services: Alternative Strategies for the 1990s*, London: Pluto Press.

Williams, K., Haslam, C., Johal, S. and Williams, J. (1995) The Crisis of Cost Recovery and the Waste of the Industrialised Nations, *Competition and Change*, 1(1): 67–93.

2 Restructuring state–economy relations

Britain under the Major and Blair governments

Peter Burnham

During the 1980s and the 1990s, a number of radical accounts were developed which sought to explain the apparent 'revolution' in state policy associated with the demise of social democracy and the rise of conservative governments around the globe. Numerous explanatory dichotomies (often cross-cutting and overlapping) were introduced such as the movement from 'keynesianism to monetarism'; from 'fordism to post-fordism'; from 'collectivist post-war consensus to neoliberalism' and from 'national to global systems of capitalism'. Alongside such characterisations there appeared other more idiosyncratic attempts to capture the novelty of political and economic change focusing on 'the free economy and the strong state' and the influence of personality in terms of theories of 'Thatcherism' and 'Reaganism' (Clarke, 1988; Kavanagh, 1990; Bonefeld, 1993; Gamble, 1994).

From the vantage point of the new millennium, many of these dichotomies and characterisations look rather tired and their utility questionable. Is it for instance profitable to ask, in relation to Britain, whether the Major administration (1990–1997) followed the precepts of keynesianism or monetarism or whether the current Blair government is 'neoliberal' or in the tradition of the post-war consensus? Given the general incoherence of economic doctrine, the uncertain relationship between economic theory and political practice and the unwillingness of major political parties to present current policy in these terms, such exercises, it appears, are of limited analytical value. Nevertheless, these characterisations persist and continue to dominate much academic discussion as there are very few attempts to develop accounts of how states since the mid-1990s have sought to manage economic policy (recent attempts include Hay, 1999 and Krieger, 1999).

The aim of this chapter, therefore, is to contribute to the development of new radical explanations of state–economy relations by focusing on how the British government has restructured such relations since the mid-1990s. In so doing it will argue that current state policies are usefully understood in terms of the *politics of depoliticisation* (for further details, see Burnham, 2001). The central argument is that during the 1990s, the Major and Blair governments fused aspects of traditional economic management (drawing in particular on some of the themes underlying Britain's commitment to the classical gold standard) with new initiatives to create a powerful tool of governing organised on the basis of the principle of depoliticisation. In essence, depoliticisation as a governing strategy is *the process of placing at one remove the political character of decision-making*. State managers retain, in many instances, arm's-length control over crucial economic and social processes whilst simultaneously benefiting from the distancing effects of depoliticisation. As a form of politics it seeks to change market expectations regarding the effectiveness and credibility of policy-making in addition to shielding the government from the consequences of unpopular policies (Burnham, 2001). Moreover, it is a process cloaked in the language of inclusiveness, democratisation and empowerment. It is, I will suggest, a potent form of ideological mobilisation which reflects and capitalises on the rejigging of domestic bureaucratic practices and changes in the wider international political economy (particularly those involving the deregulation of financial markets).

The rest of this introduction will lay bare some of the theoretical assumptions which underpin the argument. The second and main part of the chapter will explore in detail how 'politicised' forms of economic management gave way in the late 1980s to 'new' thinking on the relationship between expectations and inflation control. The idea of adopting 'credible rules' has, since 1990, formed the centrepiece of the British state's economic programme and underwrites the politics of depoliticisation. So far this technocratic form of governance is most evident in three main policy trends: (i) the reordering or reassignment of tasks from the party in office; (ii) increased accountability, transparency and external validation of policy; (iii) acceptance of binding rules rather than discretion, particularly in the area of monetary policy. Finally, the chapter will consider how this approach can help illuminate the restructuring of the public sector in Britain and it will point to some of the contradictions and limits of depoliticisation as a governing strategy.

The state and the regulation of capital accumulation

Marx's infamous comment that the 'executive of the modern state is but a committee for managing the common affairs of the whole bourgeoisie' laid the foundation for extensive enquiry into the relationship between the state and capital accumulation. Within the Conference of Socialist Economists (CSE), work on this relationship led to highly distinctive and productive debates in the late 1970s reviving some of the earlier concerns of Pashukanis[1] (see in particular Holloway and Picciotto, 1978; Clarke, 1991). The theoretical assumptions informing this chapter draw on the approach developed initially by a group of CSE theorists including Holloway and Picciotto, and Clarke (Holloway and Picciotto, 1977; Clarke, 1977, 1978, 1988; Holloway, 1995). Since this work has been reviewed in detail elsewhere, I will confine myself here to a brief discussion of fundamentals (Bonefeld and Holloway, 1991; Clarke, 1991; Burnham, 1995).

Holloway and Picciotto's seminal article (1977) posed the question: what is peculiar about the social relations of capitalism that gives rise to the rigidification (or particularisation) of social relations in the form of the state? In other words, what gives rise to the constitution of the economic and the political as distinct moments of the same social relations? (Also see Holloway, 1995: 120–121.) Their answer, drawn from Marx, focused on the distinctive character of the social antagonism on which capitalism is based:

> The specific economic form in which unpaid surplus is pumped out of the direct producers determines the relationship of domination and servitude, as this grows directly out of production itself and reacts back on it in turn as a determinant. On

this is based the entire configuration of the economic community arising from the actual relations of production, and hence also its specific political form. It is in each case the direct relationship of the owners of the conditions of production to the immediate producers... in which we find the innermost secret, the hidden basis of the entire social edifice, and hence also the political form of the relationship of sovereignty and dependence, in short the specific form of state in each case.

(Marx, 1981: 927)

In other words the struggles which abolished the directly political character of civil society, enabling the 'free' sale and purchase of labour power as a commodity on the market, also created the modern state. In this view, the origin and development of the capitalist state is to be understood as a moment of the development of the totality of capitalist social relations: 'it is part of the antagonistic and crisis-ridden development of capitalist society' (Holloway, 1995: 121). The continued existence of the state as a particular form of capitalist social relations rests fundamentally therefore on expanded accumulation.

For Marx, the state is 'based on the contradiction between public and private life, on the contradiction between general interests and private interests' (Marx, 1975: 46). By upholding the rule of law and money, the capitalist state maintains the formal discipline of the market, and thereby mediates the contradiction between the expression of general and particular interests. This discipline must necessarily be *imposed* in an 'independent form' which is divorced from private interests; 'Just because individuals seek only their particular interest, which for them does not coincide with their common interest, the latter is asserted as an interest "alien" to them, and "independent" of them... in the form of the state' (Marx, 1975: 46–47; Clarke, 1988: 124).

In this view therefore, the state has an 'autonomy' which is not political but which rests on its role of enhancing the general conditions of accumulation and managing overall economic strategy. However, to oversee the successful expansion of domestic accumulation, states must also seek to secure the reproduction of capital on an international or global level. Whilst exploitation conditions are standardised nationally, individual states via the exchange rate mechanism (ERM) are interlocked internationally into a hierarchy of price systems. This has two principal implications. First, national states provide the domestic political underpinning for the stability of global capitalist relations. Second, in order to enhance accumulation, state managers are under constant pressure to make more efficient use of available resources, particularly labour power, and maintain the value of currencies (particularly in relation to inflation). In the context of increased international financial interdependence, as I will indicate in the following paragraph, the management of the exchange rate is closely connected with the regulation of labour power, principally through wages policy. In short, state officials are faced with a situation of permanent crisis management. Whilst they seek to contain struggle and expand domestic accumulation they must guard against the danger of inflation, which threatens to undermine competitiveness and erode overseas confidence in the currency. Moreover, they must participate in international summits to maintain the global flow of capital whilst limiting any negative impact of increased openness on their governing strategies.

This approach locates the state as an aspect of the social relations of capitalist production and highlights that the management of labour and money are the central axes of state 'intervention' in capitalist societies. Discussions of government policy, however, should not be taken to indicate that the state 'controls' the 'economy' or that it is always able to successfully regulate class conflict. In this sense, 'it is not necessary to confuse the ideology of economic policy with its actual practice as a capitalist strategy even if the practices require such an ideology' (de Brunhoff, 1978: 64). The 'apparent separation' of the state from civil society, which defines the capitalist character of the state, places the management of labour power and money as central to the process of capitalist reproduction. However, large-scale public 'intervention' provokes resistance and threatens to reveal the illusory character of state 'neutrality'. Extensive and prolonged 'intervention' in the economy can, therefore, quickly produce a political crisis of the state itself. To avoid this situation state managers have been well served by strategies which attempt to disengage the state *publicly* from the process of economic policy-making (Clarke, 1990: 27). This, I shall argue in the following section, is one of the hallmarks of the politics of depoliticisation. Unlike 'keynesian' and 'monetarist' ideologies of the state, governing strategies since the 1990s are characterised by a technocratic embrace of the 'end of ideology' in the 'age of globalisation'. Behind such rhetoric lies a concerted attempt to restructure relations between labour, capital and the state to both enhance accumulation and reduce excessive claims (or 'overload') on the political executive.

Politicised and depoliticised governing strategies

Economic management in the twenty-first century bewilders those accustomed to viewing state policy in simple ideological terms. For example, whilst on the one hand Blairite social democracy seems to favour 'City' interests (via the operational independence of the Bank of England), it also seems to promote decentralisation and increased accountability. In the midst of this confusion flourish theories of the 'competition state' (Cerny, 1997; Elger and Burnham, 2001) and the politics of the 'third way' (Giddens, 1998). In one important respect, such theories are accurate inasmuch as debates centring on 'keynesianism' and 'monetarism' have been replaced by a form of technocratic managerialism. However, whilst the ideology of contemporary economic management may seek to cut across the 'left/right' divide, its underlying rationale is familiar – to promote a fundamental restructuring of the relations between capital, the working class and the state in order to enhance accumulation. In Britain in particular, Blair's strategy seeks to tackle the three most pressing problems that have confronted the British state in the twentieth century: maintaining foreign confidence in sterling; preventing inflationary wage settlements; and capping public expenditure (for a wider analysis, see Bonefeld *et al.*, 1995). The lesson which seems to have been learned by state managers since the mid-1990s is that 'politicised' forms of management fail to achieve lasting results on these fronts, regardless of whether they are wrapped in 'keynesian' or 'monetarist' garb. The rest of this section will expand on these comments first by drawing an analytical distinction between 'politicised' and 'depoliticised' forms of management and then by illustrating some of the key characteristics of the current mode of domination.

The characterisation of the politics of state management in the 1990s, in terms of the notion of depoliticisation, is best approached by drawing a contrast with the politicised management which dominated during the period of 1945–1976 (Burnham, 1999a, 2001). Box 1 indicates the principal features of the politicised mode of economic management. These features involve a discretion-based approach to governance of the economy. In contrast, Box 2 introduces the notion of depoliticised management (for a similar discussion, see Burnham, 1999b). Rather than emphasise discretion, this is a rule-based form of governance of the economy.

From the end of the Second World War to the mid-1980s, the British state adopted a series of politicised strategies to manage the economy and in particular to stabilise sterling, regulate public expenditure and control inflationary wage settlements. In the context of relatively full employment, successive governments sought to regulate labour through moral exhortation (in the national interest), increasing the exercise of centralised authority over wage determination and the creation of new surveillance and guidance machinery.

Indicative planning and official incomes policies were combined with the discretionary management of money as governments struggled to maintain the value of the pound, contain prices and stave off recurrent balance of payments crises. Notwithstanding the weaknesses of the 'political overload', 'ungovernability' and 'legitimation crisis' literature (Hay, 1996: 98–101), it is clear that, by the mid-1970s, politicised modes of economic management were deemed unanimously to

Box 1 Politicised management (discretion-based)

Characteristics

- Government publicly adopts primary responsibility for economic management
- Emphasis on direct intervention and conciliation/co-option
- Government takes credit if policies are successful but perceived 'economic' crisis can quickly become a 'political' crisis of the state

Principal features of economic management 1945–1976

- Direct controls (production, consumption, exchange)
- Incomes policies (formal, informal)
- Downgrading of exchange rate management (political control of Bretton Woods)
- Fiscal/monetary 'autonomy' (no significant interlinking)
- Centralisation of policy-making (including TU representation)
- Growth of public sector – political disputes given the 'state as employer'
- Large degree of public ownership and control
- International co-operation (rather than integration)

Box 2 Depoliticised management (rules-based)

Characteristics

- To place at one remove the political character of decision-making, through the reordering or reassignment of tasks from the party in office and the acceptance of binding 'rules' limiting government room for manoeuvre
- To restructure social relations in the guise of 'technical efficiency'
- To reassert the 'operational autonomy' of the political executive (in the face of 'overload') and establish credibility with financial markets

Principal features of economic management since the mid-1990s

- Centrality of exchange rate management – preference for fixed rate system (ERM/Convergence criteria/European Monetary Union – EMU)
- Institutional realignment to enhance policy credibility (central bank independence, Fiscal Code)
- Interlinking of fiscal, monetary and exchange rate policy
- Decentralisation and devolution of policy-making
- Privatisation and deregulation (re-regulation of financial markets)
- Legislative marginalisation of trade unions (redrawing of boundaries between the 'industrial' and the 'political'; switch focus from government to law courts)
- Recomposition of management hierarchies within states (managerial state)
- Support for agencies, user-groups and the language of 'inclusiveness'
- New public management (NPM)
- From international co-operation to regional integration (EU, NAFTA, APEC etc.)

---

have failed. As early as 1957, Peter Thorneycroft, as Chancellor, had pointed to the dangers inherent in the post-war pattern of economic management, noting:

> almost everything that has been tried has been worth trying. Often we have had a partial or temporary success or near-success. Nevertheless we must frankly admit that we have failed. On the path we are at present following we are moving down towards an economic and political disaster.
>
> (PRO CAB 129/087)

However, not until 1975, in the wake of successive balance of payments crises, devaluations and increasing inflation, did the Treasury admit that post-war management and, in particular, incomes policy 'must be judged a failure' (PRO T 267/28). The pessimistic picture painted by Thorneycroft seemed to have materialised as the

Callaghan government left office (1979) amid sterling crisis, rising unemployment and escalating inflation and public expenditure (Coates, 1980).

In terms of broad macroeconomic management, the gradual relaxation of direct controls in the late 1940s initially placed a greater burden on fiscal policy. Although during the 1950s monetary policy played an enhanced role, in the form of credit restrictions and movements in short-term interest rates, the Radcliffe Report of 1959 confirmed the view that interest rates were an uncertain tool for demand management (Dimsdale, 1991: 89; Hatton and Chrystal, 1991: 68). However, balance of payments difficulties experienced particularly under Wilson in the 1960s led to increased reliance on monetary restriction to stabilise the external balance. The collapse of Labour's politicised strategy in the mid-1970s saw monetary policy, in the form of one-year targets for monetary aggregates, assume centre stage in macroeconomic policy. By the early 1980s, the government gave a clear signal that it would no longer adjust demand to accommodate inflation. The credibility of this strategy, as Hatton and Chrystal (1991: 74) emphasise, was established by the imposition of cash limits, by the commitment to medium-term budgetary objectives and by the refusal to reflate the economy using fiscal policy in the early 1980s. Whereas in general, in the 1950s and 1960s, changes in monetary and fiscal policy were not closely related, the adoption of targets for monetary aggregates led to explicit co-ordination in the 1980s and the increased importance of exchange rate considerations dominating monetary policy (Dimsdale, 1991: 137–140).

For a short while in the early 1980s many commentators assumed that 'Thatcherism' was a coherent and possibly 'new' governing strategy. However, it is now clear that its novelty and consistency were widely overestimated (Bulpitt, 1986). By the mid-1980s, 'monetarism' had been abandoned and the British government lacked a coherent approach to economic policy (Johnson, 1991; Smith, 1993). However, out of the debates between Lawson (Chancellor) and Thatcher on how best to tackle inflation (Bonefeld *et al.*, 1995: 74–83) the beginnings of a new strategy emerged which looked not to 'keynesian' or 'monetarist' ideologies but rather back to the principles which underlay governing during the classical gold standard (and the resumption of gold in 1925) and which drew in particular on the rules-versus-discretion theory of monetary policy.[2]

In this debate on monetary policy, as Alberto Giovannini (1993: 110) clarifies, the idea that fixed rules might improve the performance of monetary authorities has been a recurrent one and was most prominently claimed by the Cunliffe Committee in 1918, which considered Britain's return to gold. Cunliffe concluded, 'Nothing can contribute more to a speedy recovery from the effects of the war, and to the rehabilitation of the foreign exchanges, than the re-establishment of the currency upon a sound basis' (Giovannini, 1993: 116). Across Europe those favouring rules rather than discretion advocated the elimination of exchange controls, the restoration of central bank independence and the creation of a common standard of value on which to base the new monetary system.

The logic underlying this preference for 'rules' is that if such rules are credible, in the sense that the government cannot easily renege on them, the public forms expectations assuming that the rules are followed. In this way, 'To the extent that monetary rules are sufficiently restraining, the public's inflationary expectations will be stemmed, and therefore equilibrium inflation will be lower than under a discretionary regime' (Giovannini, 1993: 111). In short, 'credible monetary rules are effective because they stabilise expectations' (Giovannini, 1993: 112). In terms of the operation of the classic gold standard, international monetary rules were rooted in strict convertibility regulations that were extremely visible. The visibility of the gold standard rule was accompanied by public awareness that the government and the Bank regarded the maintenance of the convertibility obligation as paramount (Giovannini, 1993: 116).

The movement from a politicised (discretion-based) to a depoliticised (rule-based) system allows state managers to establish credible rules for economic management, thereby altering expectations concerning wage claims, in addition to 'externalising' the imposition of financial discipline. The stronger (and more distant) the set of 'rules', the greater manoeuvrability the state could achieve, increasing the likelihood of attaining objectives. Leading supporters of the return to gold in Britain, in particular John Bradbury and Otto Niemeyer, were adamant that the gold standard would make the British economy 'knave-proof', free of manipulation for 'political or even more unworthy reasons' (Rukstad, 1989: 440). In effect it was judged that the gold standard with its 'automatic corrective mechanisms' was the best guarantee against inflation. Similar arguments were employed in the late 1980s, as I will indicate in the next section, by Lawson and Major favouring entry to the ERM. Before, however, considering in more detail the form taken by the politics of depoliticisation in Britain in the 1990s, it is necessary to explore the relationship between the commitment to credible rules and the re-regulation of financial markets which began in earnest in October 1979.

Between the early 1960s and the late 1980s, policy-makers, according to Helleiner (1994: 8), made three types of policy decision that produced major changes in the nature and structure of the international monetary and financial system. These involved: (1) granting more freedom to market operators through liberalisation; (2) refraining from imposing effective controls on capital movements; and (3) making moves to prevent the outbreak of major international financial crises. The most important recent transformations in financial markets are summarised by Underhill (1997: 3) as *desegmentation* – a blurring of the line, in terms of ownership and market activities between banking, securities and insurance; *marketisation* – understood as the liberalisation of traditional cartel arrangements in national sectors through domestic market-oriented reform programmes; and *transnationalisation* – the integration of financial markets across traditionally closed national jurisdictions. The result of these changes is a highly differentiated financial space consisting of an incomplete set of transitional institutions linking domestic, regional and global levels (Underhill, 1997: 314–315). Nevertheless, despite the untidiness of financial interdependence it is clear that re-regulation has undoubtedly affected the fiscal and monetary choices open to governments (Thompson, 1995: 1103).[3] Since foreign exchange dealers prefer to hold currencies backed by anti-inflationary policies, the search for counter-inflationary credibility is of paramount importance both rhetorically and materially. Whilst in the post-war era, as Helen Thompson (1995) indicates, currency markets were driven largely by current account imbalances, now interest rate differentials are the prime determinant of exchange rate movements. The 1980s and 1990s have seen a general convergence in interest rates, and any state which adopts a significantly looser monetary policy than the prevailing level risks a depreciation in its currency. Since the sheer scale of flows in the foreign exchange markets rules out reserve intervention as anything more than a short-term policy, monetary policy is, for the moment, inextricably tied to exchange rate management. The net result of this fiscal and monetary environment is that governments have a clear incentive to enhance their counter-inflationary credibility (Thompson, 1995: 1103; for further elaboration, see Thompson, 1996 and also Radice, 1997).

It is common to view these developments as giving markets 'power' over states. However, it is also possible to see the re-regulation of financial markets as providing the strongest possible public justification governments can muster for maintaining downward pressure on wages to combat inflation and thereby achieve price stability (states, of course, were responsible for the creation of the Eurocurrency markets that developed largely out of interstate rivalry focused on finance – van Dormael, 1997). In many key ways therefore, the re-regulation of financial markets enhances the 'power' of the state *vis-à-vis* labour and capital since it can be argued forcefully that price stability really is the crucial determinant in the global political economy and lack of 'competitiveness' translates directly into a loss of jobs and profits. 'Globalisation' in this sense is far from being 'merely' an ideology.

In this environment where the maintenance of price stability is publicly acknowledged as the first objective of monetary policy (and high wage settlements are seen as a major cause of inflation), governments across the world in advanced capitalist states have attempted to control inflation by adopting 'rules based' rather than 'discretion based' economic strategies. As noted earlier, 'rules based' approaches attempt to build counter-inflationary mechanisms into the economy by re-ordering part of the government's responsibility for economic policy onto non-governmental bodies. This can be achieved in two ways. First, by reassigning tasks onto an international regime, usually an international monetary mechanism, which sets definite rules (Gold Standard, ERM). This attempts to build 'automaticity' into the system, formally limiting government room for manoeuvre. Second, by reassigning tasks to a national body which is given a definite role in statute and thereby greater independence from the government (e.g. moves towards central bank independence, complemented by fiscal responsibility codes). Whereas 'rules based' strategies are attempts to 'depoliticise' the government's economic policy-making (thereby shielding the government from the political consequences of pursuing deflationary policies), 'discretion based' approaches are highly politicised since national governments play the central role in controlling inflation, usually through formal incomes policies.

Depoliticisation strategies in Britain in the 1990s

In the 1990s the shift to depoliticisation was pronounced and can be illustrated in particular with reference to the British state's management of labour and money (this section draws on Burnham, 1999b). As indicated previously, 'depoliticisation' should not be taken to mean the direct removal of politics from social and economic spheres or the simple withdrawal of political influence. Rather, depoliticisation is a governing strategy and in that sense remains highly political. In essence, depoliticisation as a governing strategy can be defined as *the process of placing at one remove the political character of decision-making*. In many respects state managers retain arm's-length control over crucial economic processes whilst benefiting from the distancing effect of depoliticisation. Furthermore, depoliticisation strategies invariably require the public rejigging of bureaucratic practices to achieve their primary aim, which is to change expectations regarding the effectiveness and credibility of policy-making. In this sense depoliticisation is not simply an ideology (unrelated to material practice) but rather is one of the most potent forms of ideological mobilisation, reflecting changes in the form in which state policy-making is carried out (capitalising thereby on the ideological effects of changed material practices).

As a governing strategy, depoliticisation took three main forms in Britain in the 1990s. First, there has been a reassignment of tasks away from the party in office to a number of ostensibly 'non-political' bodies as a way of underwriting the government's commitment to achieving objectives. The most obvious example in this regard is the government's move to grant 'operational independence' in the area of monetary policy to the Bank of England. On 8 October 1992, in a memo to the House of Commons Treasury and Civil Service Committee, Norman Lamont (Chancellor) set out the policy framework which would replace the ERM. Counter-inflationary credibility would now be sought by restructuring the institutional relationship between the Treasury and the Bank of England in order 'to make the formation of policy more transparent and our decisions more accountable' (for further details, see Jay, 1994). In November 1992, Lamont set an inflation target of 1–4 per cent and asked the Bank to assess inflation prospects in quarterly independent reports. With Kenneth Clarke as Chancellor in May 1993, the Bank was given the right of deciding the timing of interest rate changes. Finally in February 1994, Clarke outlined a new framework for monetary policy decision-making: decisions concerning interest rates would be taken at meetings between the Chancellor and the Governor (Chancellor) and minutes would be published with some time delay. Well publicised disputes between the Chancellor and the Governor questioned the ability of these moves towards central bank independence to constitute an effective counter-inflationary anchor. It is for this reason that the government in 1995 reviewed recommendations to enshrine price stability in statute as the primary objective of monetary policy and follow the Bank of France by creating an independent Monetary Policy Committee within the Bank to oversee the making of policy. In the wake of Blair's victory in May 1997, 'New Labour' completed the reforms begun by Lamont and Clarke. The move to introduce 'operational independence', broadly along the lines of the New Zealand model, has now left the Bank 'free' to set interest rates to meet the government's inflation target (for more detail, see Bonefeld and Burnham, 1996, 1998; also see Smith, 1998).

In respect of the management of labour, the reassignment of tasks away from the party in office is evident first in the legislative marginalisation of trade unions, second in government sponsored union use of the legal system, which switches attention away from government to the law courts, and third in the reorganisation of the public sector and the emergence of so-called NPM. Since most attention in industrial relations has been focused on the use of restrictive legislation, I will focus this brief discussion on the reorganisation of labour in the public sector and return to NPM in the conclusion (for a good review of the impact of the legislation, see McIlroy, 1997).

The politicised management of public sector labour established in line with the Whitley procedures of interest representation, which underwrote the increased relevance of trade unionism to state workers, resulted in mass union militancy by state workers in the 1970s (this section draws on Fairbrother, 1994 and Chapter 4). As Peter Fairbrother (1994) points out, for union leaders this meant a direct engagement with state policy and a questioning not only of incomes policies but also of other state policies concerned with the provision of state services. For successive governments the dilemma was how to implement state policies on public services as well as incomes policies without creating the conditions for direct challenges from increasingly active state sector unions.

The result in key areas of state administration has been the recomposition of managerial and worker relations through the establishment of marketised state labour processes. Moving beyond notions of privatisation where the emphasis is on ownership and the transfer of assets, it is now common for a range of public sector functions to be externalised and out-sourced. The consequence is that the public sector is best defined as 'a permeable set of relations, where there is a mix of responsibility between public sector enterprises and the private sector for the provision of public sector functions' (Fairbrother in Chapter 4: 53–54). In short, we are witnessing the creation of 'managerial states' as part of the process of depoliticising labour–management relations in the public sector, as responsibility for the operational activity of state bodies shifts from central government and is placed in the hands of managers who represent a more distant and disembodied form of regulation via financial control and restriction (Pollitt, 1990; Carter, 1997).

The second form in which depoliticisation was manifest as a governing strategy in Britain in the 1990s was in the adoption of measures ostensibly to increase the accountability, transparency and external validation of policy. Recent moves to establish a Code for Fiscal Stability (based on the fiscal responsibility codes created in New Zealand) and the government's intention to create, in conjunction with the World Bank and the OECD, a Code of Good Practice for openness and transparency in macroeconomic policy both exemplify this trend.

In July 1997, the Blair government tied fiscal policy to two rules (HM Treasury, 1998). First, over the economic cycle, the government would only borrow to invest (public consumption would therefore be paid for by taxation). Second, the government would ensure that the level of public debt as a proportion of national income would be held at a stable and prudent level. Building on this framework, the government announced in March 1998 that its fiscal rules must be seen to represent a 'credible commitment in the eyes of the public'. To make this commitment visible the Chancellor proposed that the code be enshrined in legislation, 'to rule out the possibility of profligate fiscal behaviour and so that governments can be held accountable for their policy decisions'. At the heart of the Code stand five principles of fiscal policy management: *transparency* in the setting of fiscal objectives, implementation of policy and presentation of results; *stability* in policy-making and the impact of fiscal policy; *responsibility* in the management of public finances; *fairness* not least between generations; and *efficiency* in managing both sides of the public sector balance sheet.

To achieve these objectives, and more importantly to indicate in public how specific policies relate to declared principles, the government has drawn up plans to recast the Financial Statement and Budget Report (to include its key operating assumptions and explain discrepancies between outcomes and previous budget forecasts) and to introduce an Economic and Fiscal Strategy Report (reconciling short- and long-term fiscal strategy). In addition, to enhance accountability and transparency the government proposes a closer involvement of the National Audit Office to police key assumptions and conventions underpinning economic policy. In short, through these measures, justified in terms of openness and accountability, the government aims to both alter expectations of key actors (in particular public sector trade unionists) and insulate itself from the consequences of tight fiscal policies.

Finally as indicated earlier, depoliticisation strategies have been pursued in an overall context favouring the adoption of binding credible 'rules' which limit government room for manoeuvre. Throughout Europe this is clearly seen in the preference for the fixed exchange rate management system, the centrepiece of which is the ERM, and the convergence rules governing the move to Stage 3 of EMU. I have outlined in detail elsewhere how the Major government hoped it could be insulated from the unpalatable consequences of 'economic adjustment' by shifting responsibility onto an international regime, in this case the ERM (Bonefeld *et al.*, 1995; Bonefeld and Burnham, 1996). Membership, it was thought, would force employers to compensate for the high interest rate pressure on profits by confronting their labour force to secure lower wage rates and increase output per worker. A falling exchange rate would no longer compensate sluggish productivity or enable wage negotiators to agree 'unacceptably' high claims. In essence, the ERM replayed the episode of Britain's return to the Gold Standard in 1925. The 'politics of austerity' could now be legitimated in the language of globalisation with 'external commitments' uppermost.

In a wider context the adoption of rules based strategies is evident in government support for new international institutions such as the World Trade Organization (WTO) and in particular the linchpin of the organisation, its dispute settlement mechanism, which seeks to integrate previously disparate settlement procedures and enforce the rules of the WTO (for further details, see Marceau, 1997 and Petersmann, 1997). In short, despite some dissenting voices, it seems clear that European policy-makers, within and outside the European Monetary System (EMS), now accept the idea that credible, public rules associated with fixed rate systems effectively change expectations and thereby help keep inflation low (Giovannini, 1993: 110).

Conclusion: NPM and the contradictions of the politics of depoliticisation

In the guise of 'technical efficiency' the British state, since the mid-1990s, has sought to restructure political and economic relations in order to enhance its managerial autonomy, maintain its international standing and break down the resistance of powerful groups of employers and workers. This latter point is particularly important when considering the restructuring of the public sector and the reforms often labelled, 'new public management' (NPM).

Popular perceptions of the restructuring of the public sector are often couched in terms of 'rolling back the state'. In this view the process of public sector reform and privatisation involves a simple transfer of services and assets from public to private hands. Such characterisations fail to grasp the complexity of the current constitution of the public sector and fail to accurately identify the political logic behind restructuring. Fairbrother (Chapter 4: 53, 54), as noted earlier, offers a more sophisticated starting point indicating that the public sector is now best defined as 'a permeable set of relations, where there is a mix of responsibility between public sector enterprises and the private sector for the provision of public sector functions'. This recognition of the complexity of current arrangements gives rise to a view of public service regulation involving, as Cope and Goodship (1999: 5) point out:

> both 'regulation inside government' and 'regulation outside government', with regulatory agencies (firmly located within the public sector) shaping the activities of those agencies delivering public services (located within both the public and private sector, such as central government departments, executive agencies, quangos, local authorities, private contractors and voluntary bodies).

In this context NPM as a set of formalised procedures involves, 'simultaneous moves to centralise and decentralise the management of public services' (Cope and Goodship, 1999: 6). It centralises policy-making in the hands of the core executive (Prime Minister's Office, Cabinet Office and Treasury) whilst decentralising the delivery of policy to a number of agencies, which operate within limits set by the centre. Although this can be, and often is, dressed up by ministers in terms of furthering accountability and empowering users, Cope and Goodship's research indicates that public service regulation is primarily a 'control mechanism' enhancing central government management whilst off-loading difficult issues of provision to local agencies. A useful analogy they borrow from Osborne and Gaebler (1992) is that NPM separates 'steering from rowing' (steering being the proper activity of the central government). In short:

> central steering agencies (such as central government departments) increasingly, both directly and indirectly, regulate local rowing agencies (such as executive agencies, local authorities and quangos) by setting policy goals for rowing agencies to achieve, fixing budgets within which rowing agencies must operate, awarding contracts (or quasi-contracts) to competing rowing agencies, appointing the 'right' people to head up rowing agencies to do the 'right thing', and establishing regulatory agencies (such as the Audit Commission) to monitor the performance of the rowing agencies.
>
> (Clarke and Newman, 1997; Cope and Goodship, 1999: 7)

It is hard to disagree with the conclusion reached by Cope and Goodship (1999: 7), that NPM is 'all about managerial surveillance – the ability of steering agencies to monitor and direct rowing agencies more effectively, and within rowing agencies the ability of managers to control workers more effectively'. NPM in summary is designed to enhance central government control and reduce public expenditure. In this way the current regulation of public services is perfectly consistent with the broader governing strategies outlined earlier in terms of the politics of depoliticisation.

As with all governing strategies, however, there are limits and contradictions inherent in the attempt to manage class relations. First, it is evident in particular from this brief discussion of NPM that although one important aim is to enhance government control, in practice it may reduce the significance of state managers. Cope and Goodship (1999: 11) note in this regard that not only does the establishment of regulatory agencies fragment governance but it is also possible (given the longer chain of command and the role of intermediaries) for regulators to be 'captured' (or partly captured) by the regulated. As Croft and Beresford (1996: 191) point out in a different context, notions of 'user involvement' entail the 'paradox of participation' – 'participatory initiatives can be a route to redistributing power, changing relationships and creating opportunities for influence: equally they can double as a means of keeping power from people and giving a false impression of its transfer'. Although state managers would, through depoliticisation, aim to achieve the latter outcome, arm's-length control may, in principle, result in the fragmentation of authority. Second, although a central aim of depoliticisation is to disengage the state *publicly* from the process of policy-making, the centrality of the state in the reproduction of accumulation always threatens to undermine this stance. The state has a permanent presence in the reproduction of capitalist social relations, particularly in the core areas concerning the management of labour and money, and the management of periodic crises requires the substantive intervention of the government. The strategy of depoliticisation is thus liable to be undermined particularly in the wake of financial crisis and/or widespread industrial/civil unrest when government is called upon to intervene publicly to secure the 'illusory communal interest'.

Finally, the inherently political character of depoliticisation strategies is likely to be foregrounded by government action which clearly flouts the language of stability, prudence and external constraint. This is seen most obviously in the relationship between domestic and foreign affairs in the wake of the Bush/Blair 'global war on terrorism'. In this respect New Labour's 'Third Way' foreign policy with its emphasis on international debt relief and military intervention threatens to expose depoliticisation as a class strategy by provoking a new 'guns or butter' debate in the domestic arena. The successful pursuit of depoliticisation strategies dictates that foreign policy should serve and buttress domestic economic management. In this context it is easy to understand Gordon Brown's enthusiasm for deepening the politics of depoliticisation by ensuring Britain's participation in full EMU.

Notes

1 Evgeny Pashukanis posed the question, 'why does class rule not remain what it is, the factual subjugation of one section of the population by the other? Why does it assume the form of official state rule, or – which is the same thing – why does the machinery of state coercion not come into being as the private machinery of the ruling class? Why does it detach itself

from the ruling class and take on the form of an impersonal apparatus of public power, separate from society?' Pashukanis (1978: 139).

2 For an overview of literature on rules versus discretion see Keech (1992) and Kydland and Prescott (1977). Also see the useful discussion of 'new constitutionalism' by Gill (1995, 1998).

3 The term 'reregulation' is preferred to 'deregulation' since, as Phil Cerny points out, in the past twenty years we have seen a complex process of the drafting of new regulations (often new market-oriented rules) rather than a simple lifting of regulations (see Cerny's contributions to Cerny (ed.) (1993)). Also see Eric Helleiner (1994) and Helen Thompson (1994).

Bibliography

Bonefeld, W. (1993) *The Recomposition of the British State During the 1980s*, Aldershot: Dartmouth.

Bonefeld, W. and Burnham, P. (1996) 'Britain and the Politics of the European Exchange Rate Mechanism', *Capital and Class*, 60: 5–38.

Bonefeld, W. and Burnham, P. (1998) 'The Politics of Counter-Inflationary Credibility in Britain, 1990–1994', *Review of Radical Political Economics*, 30(1): 32–52.

Bonefeld, W. and Holloway, J. (eds) (1991) *Post-Fordism and Social Form*, London: Macmillan.

Bonefeld, W., Brown, A. and Burnham, P. (1995) *A Major Crisis? The Politics of Economic Policy in Britain in the 1990s*, Aldershot: Dartmouth.

Bordo, M. and Eichengreen, B. (eds) (1993) *A Retrospective on the Bretton Woods System*, London: University of Chicago.

Bulpitt, J. (1986) 'The Discipline of the New Democracy', *Political Studies*, 34(1): 19–39.

Burnham, P. (1995) 'Capital, Crisis and the International State System', in W. Bonefeld and J. Holloway (eds), *Global Capital, National State and the Politics of Money*, London: Macmillan, pp. 92–115.

Burnham, P. (1999a) 'The Recomposition of National States in the Global Economy: From Politicised to Depoliticised Forms of Labour Regulation', in P. Edwards and T. Elger (eds), *The Global Economy, National States and the Regulation of Labour*, London: Mansell, pp. 42–63.

Burnham, P. (1999b) 'The Politics of Economic Management in the 1990s', *New Political Economy*, 4(1): 37–54.

Burnham, P. (2001) 'New Labour and the Politics of Depoliticisation', *British Journal of Politics and International Relations*, 3(2): 127–149.

Cairncross, A. (1985) *Years of Recovery*, London: Methuen.

Carter, B. (1997) 'Restructuring State Employment', *Capital and Class*, 63: 65–84.

Cerny, P. (ed.) (1993) *Finance and World Politics*, Aldershot: Edward Elgar.

Cerny, P. (1997) 'Paradoxes of the Competition State', *Government and Opposition*, 32(2): 251–274.

Clarke, J. and Newman, J. (1997) *The Managerial State*, London: Sage.

Clarke, S. (1977) 'Marxism, Sociology and Poulantzas' Theory of the State', *Capital and Class*, 2: 1–31.

Clarke, S. (1978) 'Capital, Fractions of Capital and the State', *Capital and Class*, 5: 32–78.

Clarke, S. (1988) *Keynesianism, Monetarism and the Crisis of the State*, Aldershot: Edward Elgar.

Clarke, S. (1990) 'Crisis of Socialism or Crisis of the State?', *Capital and Class*, 42: 19–29.

Clarke, S. (ed.) (1991) *The State Debate*, London: Macmillan.

Coates, D. (1980) *Labour in Power?*, London: Longman.

Cope, S. and Goodship, J. (1999) 'Regulating Collaborative Government', *Public Policy and Administration*, 14(2): 3–16.

Croft, S. and Beresford, P. (1996) 'The Politics of Participation', in D. Taylor (ed.), *Critical Social Policy: A Reader*, London: Sage, pp. 175–198.

de Brunhoff, S. (1978) *The State, Capital and Economic Policy*, London: Pluto.

Dimsdale, N. (1991) 'British Monetary Policy Since 1945', in N. Crafts and N. Woodward (eds), *The British Economy Since 1945*, Oxford: Oxford University Press, pp. 89–140.

Elger, T. and Burnham, P. (2001) 'Labour, Globalisation and the "Competition State"', *Competition and Change*, 5(3): 245–267.

Fairbrother, P. (1994) *Politics and the State as Employer*, London: Mansell.

Fairbrother, P. (2005) 'The Emergence of the "De-centred" British State', in P. Fairbrother and A. Rainnie (eds), *Globalisation, State and Labour*, London: Routledge, pp. 53–71.

Gamble, A. (1994) *The Free Economy and the Strong State*, London: Macmillan.

Giddens, A. (1998) *The Third Way*, Cambridge: Polity.

Gill, S. (1995) 'Globalisation, Market Civilisation and Disciplinary Neoliberalism', *Millennium Journal of International Studies*, 24(3): 399–423.

Gill, S. (1998) 'European Governance and New Constitutionalism: Economic and Monetary Union and Alternatives to Disciplinary Neoliberalism in Europe', *New Political Economy*, 3(1): 5–26.

Giovannini, A. (1993) 'Bretton Woods and Its Precursors: Rules versus Discretion in the History of International Monetary Regimes', in M. Bordo and B. Eichengreen (eds), *A Retrospective on the Bretton Woods System*, London: University of Chicago, pp. 109–154.

Grant, W. (1993) *The Politics of Economic Policy*, Hemel Hempstead: Harvester.

Hatton, T. and Chrystal, K. (1991) 'The Budget and Fiscal Policy', in N. Crafts and N. Woodward (eds), *The British Economy Since 1945*, Oxford: Oxford University Press.

Hay, C. (1996) *Re-stating Social and Political Change*, Buckingham: Open University Press.

Hay, C. (1999) *The Political Economy of New Labour*, Manchester: Manchester University Press.

Helleiner, E. (1994) *States and the Re-emergence of Global Finance*, New York: Cornell University Press.

HM Treasury (1998) *A Code for Fiscal Stability*, London: HMSO.

Holloway, J. (1995) 'Global Capital and the National State', in W. Bonefeld and J. Holloway (eds), *Global Capital, National State and the Politics of Money*, London: Macmillan, pp. 116–140.

Holloway, J. and Picciotto, S. (1977) 'Capital, Crisis and the State', *Capital and Class*, 2: 76–101.

Holloway, J. and Picciotto, S. (eds) (1978) *State and Capital: A Marxist Debate*, London: Edward Arnold.

Jay, P. (1994) 'The Economy 1990–1994', in D. Kavanagh and A. Seldon (eds), *The Major Effect*, London: Macmillan.

Johnson, C. (1991) *The Economy under Mrs Thatcher 1979–1990*, London: Penguin.

Kavanagh, D. (1990) *Thatcherism and British Politics*, Oxford: Oxford University Press.

Kavanagh, D. and Seldon, A. (eds) (1992) *The Major Effect*, London: Macmillan.

Keech, W. (1992) 'Rules, Discretion, and Accountability in Macroeconomic Policymaking', *Governance*, 5(3): 259–278.

Krieger, J. (1999) *British Politics in the Global Age*, Cambridge: Polity.

Kydland, F. and Prescott, E. (1977) 'Rules Rather Than Discretion', *Journal of Political Economy*, 85(3): 473–490.

McIlroy, J. (1997) 'Still under Siege: British Trade Unions at the Turn of the Century', *Historical Studies in Industrial Relations*, 3(March): 93–122.

Marceau, G. (1997) 'NAFTA and the WTO Dispute Settlement Rules', *Journal of World Trade*, 31(2): 25–57.

Marsh, D., Buller, J., Hay, C., Johnston, J., Kerr, P., McAnulla, S. and Watson, M. (1999) *Postwar British Politics in Perspective*, Cambridge: Polity.

Marx, K. (1975) 'Contribution to the Critique of Hegel's Philosophy of Law', in K. Marx and F. Engels (eds), *Collected Works*, vol. 3, London: Lawrence and Wishart, pp. 3–129.

Marx, K. (1981) *Capital*, vol. 3, London: Penguin.

Marx, K. and Engels, F. (1848) *The Communist Manifesto* (various).

Osborne, D. and Gaebler, T. (1992) *Reinventing Government*, Reading, MA: Addison-Wesley.

Pashukanis, E. (1978) *Law and Marxism*, London: Pluto.

Petersmann, E. (ed.) (1997) *International Trade Law and the GATT/WTO Dispute Settlement System*, Amsterdam: Kluwer Law.

Pollitt, C. (1990) *Managerialism and the Public Services*, Oxford: Blackwell.

PRO (various) – Public Record Office, Cabinet and Treasury documents, Kew, London.

Radice, H. (1997) 'The Question of Globalization', *Competition and Change*, 2(2): 247–258.

Rukstad, M. (1989) *Macroeconomic Decision Making in the World Economy*, London: Dryden.

Sandholtz, W. (1993) 'Choosing Union: Monetary Politics and Maastricht', *International Organisation*, 47(1): 1–39.

Smith, D. (1993) *From Boom to Bust*, London: Penguin.

Smith, D. (1998) 'Pounded by Interest Rates', *Sunday Times* (Business section), 15 March.

Thompson, H. (1994) *Joining the ERM* (PhD Thesis, LSE).

Thompson, H. (1995) 'Globalisation, Monetary Autonomy and Central Bank Independence', in J. Lovenduski and P. Stanyer (eds), *Contemporary Political Studies 3*, Exeter: PSA, pp. 1100–1111.

Thompson, H. (1996) *The British Conservative Government and the European Exchange Rate Mechanism 1979–1994*, London: Pinter.

Underhill, G. (1997) 'Introduction' and 'Conclusion', in G. Underhill (ed.), *The New World Order in International Finance*, London: Macmillan, pp. 1–13, 313–318.

Van Dormael, A. (1997) *The Power of Money*, London: Macmillan.

3 The state we are in (and against)

Al Rainnie and Peter Fairbrother

Introduction

The modern state has been the focus of attention by governments over the past two decades. This concern has involved debate about managerialism (Pollitt, 1990), the scope and remit of the state (Whitfield, 2001) and the position of the state in the international economy (Hirst and Thompson, 1999). During this period, many governments, particularly those in liberal democratic states, initiated policies aimed at recasting their states, structurally as well as in relation to policy. More specifically, in the wake of the September 11 (2001) attack on the World Trade Centre, there has been a further move to reposition the modern liberal democratic state, in particular involving an attempt to reinforce the pre-eminence of the US state, as well as to enhance the militarisation of the state. On the one hand, there appears to be a move towards a more transnational state form, militarised and increasingly undermining democracy and freedom. On the other hand, such a shift confronts moves towards a more decentralised state, engaged with the institutions of civil society. However, this tension is not new and has been recognised in debates about the direction of change that is taking place involving the modern liberal democratic state (e.g. Botsman and Latham, 2001).

What has been of lesser concern in these analyses is the question of labour, either as a state employee or in relation to resistance to the thrust of change. The neglect of labour is evident in the debates about globalisation. An emerging thesis in arguments about globalisation is that labour and labour organisation are at best marginal or at worst entirely absent (e.g. Beynon and Dunkerley, 2000; Held *et al.*, 2000). Indeed, where work and workers do make an appearance it is usually only as the object of apocalyptic visions in the snippets presented (e.g. Castells, 1996 or Rifkin, 1996). However, numerous writings do deal specifically with labour, unions and globalisation (Edwards and Elger, 1999; Waddington, 1999). Waddington is concerned with the response of labour to evolving regulatory structures and new forms of production, whereas Edwards and Elger examine the implications of globalisation for experience of and activity by labour in relation to state and supra-state forms of regulation. Thus, while one fundamental aspect of all forms of globalisation theorising concerns the changes that are taking place in the form and function of the state itself, little or no connection has been made between literatures on labour and state restructuring, on the one hand, and the globalisation debate, on the other.

The aim of this chapter is to examine how such changes have been analysed (and prescribed) and to begin an exploration of some of the (unexpected) implications of these changes. In the first part of the chapter, we examine analyses of state restructuring, outlining an apparent paradox. One influential argument focuses on the reconstitution and recomposition of the state, via new public management (NPM). A second argument is that the state is being transformed through the development of collaborative power relations, vertically and horizontally, the so-called New Institutionalist School (NIS). Although starting from different ends of the political spectrum, the analysis of (if not prescription for) the new form and function of the state emerging from the NPM and the NIS appear to be converging. There is, in fact, a growing consensus amongst commentators about the necessity of a 'hollowed out' or 'decentralised' state (OECD, 2001a,b). In the second section of the chapter we argue that both schools of thought are based on an inadequate analysis of the role of the state and put forward an alternative approach, developing and extending Burnham's 'depoliticisation' thesis (1999a; see also Chapter 2). Building on the idea that states and markets are an aspect of the social relations of production, we argue that central to an understanding of the modern state is the labour–capital relation and the politics embedded within it. In developing this argument, we designate the processes of transformation over the past three decades as one of re-politicising the modern state. This section is followed by an analysis of the implications of this re-politicisation for collective resistance. Our argument in a nutshell is that despite the apparent convergence of mainstream approaches to state restructuring and attempts to 'depoliticise' this process, the form and function of the state is becoming increasingly political and politicised, albeit in a nuanced and relatively subtle way.

New public management: from the Keynesian to the Washington consensus

The 'hollowed out' state is characterised by NPM, as a distinctive form of state managerialism (Pollitt, 1990). Much has been written about the emergence and development of NPM in particular national contexts. Here we are more concerned with the process by which the original neo-liberal prescription appeared to operate in a global context, a process that we might describe as 'capitalist internationalism'. The new orthodoxy spread through the active intervention of important actors, a process that Thrift (1998) has described as soft capitalism. In this case, the idea that the public sector must ape the private sector was driven hard by major institutions such as the International Monetary Fund (IMF), World Bank and the Organisation for Economic Co-operation and Development (OECD) (e.g. World Bank, 1999, 2000).

Reconstituting state and capital

The Keynesian consensus had over a number of decades (1940s–1960s) institutionalised practices and structures which were anathema for the new market revolutionaries of the last quarter of the twentieth century (such as Bacon and Eltis, 1976). The crisis of the welfare state was based, it was stated, on 'excessive' public spending, too rigid public sector structures and the arrival of global markets, defined by some as a fiscal crisis (Brenner, 1998). More broadly, the developmental state or state monopoly capitalism, a model which in a number of variants had dominated economic development and state formation up to the end of the short 'long boom', had been undermined by the internationalisation that successful autarchic development itself had promoted and a falling rate of profit evident from the end of the 1960s (Bramble and Kuhn, 1999; Upchurch, 1999). This internationalised economy provided the context for the collapse of the Keynesian consensus but more particularly increasingly constrained the room for manoeuvre that social democratic parties in particular found available to them.

However, there was not a simple and uniform transition to the new orthodoxy about the emergent state. If we take the influential OECD Public Management Programme (PUMA) as an example, for Premfors (1998), this approach is best described as rational choice institutionalist (more generally drawing on public choice theory and principal–agent theory). Premfors sees the OECD approach as going through a three-phase developmental sequence:

> 1970s: Crisis of the welfare state
> 1980s: A transitional state
> 1990s: Arrival of the management state.

> (1998: 142)

In response to a perceived crisis in the welfare state in the 1970s, a series of piecemeal and partial measures were introduced in the 1980s focused on restructuring the state and opening it up to the private sector under the rough title of '*let* managers manage'. This move is just one aspect of the new managerialist discourse that was becoming all pervasive (Thrift, 1998). But, it was argued by governments of the period that this did not go far enough. In order to fully transform rigid and entrenched state structures of the welfare period, it was necessary to *make* managers manage, through centrally driven restructuring of incentives for managers (on Britain, see Fairbrother, 1994). The normative ideal was the market, and where outright privatisation was not possible then the creation of quasi-markets was the order of the day (Premfors, 1998: 143). For Premfors, the OECD/PUMA story had heroes or leaders, in particular New Zealand and, to a lesser extent, the United Kingdom, and implied a necessary convergence of state formations, through the ubiquitousness of the purchaser:provider split (Kelsey, 1999; Whitfield, 2001).

It is important here to note that in some headline cases, changes were being driven by supposedly centre-left political parties (Labour in New Zealand) as well as more straightforwardly Thatcherite/Reaganite governments in the United Kingdom and the United States. Peck (2001: 445) argues that though this policy medicine might be administered in a number of different ways – from the shock treatment of Structural Adjustment Programmes to the sweetened pills of Third Way politics as elaborated by Prime Minister Blair (UK), President Clinton (US) and Chancellor Schroeder (Germany) during the late 1990s – never mind what it says on the bottle, the treatment remains pretty much the same. Doses vary but the prescription includes purging the system of obstacles to the operation of free markets; restraining public expenditure and any form of collective initiative; celebrating the virtues of individualism, competitiveness and self sufficiency; abolishing or weakening social transfer programmes while actively fostering the 'inclusion' of the poor and marginalised into the labour market on the markets terms (see also Baumann, 1998). In this regard, the New Zealand experience was not only seminal but also iconic (see Kelsey, 1999: 8–19; as well as Walsh *et al.* Chapter 7 in this volume).

One strand of argument is that there was no choice. For O'Tuathail and others (1998: 6), this shift meant first that the state must be 'seized' by NPM proponents so that it might be used to liberate markets and second that far from being a period of deregulation, the ensuing revolution would be highly regulatory. Held argued that the state was 'trapped within webs of global interconnectedness permeated by quasi supra-national, intergovernmental and transnational forces, and unable to determine its own fate' (quoted in O'Tuathail *et al.*, 1998: 6). This approach, which sees states simply as conduits for the new rules determined by organisations such as the OECD, World Trade Organisation (WTO), IMF, World Bank, European Union (EU) and North American Free Trade Agreement (NAFTA) is, as we shall see, too simple, but it does point to a new framework designed to regulate the New World Order. The neo-liberal dream of a free market world is simply that, a dream that exists only in hyper-reality, but the reality of restructuring requires a new and complex regulatory framework to oversee its implementation. Within this reading, states are expected to localise the prevailing liberal orthodoxy by reinventing government as a flexibly specialised ensemble of institutions that facilitate, enable and enhance globalisation (Osborne and Gaebler, 1993). As noted:

> The govern-mentalities of state managers become globalized as they downsize the state, deregulate its economy and reconceptualized its citizens as human resources and clients in need of management and service ... [states were] ... also forced to restructure the internal social bargain to attract global flows of capital.
> (O'Tuathail *et al.*, 1998: 15)

Kelsey (1999: 30), in particular, points to the coercive effects of WTO agreements in this process of re-regulation.

But, this is a duplicitous process, with the US as the most active participant in determining the needs of the world economy. While this observation is a statement of the obvious, it bears repeating insofar as the political response to restructuring at national level is, to a degree, dependent on where in the hierarchy of influence the particular state finds itself. Therefore, defence of indigenous capital for dominant or hegemonic states, such as the United States, may translate into an aggressive attack on other states to open up markets or the manipulation of quasi-independent agencies to achieve the same ends. For lower tier states these forces translate into attempts to resist the predations of dominant states whilst attracting foreign direct investment (FDI) on the best terms possible and simultaneously attempting to block cherry picking of particular companies or the privatisation of strategic sectors such as defence industries (Hardy and Rainnie, 1996). Thus deregulation and privatisation is driven by accumulation and profit, as a way to resolve problems of government spending. Bramble and Kuhn (1999: 26) outline the shift in Australia from direct state regulation of the assets of the banking sector to open market operations through trading in currencies and government bonds. Further, while governments may no longer construct or even own public infrastructure projects or directly provide public services themselves, they set the terms for the provision of public services through regulation, performance criteria or out-sourcing. While pathways vary, from the enthusiastic embrace of deregulation by Australia to the more circumspect approach of Poland, the unifying factor to varying degrees is the dominance of the US.

The OECD has been an influential determinant of public sector restructuring through its PUMA. For the OECD, up to the late 1990s, there was not only no alternative to public sector reform but also only one effective path down which reform could go. Five elements were outlined:

- A focus on results in terms of quality, efficiency and effectiveness.
- Decentralised structures replacing highly centralised hierarchical structures.
- Flexibility to explore alternatives to direct public provision.
- Greater focus on efficiency in services directly provided by the public sector.
- Strengthening of strategic capacities at the centre, allowing for response to external changes, flexibly and at least cost.

(OECD, 2001a)

At the heart of state restructuring lay a cost-driven 'purchaser:provider split', the outcome of which tends to be described in two pieces of jargon as 'public–private partnership' leaving the public sector 'to steer rather than row'. This fitted neatly into the Washington consensus, described as a policy fix comprising a complex of reforms:

- *Fiscal discipline* – the effective capping of government budget deficits.
- *Public expenditure priorities* – focused on supply-side investments not on social amelioration or progressive redistribution.
- *Tax reform* – rates held down and incentives sharpened.
- *Financial liberalisation* – interest rates and capital flows market determined.
- *Exchange rates* – competitive to promote traditional exports.
- *Trade liberalisation* – remove import restrictions.
- *Foreign Direct Investment* – barriers to entry removed.
- *Privatisation* – of state-owned enterprises (SOEs).
- *Deregulation* – abolish restrictions on competition.
- *Property rights* – legal system to ensure property rights without excessive costs.

(Peck, 2001: 448)

The OECD in particular viewed the neo-liberal experiment in New Zealand as a star act (Kelsey, 1999: 68). During the 1990s, Ruth Richardson and Roger Douglas, both former finance ministers, were employed by the World Bank to inspire client governments. The Commonwealth Secretariat and the OECD also sought their help. Richardson's prescription for public sector reform was outlined to a group of 'opinion formers' in Iceland:

- Make all the changes they were going to do fast, and as many at the same time as possible.
- Don't discuss them with the labour movement.
- Don't listen to any protests made by the labour movement and others.
- Make the changes as soon as possible as there are nearly four years to the next election.

(Kelsey, 1999: 101)

By default, if nothing else, Richardson acknowledged the processes of the importance of labour in state restructuring.

Tours of New Zealand organised by the World Bank Learning Leadership Centre for government officials, journalists, politicians and bank staff from around the world emphasised the New Zealand model as 'conventional Washington consensus reforms' with four special characteristics: first the changes were comprehensive across all sectors; second, without exception, the best possible policies were implemented; third, the approach was non-ideological, initiated by a left of centre government; and fourth, the separation of desired general outcomes from specific outputs with performance contracting of civil servants was novel (Kelsey, 1999: 109). While the claim that this process was 'non-ideological' may seem, at first sight, to be straining credibility, it does reinforce the importance of former social democratic parties in providing an ideological cover for the introduction of NPM. The collapse of the Keynesian consensus and the ensuing crisis in social democratic ideology ushered in the embrace of the Washington consensus, more recently and briefly wrapped in the flimsy rags of the Third Way (Giddens, 1998; Latham, 1998).

Uncertainties about the thrust of change

By the late 1990s, it became apparent that all was not well with the embrace of NPM and related policies. A series of events took place that represented a challenge to the Washington consensus; however, at no point was reconstitution of the state questioned. While it had been acknowledged that labour acquiescence was central to the reconstitution of the state apparatus, labour was defined very broadly rather than in relation to the state as employer. More generally, it was not at all clear how best to secure continued compliance from the broader population for public sector reform.

The restructuring of state regimes was questioned in two ways. First, the emphasis on policy (e.g. privatisation strategies) rather than the composition of regimes was challenged by the Asian financial crisis of 1997. The IMF's initial intervention in Asia, imposing fiscal austerity, high interest rates and deregulation of the financial sector only served to provoke a deepening recession. Cuts in subsidies on food and fuel alongside company bankruptcies and rising unemployment drove 60 per cent of the population of Indonesia, the world's third most populated country, into poverty.

Russia defaulted on its IMF repayments in September 1998 and by 1999, financial instability was flowing through Latin America.

Second, the acquiescence of labour could no longer be taken for granted by governments or the supra-national agencies that promoted policies for a hollowed-out state. McNally (1998), ruminating on the emergence of a new 'Asian model' – of working class resistance to capitalist globalisation – identified strikes by young women in garment factories in Bogor and electronics plants in Kuala Lumpur and by aircraft workers in Bandung against IMF directed lay-offs, mass demonstrations by thousands of workers in Surabaya and weeks of strikes by workers at Kia in South Korea as signs of resistance to downsizing, privatisation and poverty (McNally, 1998: 13). Writing before the uprising in Indonesia, Moody (1997: 10) pointed to more than twenty mass political strikes around the world between 1994 and 1997. And even before the 1999 problems arose, commentators had noted the incidence of what have become known as IMF riots throughout much of the Third World (Rees, 1998: 10).

The end of consensus

In January 1998, the Washington consensus started to break. The World Bank's chief economist, Joseph Stiglitz, attacked the IMF approach to the Asian crisis. He described the Washington consensus as neither necessary nor sufficient either for macro-stability or longer-term development (Stiglitz, 2002). Stiglitz was closely followed by Ravi Kanbur, head of the World Development Report task force. Former guru of shock therapy transformation Jeffrey Sachs jumped ship and launched a virulent attack on the Bretton Woods institutions and their policies. O'Brien (2000: 9) remarks on the unlikely sources of some of these critical voices and points to a significant shift from earlier agendas of preaching rapid liberalisation as the solution to the world's problems.

In 1998, President Bill Clinton and WTO Director, General Ruggiero, had already called for greater dialogue with civil society. Clinton wanted to set up a forum where business, labour, environmental and consumer groups could speak out (Kelsey, 1999: 277). The most bizarre example of attempted accommodation came at the 2001 World Economic Forum meeting in Davos, where, protected by riot police inside a 30 kilometre exclusion zone, the world's economic and political elite offered to debate via a television link with delegates at the 'alternative Davos' organised by the World Social Forum and held in the Brazilian city of Porto Alegre (Rees, 2001: 8).

By 1999, the World Bank's *World Development Report* was advocating decentralisation of government structures because this 'improves the efficiency and responsiveness of the public sector while accommodating potentially explosive political forces' (1999: 107). But decentralisation alone was not enough. The report acknowledged that this could simply transfer power from national to local power elites – equity would require both the ability and willingness of local government to engage in income redistribution (1999: 110) – and further that local officials and community groups are best placed to identify and reach the poor rather than central authorities. The report goes on to argue that a multitude of actors outside the public sector – including unions, grassroots organizations, non-government organisations

(NGOs) and neighbourhood groups – hold local governments accountable, and in particular these groups, including unions, have played a fundamental role in restoring democracy and building civil society (1999: 122).

In the 2000/2001 report, promoting a Comprehensive Development Framework, the Bank recommended three areas of action:

- *Promoting opportunity* – expanding economic opportunity for poor people.
- *Facilitating empowerment* – making state institutions more accountable and responsible to poor people.
- *Enhancing security* – reducing poor people's vulnerability.

(2000: VI)

This recommendation was based on the assumption that facilitating the empowerment of poor people through making state and social institutions responsive to them is a key to reducing poverty (2000: 3). Achieving access, responsibility and accountability is, according to the report, intrinsically political and requires active collaboration among poor people, the middle class and other groups in society (2000: 7). Even the OECD had shifted ground. By 2001, the PUMA Policy Brief was singing a slightly amended tune. Although still arguing that there were few alternatives to reform (2000: 1), the concern was now with consensus. Arguing that people want more government that does less, the belief now was that government needed to re-earn public trust by providing more choice, democracy and transparency. The necessity was now to work with media, industry and non-profit groups to serve better as mediator, coordinator, policy-maker and regulator (2000: 2). Such a common vision, it is suggested, unifies political leaders, senior officials, front line workers and the general public. Government should now consult with all stakeholders and bring together their many varied visions.

However grudging and slight, there has been a growing acceptance of the political necessity to engage with the institutions of civil society, albeit in a limited way. Equally, engagement was as much about selling a slightly softer version of the original medicine as it was a Damascene conversion to inclusive democratic structures. Nonetheless, there is a simplification to the argument where it is claimed that the problem is one of poor communication (OECD, 2001a). Thus, while policy elites and overseas commentators viewed the New Zealand experiment as a success, the public did not share the enthusiasm, because of poor communications. If only communications had been better the victims would have realised just how lucky they actually were!

Thus, by the time the World Economic Forum met in 2002, Kofi Annan, United Nations Secretary General, was arguing that 'None of us, I suggest, can afford to ignore the conditions of our fellow passengers on this little boat. If they are sick, all of us risk infection. And if they are angry, all of us can easily get hurt' (*Australian Financial Review*, 6 February, 2002).

Globalisation and its discontents

At the same time, from a different position in the political spectrum, the emergent NIS was reaching much the same policy prescription, if by a somewhat different route.

The New Institutionalists, drawing on Polyani (1944), argue that unfettered markets create social and political trouble; therefore market economies need to be appropriately governed if they are to successfully meet the needs of a wide range of groups in society. Markets must be embedded in a variety of non-market social institutions and regulating mechanisms if they are to produce efficient outcomes. The rediscovery of Karl Polanyi and in particular his impressive work *The Great Transformation* is no accident. It appears to provide a way back into debate on economic and social policy for those opposed to the dominant free market ethos of the 1980s and 1990s. Polanyi's work is a devastating critique of the political and social disaster that free markets bring with them. For Polanyi, the reduction of all factors of production (labour, land and money) to simple commodity status to be traded on free markets was both undesirable and unstable. His argument was that lurches in the direction of deregulation inevitably led to instability and eventually a return to regulation. For many, Polanyi provides a framework for arguing for reregulation in the twenty-first century, in the face of the enthusiasm for privatisation and deregulation. However, it is a framework which allows distance to be put between new institutionalist prescriptions and more radical agendas; it constitutes an accommodation, or surrender, to the perceived primacy of markets.

Hollowing out the state

For Hirst and Thompson (1999), globalisation is a myth suitable for a world without illusions, but it is one that robs workers in particular of any hope, leaving only defensive strategies in the enclaves where the labour movement still exists. Against this, and the important point as far as this chapter is concerned, Hirst and Thompson argue that Keynesianism is not dead. They suggest that the EU itself along with state action at the national and sub-national level could initiate a form of Euro-Keynesianism that could revive the social democratic agenda. The conclusion that Hirst and Thompson draw is that, because international businesses remain embedded in their home territories, they remain multinational rather than transnational corporations (TNCs). This implies that it is not beyond the powers of national governments to regulate these companies. In developing this analysis, Hirst and Thompson draw on Polanyi, as does Jane Kelsey in her brilliant analysis of the New Zealand experiment (Kelsey, 1999). Crucially, for Kelsey and others, there are alternatives although a degree of political will is required to generalise this possibility. Further, the state is not dead, and though its role may have changed it still has a crucial part to play.

Despite arguing the continuing importance of the nation state, Hirst and Thompson argue that there can be no return to old modes of state intervention. Classical national economic management now has limited scope. New agencies of governance are now likely to be international and herein lies the potential importance of the EU. The authors argue that the triad of the EU, Japan and NAFTA dominate the world economy. Therefore, if they so chose, the triad could effectively control the direction of the world economy if they acted in concert. The strong governance of the world economy towards ambitious goals (e.g. promoting employment) requires highly coordinated policies on the part of triad members. If they did embrace such ambitious goals then they could impose a new tripartite hegemony on world financial markets, international regulatory bodies and other nation states comparable to that exercised by the United States between 1945 and 1973. Weiss has a stronger version of this thesis, arguing for the emergence of what she calls the 'catalytic state' (Weiss, 1998: 209). This involves building or strengthening power alliances, first upwards via inter-state coalitions at the regional and international level, and/or downwards via state–business alliances in the domestic market. Far from relinquishing roles, states are increasingly using collaborative power arrangements to create more real control over their economies, by playing a dominant role in coalitions of states, transnational institutions and private-sector groups and relying less on their own resources. Elsewhere it has been argued that this represents little more than social democratic utopian dreaming (Rainnie, 1997); however, we have the emergence of a new orthodoxy wherein the role of the state is still important but is undergoing a profound transformation.

In stressing the link between the supra- and sub-national governance structures, Hirst and Thompson (1999) are following the standard line of argument emanating from the flexible specialisation school. They have little to say about the actual form of the state that this implies, although Jessop (1994), developing a similar line of argument, does analyse the state form. For Jessop, the Keynesian Welfare State, appropriate to Fordist times, is now being replaced by a Schumpetarian Workfare State. Furthermore, and echoing Hirst and Thompson, the state itself is being 'hollowed out', with state capacities, new and old, being reorganised on supranational, regional, local or trans-local levels. Three forces are driving this shift. First, the growing competitive pressures from newly industrialised countries (NICs) in low-cost, low-tech production, forcing advanced capitalist economies to move up the technological hierarchy. Second, the pace of internationalisation shuts down the possibility of closed, protected and autocentric growth models. Thus Keynesian macroeconomic policies lose their efficacy. Third, the flexibility demanded by post-Fordism encourages the state to concentrate on supply side problems of international competitiveness and attempts to subordinate welfare policy to the demands of flexibility. Whilst arguing that national governments remain important, Jessop stresses supra- and sub-national governance structures. He talks of a shift from local government to local governance, with local trade unions, chambers of commerce, education and research centres all entering arrangements to regenerate local economies. Furthermore, elsewhere Jessop talks about globalisation bringing about a relativisation of scale, with new places emerging, new spaces being created and new scales of organisation being developed (1999: 25). Crucially, the sub-national or regional level is promoted as a major site for new space activity and state restructuring.

If NPM proponents had initially hoped for a convergence of social systems towards a minimalist state structure, NIS advocates argue for a slightly more inclusive model. Based on approaches that emphasise the importance of history, path dependency and the important mediating effects of socio-economic institutions, New Institutionalism stresses difference in outcome. Waddington (1999), for example, argues that the emergence of NIS thought within economics and sociology has been important in rejecting the convergence hypothesis:

> Whereas the convergence thesis assigns to technology and markets the position of determinants, new institutionalists recognize the influence of several other factors. Principal among these are the varied roles of the state in economic management, which results in different 'state traditions'; the role of informal communities and networks in influencing patterns of regulation; and the activities of formal associations, including trade unions, in concluding negotiated settlements between groups with opposing interests. . . . For the new institutionalists it is the various interactions between these factors and those identified within the convergence thesis that explain the emergence and resilience of different regulatory regimes.
>
> (Waddington, 1999: 17)

Waddington points to the distinction between the Rhine and Neo-American models, contrasting Atlantic short-termism with highly sophisticated levels of interest mediation between states, employers and unions emphasising long-term calculations over investment, jobs and economic growth. However, critics from the left have pointed to inherent problems with the institutionalists' favoured models of Germany (Mahnkopf, 1999) or Sweden (Coates, 1999), although Lubanski and Andersen (Chapter 5) argue that the Scandinavian model is both more equitable and resilient than Coates would allow. Hay and others (1999: 18), on the other hand, argue that the marginalisation of the European social model and the almost total dilution of the notion of social partnership suggest that EU harmonisation and regulation may have a further corrosive effect on national social models, driving a residualisation process by which social policy is increasingly subordinated to the perceived imperatives of competitiveness and of labour market flexibility, in particular.

However, even in the institutionalist schools labour enters the equation only as an element in corporatist structures or as a victim in the Anglo-Saxon model, and the state itself remains inadequately theorised. Waddington confronts some of these problems and points to the role that some analysts argue that labour played in triggering the crisis of the regulatory regime that was supposedly to have characterised the long post-war boom (1999: 1). However, even the institutionalist critics of NPM convergence appear to be arguing for a picture of fairly uniform pressures to restructure state formations and functions in a particular direction mediated and therefore differentiated in pace and pattern of restructuring only by national social formations.

The global region

Globalisation has brought with it a new key to regional development, knowledge-intensive innovation and flexibility. The 'new regionalism', drawing its intellectual backing from the new institutionalism, points to localities as the emerging focus of economic and political activity. Storper (1998), for example, has suggested that dense local tissues of corporate and institutional interaction are important in explaining the apparent success of industrial agglomerations. These firm–institution relations have been described as 'untraded dependencies', that is conventions and norms that foster collective and localised learning and promote trust between economic actors. Arising from this work has been an argument that an explanation of regional success lies in the way that local resources and institutions (including trade unions) are mobilised to enhance competitiveness, trust and innovation (for critiques see Lovering, 2001; Smith *et al.*, 2001).

The forces driving restructuring are inevitable (or at least appear to be so). Keynesian intervention is dead, to be replaced particularly at the local level by associative democracy. This localised third way attempts to attract FDI, promote small firms and encourage labour market flexibility in partnership agreements in local governance structures. Workers and their unions have a role only in positive participation in such structures. For Murray *et al.* (2000: 248), the result moves towards some sort of functionalist voluntarism in which unions and managers are somehow condemned to come to some agreement – a veritable co-operative over-determination! In one of the major texts outlining this approach (Cooke and Morgan, 1998), Nissan in North-east England is put forward as an exemplar of the new work relations, having apparently created an unprecedented degree of worker involvement and commitment, despite evidence to the contrary (Garrahan and Stewart, 1992). The focus is on a pluralistic notion of trust as the cement holding the new systems together, both in intra- and inter-work organisation relations.

The new regionalism stresses the importance of the creation of socially inclusive entrepreneurship and employment to nurture skills, expertise and capabilities rather than simply focusing on the number of jobs created. Firms need to draw on the active participation of their workers, suppliers and customers as well as building long-term relationships with providers of public goods such as training and education. This forms the basis of what Amin and Thrift (1995) have termed associative democracy, defined (inevitably) as a third way between state and market. The third way:

> is an attempt to set up networks of intermediate institutions between market and state.... Its emphasis is on forms of governance which integrally involve institutions in civil society, especially those without hegemonic power.
>
> (Amin and Thrift, 1995: 50)

Competitiveness requires associationalism and, as successful regions show, networking is the way to achieve it – once again a resurrection of the social democratic dream in the face of apparently horrendous odds. Unsurprisingly, Phelps and others (1998) and Lovering (1999) argue that the new regionalism tends to prioritise the interests of TNCs and ignores issues of poverty and inequality. Indeed Lovering (2001) argues that arguments about the empowering nature of the new regionalism are at best romantic readings of only one small part of the story. Regionalisation can be a key component of a strategy of state restructuring aimed at realising a broadly neo-liberal model of globalisation (for an argument supporting this view in the Australian context see Rainnie, 2001).

The analysis does not have much to say about how the state might achieve these ambitions and what a restructured state might look like. Nonetheless, Cooke and Morgan (1998: 79) suggest that accomplished regional systems are likely to display strong socio-cultural annealing mechanisms in their collective social order, institutions and organisation. They quote approvingly from a description of Danish associative democracy, which is taken to hold within it the necessary elements:

- A high level of interest representation and organisation of public life across economy, politics and society.
- A considerable spread of decisional autonomy and authority.
- The state as arbitrator and facilitator as well as rule maker and service provider.
- The evolution of a dense network of vertical and horizontal policy channels for decision-making.
- Iterative dialogue for conflict resolution and policy consensus via policy networks and co-representation.

(Cooke and Morgan, 1998: 81)

What is emerging is a variety of the 'one best way' approach which has echoes in the works of the OECD and American gurus who suggest that the detailed restructuring of the state is driven by the same forces outlined here and equally will result (or should result) in a unity of outcome – the NPM, but now a more democratic and inclusive variation on the original model. In the new regionalism we have decentralised state institutions which, if not actually privatised, then involve much more closely public–private partnerships and a heightened role for the third or voluntary sector. In other words associative democracy assumes a more active engagement with the institutions of civil society than old planning models encompassed. Associative democracy on this reading bears startling resemblances to a new socialised form of NPM.

State and labour

One of the issues that remains unexplored in either the NPM or NIS related debates is the question of the evolving relations between state and labour. Instead of focusing on trust and associative democracy, we examine the state as the site of the complex of relations between state and labour in general. These issues have been addressed in recent debates about international political economy (IPE). They also raise questions about the forms of struggle and resistance that may be emerging in relation to the globalised state.

The capitalist state

One of the major IPE theorists, Robert Cox, argues that we are currently witnessing 'the internationalisation of the state'. This involves the internal and external restructuring of the state rather than its destruction as in the more extreme forms of globalisation analysis. There are three elements to the analysis; first, states have historically acted as buffers and bulwarks protecting national economies from disruptive external forces in order to sustain domestic welfare and employment. Since 1973, this priority shifted to one of adapting domestic economies to the perceived exigencies of the world economy. Second, this shift has affected the structures of national governments; with agencies that act as conduits for the world economy becoming pre-eminent within governments, ministries of industry and labour are subordinated to ministries of finance. Finally, as indicated there is a transnational process of consensus formation (OECD, IMF, Group of Seven major economies – G7; now G8) that transmits guidelines to dominant state agencies which in turn enact national policies. The state's role therefore becomes one of helping to adjust the domestic economy to the requirements of the world economy. The state is a trans-mission belt from the world to the domestic economy; it is 'internationalised' from the outside in.

In a critique of this position, Burnham (1999b) argues that IPE fails to conceptualise the role of the state in capitalist reproduction. Further, he argues that:

> The . . . sense in which much mainstream international political economy literature eschews the 'political' is in respect of its conceptualisation of labour. This is most evident in popular treatments of the state–market dichotomy. Although some neoGramscians take seriously Polanyi's assertion that markets are political creations, in general markets are fetishised as discrete, technical economic arenas and the overwhelming tendency is to view them in terms of trade, finance and the application of new technology. Not only are labour markets generally ignored, but much more significantly, the category of labour itself is often viewed as external to state/economy restructuring and is equated simply (in a pluralist sense) with trade union bargaining power. In other words, in orthodox (and much heterodox) international political economy there is no systematic conceptualisation of the internal relations between state, labour and capital.
>
> (Burnham, 1999b: 38)

For Burnham, Cox underplays the role of labour. Class relations are seen to be external to the process of restructuring, and labour and the state itself are depicted as powerless, passively responding to the demands of the post-Fordist economy. Furthermore, such an approach underplays the extent to which globalisation may be authored by states and be regarded by state agents (both liberal and social-democratic) as one of the most efficient means of restructuring labour–capital relations in a time of economic crisis. The mistake Cox makes is to view the state and the market as opposed forms of social organisation by equating the defining characteristic of capitalism with private property rather than the commodification of labour.

Instead, Burnham views the relationship between states and markets not as exter-nal and contingent but as internal and necessary. States are an aspect of social relations of production and their power derives from their ability to reorganise capital–labour relations within, and often beyond, their boundaries, to enhance the accumulation of capital. Recent changes in global political economy are therefore predominantly about reorganising rather than bypassing states and this recomposition is actively undertaken by state managers as part of a broader attempt to restructure and respond to a crisis of labour–capital relations.

For Burnham, the form that this restructuring takes is the 'depoliticisation' of the state. Depoliticisation is a government strategy of placing at one remove the political character of decision-making, and is therefore a highly political process (see Chapter 2). Depoliticisation, for Burnham, is important precisely because of the highly political pressures that capitalist states are now under. State restructuring had produced a growing reaction and opposition during the 1990s. The strength of Burnham's analysis is that it unites the form and function of state restructuring (marketisation of the public sector) with analysis of work and workers.

The re-politicisation of the modern state

The capitalist employment relation is inherently exploitative and based on a structural antagonism between capital and labour. However, this antagonism is mediated through a series of institutions that mix coercion with cooperation, and further, this mediation has to be constantly reworked and reformed. The liberal democratic state is a capitalist state and as such is as much a structure of competition reflecting the competing and often contradictory demands of differing fragments of capital as it is a structure of class domination. The state is therefore both an apparatus of class domination and an apparatus of competition between segments of the bourgeoisie. This latter element is packed full of complexities, particularly in the current situation. Calls on governments to defend the jobs of workers made redundant by international capital, to resist takeover of domestic capital by foreign companies or to resist offshoring of local companies are relatively common. One outcome is argument that moves in such a direction would damage the country's standing in the eyes of the international financial community and thus make it less attractive as a site for investment.

In this analysis of the liberal democratic state as a capitalist state, labour becomes both object and subject. As Dick Bryan has pointed out:

> In a world of international mobility (and pricing) of capital and commodities, national costs come down predominantly to labour as the economic factor which, by its relative immobility internationally, is the one most imbued with the characteristics of 'nationality'. Labour costs become the key to national success. They also become the zone of sacrifice in order to achieve that success.
>
> (2000: 5)

The point is that even when contradictions or complexities arise for the state at the level of the capital–capital relationship, relief is sought at the site of the capital–labour relationship, either directly through job loss or wage cuts or indirectly through attacks on the social wage and welfare state. However, hostility between capitals not only manifests itself within states, depending on the dominant fractions of capital, but also between states. The state's ability to compete depends on the relative size, composition and quality of the sections of capital that fall within its orbit. A number of conclusions flow from this feature, the most important being that the limits and scope of state action will depend on its relative strength and therefore place in the hierarchy of states.

For Ellen Meiksins Wood, the growing role of the state in the anti-social purposes of capital means that the state would increasingly become a prime target for resistance:

> if anything, the state is the main agent of globalisation. US capital in its quest for competitiveness demands a state that will keep social costs to the minimum, while keeping in check the social conflict and disorder generated by the absence of social provision. In the European Union, which is supposed to be the model of transnational organisation, each European state is the principal agent, for instance, in the creation of conditions for monetary union. Each state is the main agent forcing on its citizens the austerities and hardship needed to comply with the stringent requirements of the currency, and each state is the main instrument for containing conflicts engendered by these policies, the main agent for maintaining order and labour discipline.
>
> (1997: 12)

At the same time the dominant political orthodoxy increasingly attempts to lay the blame for political and social problems on the individual 'failings' of the poor and oppressed (Baumann, 1998). This assessment places politics at the heart of the equation.

To make sense of these processes, it is helpful to distinguish between depoliticised relationships and politicised ones. By depoliticisation is meant the formal disengagement of the state politically from the economy, defining problems as technical and 'economic' questions, as if these issues are not associated with the structuring of class relations (Burnham, 1999a, Chapter 2; Fairbrother, 2000). However, as indicated, this analysis can be elaborated to capture the complex processes of change that are taking place. Thus, in contrast, politicisation refers to the ways in which governments seek to regulate state policy and practice via highly mediated policies of intervention and involvement in the organisation and operation of the state and civil society. Specifically, the state is caught in two crosscutting relationships. As Bryan (2000) intimates, the state is defined by complex and mediated relations between labour and capital. These relations are mediated as both depoliticised relations (defining critical aspects of economic organisation in economic and technical ways, once removed from direct political control) and politicised ones (reflected in centralised control and direction of the economy). These relations are not bi-polar, but are part of the same process of regulation and control, involving increased porosity in these relations between national and international, although often played out in the ways suggested by Meiksins Wood (1997). The implications for labour organisation and regulation are profound, indicating a shifting terrain of relations, both within the national state and beyond.

Thus, there are three points to note about the analyses of state and labour. The first is that the focus of the emergent critique of globalisation is that the market in a globalised world does not operate perfectly and rests on inequalities between different areas of the world, and resulted in self-serving supra-national agencies and particularly the IMF, which increasingly acts as an arm of the US Treasury (Stiglitz, 2002). The second point to note is that those accounts that focus on the state in the context of globalisation provide an opening to the analysis of globalisation and the market that underwrites the continuing importance of the state as a focus for the form and effect of economic globalisation (Hirst and Thompson, 1999). This analysis allows an assessment of the politics of globalisation, taking into account the explicit hierarchy between the US and other states. The third point to note is that the analysis that addresses the class basis of state rule, pointing to the processes of depoliticisation that ideologically underwrite the supposed neutral intervention of the state in market relations, reveals a dimension of globalisation that is usually underdeveloped (Burnham, Chapter 2: 22, 25, 1999a,b). However, while the Burnham analysis is critical it should also be extended, since paradoxically it does not centre-stage the state as a site of contested social relations. As a result it is an analysis that overlooks the way in which state relations are emergent as the site for labour struggle, both within and against the state. As part of the processes of depoliticisation, there is a process of re-politicisation taking place, at the level of the state, both internally and as a node of capitalist relations within the globalised economy and polity.

Renewal and resistance

Emphasising the complexities of both the capital–capital as well as the capital–labour elements of the state reinforces the point regarding the highly politicised nature of current state restructuring. It is an apparent paradox that at a time when the dominant analyses of state restructuring emphasise a social democratic pluralist consensus, the activities of the state are becoming increasingly (de)politicised and contested. If the state is a site of contested social relations, one aspect of such contestation will be through the institutionalised relations between labour and capital, via trade unions and related organisations.

An understanding of the role of the state in shaping employment regulation is central to understanding the rapidly changing political economy of industrial relations in the context of globalisation (Treuren, 2000: 75). The ongoing integration of domestic markets into the international marketplace is placing unprecedented pressure on domestic institutions of economic, political and social management. Treuren points to the error of conflating 'state' and 'government' in much industrial relations literature (including one of the authors of this chapter in the list of criminals!). More generally he points to three levels of analysis (micro, meso and macro) and argues that most work has concentrated on the first and second, thus reinforcing the error of conflation. Further he questions whether the disciplinary boundaries of industrial relations are too tightly drawn to cope with issues of state and globalisation.

It is important to extend this analysis so that the state is seen as an integral aspect of the processes towards globalisation. For Giles (2000), industrial relations remain fixated with the centrality of national systems approaches, viewing globalisation as an external factor in both analytical and spatial terms, constituting discrete pressures on national systems, and seeing globalisation only in economic or technological terms and thereby ignoring social, political or cultural dimensions. Giles argues that an IPE-based approach is preferable, which would have six characteristics:

- An insistence on the artificiality of the separation between economy and polity.
- An insistence on the capitalist character of contemporary IPE.
- Capitalism changes, not just in the sense of being a dynamic system, but also as a series of waves or phases.
- Analytical priority is accorded to production and the social relations that spring from production.
- The IPE is a structure of deep and persistent inequality fissured by deep diversity.
- Social conflict is the motor of development.

On this reading then it is incorrect to see the state as increasingly constrained by international competition and capital mobility. Echoing our earlier argument, for Giles an IPE perspective views individual states as important authors of these self same constraints, which do not just drop from the sky onto unsuspecting governments.

In a sharper reading of these issues, Burnham argues that with the recomposition and reconstitution of the modern liberal democratic state managerial and worker relations have been recast, with implications for struggles by state labour (1999a and Chapter 2). Analysts such as Fairbrother (2000 and Chapter 4) have used Burnham's approach to theorise on the possibility of the renewal of trade union organisation in the public sector as a direct outcome of the restructuring that Burnham outlines – the renewal hypothesis (Fairbrother, 1996, 2000; see also Fairbrother and Yates, 2003). However, we now want to argue that the implications are deeper and wider than simply the possibility of resurrecting active trade union organisation, particularly at a workplace level, though this is important enough in its own right.

There are two points to note. First, a series of arguments have been developed focusing on the restructuring and transformation of work and employment relations over the past two decades. It would appear that capitalist forms of production are in a moment of transition and that the previous patterns of production, with their implications for how workers organise are coming to an end (Abreu *et al.*, 2000; Appelbaum *et al.*, 2000; Cohen and Kennedy, 2000: 60–77, 121–131). The background to these debates is that what came to be regarded as the dominant form of work organisation in the twentieth century is in transition. The previously nationally based and focused forms of production have been transformed so that a complex division of labour has emerged, with workers in one part of the world producing goods and services for use elsewhere in the world (Gereffi, 1999).

The second point to note is that accompanying these developments, public services have become a focus of attention for successive governments, concerned to reduce public expenditure and to improve the delivery of public services, often designated as the modernisation of the state (e.g. for the United Kingdom, see Cabinet Office, 1999). The outcome is that the boundaries of the modern state have been redrawn and relations within the state recomposed. Such changes have had a major impact on work and employment in the public services in the liberal democracies. For many commentators, this restructuring and reorganisation is characterised by a shift in public sector institutions and recently privatised state industries towards a new managerialism and the marketisation of workplace relations (e.g. Carter *et al.*, 2002). The critical aspect to note in relation to these developments is that they are part of a worldwide shift, with the transfer of ideas and policies about the restructuring of the modern state and the implementation of a suite of policies promoting deregulation and competitiveness, within and between states (Fairbrother and Poynter, 2001; Whitfield, 2001). Unless these changes are understood, the analyses of state and labour are underdeveloped and narrowly focused.

For trade unions more generally, it is argued that the traditional bases and form of trade unionism no longer suffice (Bronfenbrenner *et al.*, 1998; Fairbrother and Yates, 2003). In addressing this circumstance, two contrasting arguments prevail. The first is that trade unions in the modern world will increasingly reconstitute themselves as nationally based organisations, addressing questions relating to recruitment and organisation (Waddington and Kerr, 1999) and/or the 'politics of production' (Stewart and Martinez Lucio, 1998). As part of this focus, many commentators have explored the dynamics of partnership and social dialogue, assuming that national states remain the critical actors in the globalised world (in an American context, see Kochan, 1999 and on the United Kingdom, see Knell, 1999; for a critical assessment, see Danford *et al.*, 2003: 17–20). The second, less frequently acknowledged point is that trade unions could begin to recast themselves both as participative and locally based organisations (Fairbrother, 2000; Danford *et al.*, 2003) as well as globally relevant unions (Moody, 1997; Waterman, 1998). In the changing terrain of internationalised economies and polities, trade unions face the danger of being ring-fenced, as predominantly nationally based and nationally focused. Such an analysis draws attention to the way that work and employment relations are becoming internationalised and the way that unions may be stimulated to adapt and change as locally active but also prominent global unions. The question is how and under what circumstances might these forms of collective organisation develop.

It can be argued that unions have taken the first somewhat embryonic steps to revive their international organisation, through more active global union federations, as well as via forms of networking and inter-union organisation (for one account, see Waterman, 1998). With the internationalisation of economies, and the globalisation of the world, the formerly moribund international union federations are gaining prominence as the international voice of nationally based trade unions; a union problem in part of the world (e.g. the attempt in 2002 to derecognise the government employees' union in South Korea) becomes a problem for state-sector unions worldwide (in the Korean case via the global union federation, the Public Services International). Resistance in one country and one sector has implications for like worker struggles elsewhere. The result is that opposition to the form of state restructuring that is taking place in one country (e.g. the disputes by French civil servants over civil service restructuring in spring 2000) have echoes elsewhere (e.g. municipal workers opposing privatisation in South Africa). It is not that there is necessarily a unity between the struggles that is recognised and acknowledged; rather it is that these events are part of the same concern with the thrust and direction of state restructuring both nationally and internationally.

Conclusion

The modern liberal democratic state remains a site of class struggle and a critical node in an increasingly internationalised economy. It is thus possible to argue that this form of state is becoming increasingly globalised. These developments involve a complex and highly mediated process of change, at the level of recomposing and re-organising state structures. The result is that a managerial state is in the process of realisation, although not in the way anticipated by many commentators.

The current debates about the modern liberal democratic state focus on the recomposition of the state (NPM) and the development of collaborative power relations within the modern state (NIS). The first set of arguments were advanced in response to the crisis of welfare state rule, arguing that laying the foundation for a managerial state is critical for the repositioning of the modern liberal democratic state. This set of arguments founders on the partiality of the solution, emphasising managerialism as such and failing to take account of the complex relations between state and labour. The second set of arguments rest on an analysis of the state and market relations, advocating a re-regulation of economies, re-emphasising the importance of the state as a regulator. This type of analysis is given a particular force with the debates about the global region. Paradoxically, this strand of argument becomes a socialised form of NPM, subject to the same inadequacies. While both strands of argument take up key aspects of the changes taking place they are both one dimensional, in that they overlook the politicised ways in which the modern state is being reconfigured.

The complexity of the modern state is captured by the idea of the state as both an apparatus of class domination and an apparatus of competition. However, while this observation has been disentangled in a variety of ways, what is missing in most analyses is recognition of the state as an employer. As a result, it is unclear quite how the modern state has been transformed as a class-based organisation, defined by complicated class relations, and encapsulated in the notion of NPM (for an early statement, see Carter and Fairbrother, 1995). One implication of this transformation is that state employees are part of the modern working class, with the prospect of both exploitation and resistance.

An important critique of these arguments has been the Burnham thesis of depoliticisation. The premise of this analysis is that the modern liberal democratic state is and remains a capitalist state. Central to the argument is the 'conceptualisation of the internal relations between state, labour and capital' (Burnham, 1999: 38). While Burnham brings the question of labour to the forefront, thereby providing the platform for analyses that address themes relating to labour organisation and renewal (e.g. Fairbrother, 2000 and this volume), his account of depoliticisation can be extended by a recognition of the state as the site of contestation and struggle, at the level of state relations and in terms of capital and labour.

It is also the case that there has been little consideration of the bases of collective organisation in and against the modern state. There are three points to make about these relations. The first is that the state workers in the modern liberal democracies have been and remain the object and subject of state policy. The state is a site of control and exploitation and thus a moment of contestation. Second, trade unions as the voice of state workers have found it difficult to shift from a situation where they were relatively integral to the class rule that characterised the welfare state to one where they were marginalised. It is in this specific domain of concern that arguments about union renewal have been advanced. Third, a more broadly based notion of renewal is one that addresses the complexity and specificity of local circumstance but within the panorama of a globalised world, where the state is the site for contestation and conflict, involving state workers and others. It is for these reasons that there is an international basis to struggle, involving workers *qua* workers and citizens more generally

Bibliography

Abreu, A., Beynon, H. and Ramalho, J. (2000) 'The Dream Factory: VW's Modular Production System in Resende, Brazil', *Work, Employment and Society*, 14(2): 265–382.

Amin, A. and Thrift, N. (1995) 'Institutional Issues for the European Regions', *Economy and Society*, 24(1): 41–66.

Amin, S. (1997) *Capitalism in the Age of Globalization*, London: Zed Books.

Appelbaum, E., Bailey, T., Berg, P. and Kalleberg, A. L. (2000) *Manufacturing Advantage: Why High-performance Work Systems Pay Off*, New York: Cornell University Press.

Australian Financial Review, 6 February 2002, p. 14.

Bacon, R. and Eltis, W. (1976) *Britain's Economic Problem: Too Few Producers*, London: Macmillan.

Baumann, Z. (1998) *Work, Consumption and the New Poor*, Milton Keynes: Open University Press.

Beynon, J. and Dunkerley, D. (eds) (2000) *Globalization – The Reader*, London: Athlone Press.

Botsman, P. and Latham, M. (eds) (2001) *The Enabling State: People before Bureaucracy*, Sydney: Pluto Press.

Bramble, T. and Kuhn, R. (1999) 'Social Democracy after the Long Boom: Economic Restructuring under Australian Labor, 1983 to 1996', in M. Upchurch (ed.), *The State and 'Globalization': Comparative Studies of Labour and Capital in National Economies*, London: Mansell, pp. 20–55.

Brenner, R. (1998) 'The Economics of Global Turbulence: A Special Report on the World Economy, 1950–98', *New Left Review*, 229(May/June): 1–265.

Bronfenbrenner, K., Friedman, S., Hurd, R., Oswald, R. and Seeber, R. (eds) (1998) *Organizing to Win: New Research Strategies*, Ithaca, NY: ILR Press.

Bryan, D. (2000) 'National Competitiveness and the Subordination of Labour', *Labour and Industry*, 11(2): 1–16.

Burnham, P. (1999a) 'The Recomposition of National States in the Global Economy: From Politicised to Depoliticised Forms of Labour Regulation', in P. Edwards and T. Elger (eds), *The Global Economy, National States and the Regulation of Labour*, London: Mansell, pp. 42–63.

Burnham, P. (1999b) 'The Politics of Economic Management in the 1990s', *New Political Economy*, 4(1): 37–54.

Cabinet Office (1999) *Modernising Government*, Cm 4310, London: Stationery Office.

Carter, B., Davies, S. and Fairbrother, P. (2002) 'The Rise and Rise of Market Relations in the British Public Sector: Implications for Industrial Relations', *Economic and Labour Relations Review*, 13(1): 36–59.

Carter, R. and Fairbrother, P. (1995) 'The Remaking of the State Middle Class', in T. Cutler and M. Savage (eds), *The New Middle Class*, University College London Press, pp. 133–147.

Castells, M. (1996) *The Rise of the Network Society*, three volumes, Oxford: Blackwell.

Coates, D. (1999) 'Labour Power and International Competitiveness', in L. Panitch and C. Leys (eds), *Socialist Register*, Rendlesham: Merlin Press, pp. 105–142.

Cohen, R. and Kennedy, P. (2000) *Global Sociology*, Basingstoke: Macmillan.

Cooke, P. and Morgan, K. (1998) *The Associational Economy*, Oxford: Oxford University Press.

Danford, A., Richardson, M. and Upchurch, M. (2003) *New Unions, New Workplaces: A Study of Union Resilience in the Restructured Workplace*, London: Routledge.

Edwards, P. and Elger, T. (eds) (1999) *The Global Economy, National States and the Regulation of Labour*, London: Mansell.

Fairbrother, P. (1994) *Politics and the State as Employer*, London: Mansell.

Fairbrother, P. (1996) 'Workplace Trade Unionism in the State Sector', in P. Ackers, P. Smith and C. Smith (eds), *The New Workplace and Trade Unionism*, London: Routledge, pp. 110–149.

Fairbrother, P. (2000) *Trade Unions at the Crossroads*, London: Mansell.

Fairbrother, P. and Poynter, G. (2001) 'State Restructuring: Managerialism, Marketisation and the Implications for Labour', *Competition & Change*, 5(3): 311–333.

Fairbrother, P. and Yates, C. (2003) 'Unions in Crisis, Unions in Renewal', in P. Fairbrother and C. Yates (eds), *Trade Union Renewal and Organising: A Comparative Study of Trade Union Movements in Five Countries*, London: Continuum, pp. 1–31.

Ferlie, E., Ashburner, L., Fitzgerald, L. and Pettigrew, A. (1996) *The New Public Management in Action*, Oxford: Oxford University Press.

Fosh, P. (1993) 'Membership Participation in Workplace Unionism: The Possibility of Union Renewal', *British Journal of Industrial Relations*, 31(4): 577–592.

Garrahan, P. and Stewart, P. (1992) *The Nissan Enigma*, London: Mansell.

Gereffi, G. (1999) 'International Trade and Industrial Upgrading in the Apparel Commodity Chain', *Journal of International Economics*, 48(1): 37–70.

Giddens, A. (1998) *The Third Way: The Renewal of Social Democracy*, Cambridge: Polity Press.

Giles, A. (2000) 'Globalisation and Industrial Relations Theory', *Journal of Industrial Relations*, 42(2): 173–194.

Hardy, J. and Rainnie, A. (1996) *Rethinking Krakow: Desperately Seeking Capitalism*, London: Mansell.

Hay, C., Watson, M. and Wincott, D. (1999) 'Globalisation, European Integration and the Persistence of European Social Models', *POLSIS Working Paper 3/99*, University of Birmingham.

Held, D., McGrew, A., Goldblatt, D. and Perraton, J. (eds) (2000) *Global Transformations*, Cambridge: Polity Press.

Herod. A., O'Tuathial, G. and Roberts, S. (eds) (1998) *An Unruly World?* London: Routledge.

Hirst, P. and Thompson, G. (1999) *Globalisation in Question: The International Economy and the Possibilities of Governance*, Second edition, Cambridge: Polity Press.

Jessop, B. (1994) 'Post-Fordism and the State', in A. Amin (ed.), *Post-Fordism – A Reader*, Oxford: Blackwell, pp. 251–279.

Jessop, B. (1999) 'Reflections on globalisation and its (il)logic(s)', in K. Olds, P. Dicken, P. Kelly, P. Kongh and H. Yeung (eds), *Globalisation and the Asia Pacific: Contested Territories*, London: Routledge, pp. 19–38.

Kelsey, J. (1999) *Reclaiming the Future*, Toronto: University of Toronto Press.

Knell, J. (1999) 'Participation at Work', *Employment Relations Research Series 7*, DTI/Industrial Society.

Kochan, T. (1999) 'Rebuilding the Social Contract at Work: Lessons from Leading Cases', *Institute for Work and Employment Research*, Sloan School of Management.

Latham, M. (1998) *Civilising Global Capital: New Thinking for Australian Labor*, St Leonards, NSW: Allen & Unwin.

Lovering, J. (1999) 'Theory Led Policy: The Inadequacies of "the New Regionalism" (Illustrated from the Case of Wales)', *International Journal of Urban and Regional Research*, 23(2): 379–395.

Lovering, J. (2001) 'The Coming Regional Crisis (And How to Avoid It)', *Regional Studies*, 35(4): 349–354.

McNally, D. (1998) 'Globalization on Trial', *Monthly Review*, September, pp. 1–13.

Mahnkopf, B. (1999) 'Between the Devil and the Deep Blue Sea', in L. Panitch and C. Leys (eds), *Socialist Register*, Rendlesham: Merlin Press, pp. 142–178.

Meiksins Wood, E. (1997) 'Labour, the State and Class Struggle', *Monthly Review*, 49(3): 1–17.

Moody, K. (1997) *Workers in a Lean World*, London: Verso.

Murray, G., Lévesque, C. and Vallée, G. (2000) 'The Re-regulation of Labour in a Global Context: Conceptual Vignettes from Canada', *Journal of Industrial Relations*, 42(2): 234–258.

O'Brien, R., Goetz, A., Scholte, J. and Williams, M. (2000) *Contesting Global Governance: Multilateral Economic Institutions and Global Social Movements*, Cambridge: Cambridge University Press.

OECD (2001a) 'Public Management (PUMA)', *Policy Brief*, No. 9.

OECD (2001b) *Devolution and Globalisation: Implications for Local Decision-Makers*, Paris: OECD.

Olds, K., Dicken, P., Kelly, P., Kongh, P. and Yeung, H (eds) (1999) *Globalisation and the Asia Pacific: Contested Territories*, London: Routledge.

Osborne, D. and Gaebler, T. (1993) *Reinventing Government: How the Entrepreneurial Spirit is Transforming the Public Sector*, New York: Penguin Plume Books.

O'Tuathail, G. and Luke, T. (1998) 'Global Flowmations, Local Fundamentalism, and Fast Geopolitics: "America" in an Accelerating World Order', in A. Herod, G. O'Tuathial and S. Roberts (eds), *An Unruly World? Geography, Globalization and Governance*, London: Routledge, pp. 72–94.

Peck, J. (2001) 'Neoliberalizing States: Thin Policies/Hard Outcomes', *Progress in Human Geography*, 25(3): 445–455.

Phelps, N., Lovering, J. and Morgan, K. (1998) 'Tying the Firm to the Region or Tying the Region to the Firm? Early Observations on the Case of LG in South Wales', 5(2): 119–138.

Polanyi, K. (1944) *The Great Transformation*, Boston, MA: Beacon Books.

Pollit, C. (1990) *Managerialism and the Public Services*, Oxford: Blackwell.

Premfors, R. (1998) 'Reshaping the Democratic State: Swedish Experiences in a Comparative Perspective', *Public Administration*, 76(1): 141–159.

Rainnie, A. (1997) 'Globalization and Utopian Dreams', *Contemporary Politics*, 3(3): 277–285.

Rainnie, A. (2001) *Globalization – The Implications for Country Victoria*, Monash University, Faculty of Business and Economics, Working Paper 73/01.

Rees, J. (1998) *The Algebra of Revolution*, London: Routledge.

Rees, J. (2001) 'Anti-capitalism, Reformism and Socialism', *International Socialism*, 90: 3–40.

Rifkin, J. (1996) *The Future of Work*, New York: Tarcher/Putman Books.

Smith, A., Rainnie, A. and Dunford, M. (2001) 'Regional Trajectories and Uneven Development in the "New Europe"', in H. Wallace (ed.), *Interlocking Dimensions of European Integration*, London: Palgrave, pp. 122–145.

Stewart, P. and Martinez Lucio, M. (1998) 'Renewal and Tradition in the New Politics of Production', in P. Thompson and C. Warhurst (eds), *Workplace of the Future*, London: Macmillan, pp. 65–83.

Stiglitz, J. (2002) *Globalisation and Its Discontents*, London: Penguin.

Storper, M. (1998) *The Regional World*, New York: Guilford Press.

The Age, 6 February, 2002.

Thirkell, J., Scase, R. and Vickerstaff, S. (1994) *Labour Relations and Political Change in Eastern Europe*, London: UCL Press.

Thrift, N. (1998) 'The Rise of Soft Capitalism', in A. Herod, G. O'Tuathial and S. Roberts (eds), *An Unruly World? Globalization, Governance and Geography*, London: Routledge, pp. 25–71.

Treuren, G. (2000) 'The Concept of the State in Industrial Relations', *Labour & Industry*, 11(2): 73–98.

Upchurch, M. (ed.) (1999) *The State and Globalisation*, London: Mansell.

Waddington, J. (ed.) (1999) *Globalisation and Patterns of Labour Resistance*, London: Mansell.

Waddington, J. and Kerr, A. (1999) 'Trying to Stem the Flow: Union Membership Turnover in the Public Sector', *Industrial Relations Journal*, 30(3): 184–196.

Waterman, P. (1998) *Globalisation, Social Movements and the New Internationalisms*, London: Cassell.

Weiss, L. (1998) *The Myth of the Powerless State*, Ithaca, NY: Cornell University Press.

Whitfield, D. (2001) *Public Services or Corporate Welfare? Rethinking the Nation State in the Global Economy*, Sterling, VA, London: Pluto Press.

World Bank (1999) *World Development Report 1999/2000: Rethinking Government*, WB/OUP.

World Bank (2000) *World Development Report 2000/2001: Attacking Poverty*, WB/OUP.

4 The emergence of the 'de-centred' British state

Peter Fairbrother

Introduction

Since 1980, the British state as an employer has changed in complex and contradictory ways. In the context of increasing difficulties with private capital accumulation, growing trade union militancy in the state sector and a shift in government ideology, governments began to impose more stringent financial regimes on state services and to restructure the control of the work process. These changes involved the recomposition of public sector managements with the emergence of the practice of 'new public management' (NPM). Of increasing importance, the structure and organisation of the public sector has been recomposed, the boundaries of the public services were redrawn, via privatisation policies, and public service provision has been reorganised so that combinations of public and private institutions increasingly provide these services. The result is a de-centred state, where institutional unity and universal provision have been replaced by institutional fragmentation and uneven provision, according to various and varied criteria.

In key areas of state administration, managerial hierarchies were recomposed, amounting to a major qualification of bureaucratised relations, characterised by layered relations of responsibility and attenuated lines of seniority. One strategy of change involved the recomposition of managerial and worker relations, within a neo-liberal framework, through the establishment of marketised state labour processes. This has been a complicated process, involving both routinised administrative workers as well as professionals, who have some degree of autonomy and discretion in the course of their work and employment. The class composition was reconfigured, so that a stratum of the public service was defined as 'management' and the remainder as state workers (Carter and Fairbrother, 1995; Foster and Scott, 1998; Carter and Fairbrother, 1999; Fairbrother and Poynter, 2001).

A second strategy involved both the reconfiguration of management structures and privatisation, redefining the boundaries and reorganisation of the state apparatus. Moving beyond definitions of privatisation where the emphasis is on ownership and the transfer of assets from the public sector to the private sector, a range of public sector functions have been externalised and out-sourced (for a further refinement of this argument, see Carter *et al.*, 2002). The result is a permeable set of relations defining the public sector, where there is a mix of responsibility between public sector enterprises and the private sector for the provision of public sector functions. In addition, there is the further complication that sections of the public sector have entered into market relations with each other, for the provision of public sector goods and services.

The context for such a reconfiguration of employment relations in the state is a developing concern by successive governments with the financial basis of public services (Whitfield, 2001). Governments attempted to ease the taxation burden through restrictions on government expenditure and the selling of assets aimed at reducing the public sector borrowing requirement (Farnham and Horton, 1993). Governments also took steps to recast work and employment relations, giving increased attention to public sector pay and working practices, against the backdrop of a more militant public sector unionism in the 1970s and 1980s (Fairbrother, 1989). More recently, during the 1990s and into the new millennium, governments have attempted to redraw the relations between the state as employer and trade unions, the aim being to narrow the scope of industrial relations and marginalise public service trade unionism (cf. Carter and Fairbrother, 1999). Such developments raise questions about class relations within the state and the bases of political mobilisation, questions that are addressed below.

There are three stages to the argument. In the first, the way in which the state has been restructured is reviewed. This process has resulted in the distancing of state responsibility for the direct management of labour while at the same time maintaining control over the provision of public services via budgetary mechanisms. In the second, the implications of these developments for workers and their trade unions in the provision of public services are explored. Finally in the last stage of the argument, the analysis is drawn together and prospects identified.

The 'de-centred' state

The modern state has been transformed over the past twenty-five years, from a bureaucratised state, underpinned by social democratic themes, to one where the state has been de-centred, in accordance with the prescriptions of liberal market ideologies. In this process of restructuring there are three motifs of change – modernisation, marketisation and non-state provision.

Modernisation

A major theme that has increasingly informed the debates about managerialism is that of 'modernisation', most clearly illustrated and articulated with reference to central government (elaborated more extensively in Carter and Fairbrother, 1999 and Carter *et al.*, 2002). While the structure and focus of central government had long been subject to enquiry and debate, in the 1980s this took a particular twist. The core idea in the 1980s was that there must be improved management so as to deliver better services within available resources, and that the most appropriate way to accomplish this objective was to draw on the private sector example. This assessment was supported by an emergent view that central government was not equipped to meet the demands of an increasingly internationalised economy.

The first stage of this process, by a series of Conservative governments during the 1980s, was to impose a sharper financial regime on state services and further the imposition of direct managerial control. Building on earlier initiatives (such as the Priestley Report, 1955; Maud Report, 1967 and the Bains Report, 1972), these governments introduced a sea change, with the result that over a decade the civil service, for example, was refashioned as an increasingly managerial employer. The principal means of achieving this goal was two-fold. First, the organisation of the civil service as a universal provider of services was increasingly qualified by measures aimed at introducing layered responsibilities for the provision of these services. The government introduced a series of measures aimed at securing financial assessments of the effective and efficient provision of services, known as the Financial Management Initiative (White Paper, 1982). Second, these governments built on these procedures and recast the civil service in terms of agencies and executive offices, semi-autonomous managerial structures, with discretion to provide services or goods according to proxy market criteria and indicators, known as the Next Steps programme (Ibbs Report, 1988). In the 1990s, the establishment of agencies fragmented state structures, so that the service-wide standards and practices of the past were no longer applicable. The outcome was a restructured labour process and a change in the dominant mode of control of labour in this sector. Class relations at the point of production were recomposed, so that a differentiation between a middle class and a working class became more apparent (Carter and Fairbrother, 1995).

While Conservative governments during the 1980s and the first half of the 1990s initiated and elaborated these measures, with the election of New Labour in 1997 the restructuring of the civil service continued and in some ways intensified. There was further privatisation of the civil service and continuation of the Next Steps project; although of even more significance was the elaboration of the Modernising Government Programme (Cabinet Office, 2001). One feature of the New Labour programme is that the government pursued a policy of extending the lessons of the civil service to public services in general. Thus, while change had been introduced across the board during the Conservative period, it tended to be sector by sector – health services, local government, civil service and so on – whereas under New Labour a more wide-ranging and integrated conception of modernisation was embraced.

Promoted by Prime Minister Blair, the modernisation programme outlines a form of public service management that rests on an adaptation of private sector business practices. The result is an attempt to graft onto the civil service a process of governance that encompasses a form of public administration that is cast as more responsive to citizens and, perhaps more significantly, to 'business'. This twin focus guides the continued construction of the managerial state under New Labour.

There was a claim by the New Labour government that the reforms of the Conservative period had been positive, even if cast in a framework of hostility to the public sector. Thus the White Paper on modernising government stated:

> Public service has for too long been neglected, undervalued and denigrated. It has suffered from a perception that the private sector was always best and the public sector was always inefficient. The Government rejects these prejudices. But their legacy remains.

Despite that, public services have responded. The reforms of the last two decades in the civil service, for example, have done much to develop a more managerial culture. The quality of management has improved, there is a better focus on developing people to deliver improved performance and there is greater professionalism.

(Cabinet Office, 1999)

For the Prime Minister:

Modernising government is a vital part of our programme of renewal for Britain. The old arguments about government are now outdated – big government against small government, interventionism against laissez-faire. The new issues are the right issues: modernising government, better government, getting government right.

(Cabinet Office, 1999)

These reforms involved a range of measures, across the public services, including competition for senior management positions, the introduction of more comprehensive performance management and performance-related pay systems and in the case of the civil service the re-examination of business planning systems in the main departments (Cabinet Office, 2001).

The pattern of restructuring the public services thus took three steps. First, there was a relatively limited attempt to reform managerial practice, involving the beginning of devolution of managerial responsibility to a localised level, across the public services. Second, this was followed towards the end of the 1980s, and into the 1990s, with a comprehensive re-institutionalisation of the public services, in the case of the civil service, with the creation of Agencies, as semi-autonomous and discrete managerial bodies. Finally, with the election of New Labour in 1997, the organisation and focus of the public services was addressed, with a view to creating a managerial state. Each stage had different but cumulative consequences for management–worker relations, and thus for state sector trade unions.

Marketisation

The moves to create managerial public services were accompanied by the increased marketisation of workplace relations (for a more developed and extensive account, see Fairbrother and Poynter, 2001 and Carter *et al.*, 2002). In part reflected in the early programmes of privatisation, but more critically a feature of the provision of public services, irrespective of ownership, successive governments during this period, and particularly during the 1990s and the early part of the twenty-first century, refashioned the public sector. Drawing on concepts relating to public choice theory, and interestingly elaborated in a most cogent way by the New Zealand governments of the 1980s, market relations became a feature of the British public services (Treasury, 1984, 1987; see also Chapter 7 in this volume).

One aspect of the argument about public choice that was embraced by successive governments was that the formerly 'bureaucratised' public services were both ossified and subject to 'producer capture' (on local government, see Foster and Scott, 1998: 109–115). Although of general applicability, the 'producer capture' argument was developed specifically in relation to education, health and welfare and less so central government. The core idea in this argument enabled governments to justify a range of *reforms* that were aimed at the marketisation of these services. It was argued that the provision of public services would be more efficient, effective and accountable if the assumed authority of professionals in decision-making was curtailed to purely technical or 'professional' matters (e.g. on the National Health Service – NHS, see the Griffiths Report, 1983, and on education, see Barber, 1992). The key point is that the move to disenfranchise professional and staff input was a condition for the marketisation of these services.

Complementing the de-professionalisation of public services, governments of this period developed a comprehensive privatisation programme, which in a number of ways became the benchmark for countries such as New Zealand and Australia (see Chapters 5 and 6). There were two sides to this process, both of which facilitated the marketisation of the public services. On one side, the privatisation of key areas of the public sector, such as the utilities and other state-owned enterprises (SOEs), during the 1980s was the occasion for repositioning these enterprises in a market context, with the conventional managerial and shareholding structures that are associated with the private sector. On the other side, and in turn, the remaining public sector (central government, local government, education and health) was marketised from within. As indicated, the civil service, as the core of the public sector, was transformed in a sequential way, initially by reconstituting class relations within the civil service (Carter and Fairbrother, 1995), followed by an opening up of service provision within the public sector to market relations (Fairbrother and Poynter, 2001). These *reforms* took the form of out-sourcing, market-testing and eventually public–private partnerships (PPPs), or a cumulative process of incorporating 'business practices' into the heartland of public service provision (Davies, 1991; Poynter, 2000).

The outcome of these changes is that the public services became in effect profit-oriented enterprises (Farnham and Horton, 1993). The outward signs of this recomposition of work relations involved business units or profit centres in the privatised sector, cost centres and the like in central and local government, internal markets in the health sector and localised budget-holding in education. Irrespective of the form of accounting in each sector, the crucial point to note is that public services were provided via a series of measurable financial indicators. Associated with this shift in practice, the work relations in each sector were recomposed with more visible and formerly accountable managements in place. The result was a marketised public service.

Public–private providers

These changes were not restricted to the public services alone, and there has been an increasing opaqueness in the relations between the public and private sectors. Apart from modelling the managerial reorganisation on the supposed advantages of the business management, there has been a cumulative embrace of the private sector, as the source of finance, the model of good practice and the exemplar of efficiency and *market* needs. The sequence has been out-sourcing and contracting-out in the 1980s, the Private Finance Initiative (PFI) in the early 1990s, followed by the PPP in the late 1990s and early 2000s. Rather than discreteness between the public and private sectors, there has been an increased permeability between the two in the provision of public services.

Thus, the outcome of twenty years of public service reform is a new form of public service provision. Theoretically, there has been a shift in public service provision from a universalistic system based on notions of welfare redistribution and citizenship rights to one where the focus is on market-based outcomes (Pollitt, 1990). These ideas have had a relatively long gestation period, initially elaborated in the 1980s, but retained as the core idea and indeed elaborated in distinctive ways by the New Labour Government elected in 1997 and re-elected in 2001 (Cabinet Office, 1999). The distinctiveness derives from the rhetoric of social responsibility and inclusion, while in practice the market remains central to the provision of public services in the New Labour world (Whitfield, 2001).

At a practical level, these changes have meant a markedly new experience for citizens who are dependent on or are beneficiaries of public services. For those who rely on public services, eligibility is no longer straightforward and rests on conceptions of the beneficiary as a potentially productive citizen or a rather selfish dependent and the provider as an 'efficient' and 'economical' supplier (Wilson and Game, 1998). For others wanting to use services such as transport or the utilities, they have become customers with all the peripheral language and experience that this term implies (for an extensive discussion of such developments, see Fairbrother and Poynter, 2001). The slow evolution of this practice received a fillip with the election of New Labour. While initially the Labour government retained the infrastructure of a managerial and marketised public sector, complemented by a privatised former public sector, the policies have been developed in such a way that public services have been redefined as a necessary but privately financed and non-accountable provision. Whether transport, health services, education, local government or central government services, the *leitmotif* is a 'pragmatic', supposedly non-ideological provision of services that is financially based and defined (Blair, 2001a). Such an elaboration is the opposite of the universal, socially humane rhetoric of the past (Crossland, 1956). Rather, the embrace of private sector interests has resulted in the gradual construction of 'instrumental, fragmented and financially-based public services which are accountable to private interests' (Carter *et al.*, 2002: 46).

The de-centred state

There are three decisive developments to this reconceptualisation of the public services, theoretically and in practice. First, public services should be provided by the private sector, as an integral part of a transformed public sector. Second, there has been a fragmentation of public service provision, reflected in two ways, as a set of institutions that have increasingly divergent remits and in terms of policy where there is little sign of co-ordinated and coherent approaches to the provision of public services. Third, the idea of public accountability has been narrowed, so that it no longer resides in democratically elected forums but in appointed public bodies and/or stakeholders, usually shareholders.

The first point to note is that the decisive step in laying the foundation for the prevalence of private sector interests came with the introduction of the PFI programme, introduced by a Conservative government in 1992 (Treasury, 1992) as the next step for the public services as a whole. This initiative was taken up by public sector managements as a way of ensuring capital project development in the civil service, education, health and local government (Kerr, 1998). However, the PFI remained a limited programme until New Labour, when it became the preferred one, if not the only option for capital projects across the public sector (Gershon Report, 1999; Treasury Select Committee, 2000). These programmes now fall under the label of the PPP.

The second feature of the past twenty years of state restructuring has been the affirmation of a fragmented and divided public service provision. Under successive Conservative governments, the modernisation and marketisation of the public services took place in a series of discrete and relatively self-contained initiatives, although throughout the Conservative period (1979–1997), there was an over-arching view that private sector organisation and approach was the exemplar of change. With the election of a New Labour government this thrust was not only maintained but also developed despite a rhetoric on joined up governance. In a series of statements, Prime Minister Blair has focused on the organisation and operation of the public services as a problem and the improvement of the public service as a key goal of the government (e.g. Blair, 2001a,b).

Thus, one key aspect of the 'modernising government' agenda is the need to overcome the debilitating consequences of fragmentation and the solution is deemed to lie in holistic or joined-up governance. The findings of a recent parliamentary inquiry succinctly sum up the problem:

> The focus of joining-up government has largely been on the centre, concentrating on how Whitehall departments can be persuaded or cajoled to abandon their 'silo' mentality and to work together to produce better and more co-ordinated policy-making and service delivery. We heard evidence about the difficulties in co-ordinating service delivery due to the vertical organisation of departments (a function both of traditional measures of public accountability and of bureaucratic hierarchy). Many of the most intractable problems of modern government have a horizontal or inter-connected nature – for example, social exclusion encompasses a range of issues and multiple departmental responsibilities.
>
> (House of Commons Public Administration Select Committee, 2001: vi)

A second set of problems relate to the pressures on government to develop policy initiatives from the top down, often at the cost of local involvement, participation and ownership, as stated:

> Government in Britain is distinguished by a culture of administrative centralism, which – along with departmentalism – presents a key challenge to any sustained attempt to make the machinery of government work better. Programmes driven

top-down from the centre often seem to offer the opportunity for speedy delivery, and hence fit with the imperatives for individual Ministers to be seen to make a difference to policy-making in relatively short time periods. But this approach can be at the expense of building up the local strategic capacity that will be required for durable results, and where new top-down programmes are initiated in rapid succession, and without much genuine evaluation of what is working and what is not, the result can be actively inimical to the sustained development of good public service delivery on the ground. It is essential that there is local ownership of programmes, including shared ownership of performance measures that are used to evaluate them. There is also the danger that a top-down and centrally-driven approach will worsen the already considerable problems of co-ordination at local and regional level...It is essential that joining-up at the centre is matched by equivalent joining-up as initiatives pass through the system.

(House of Commons Public Administration
Select Committee, 2001: vii)

However, while the problem is specified, albeit in terms of structures and procedures, the solution is not promoted. One of the main reasons for the poor record of delivery, according to the director of the government's Performance and Innovation Unit, is because 'practical experience' has been consistently under-valued relative to the formal skills of 'writing elegant minutes and memoranda or legislation'. To overcome these barriers of delivery, he recommended a number of urgent reforms – in particular the need to reward front-line experience and the need to introduce more practitioners into the early stages of the policy-making process so as to reduce the gap between design and delivery (Mulgan, 2001, Question 840). Such a suggestion, of course, is the opposite to the supposed dangers of 'professional capture'. Instead of embracing a different trajectory, with its emphasis on integrated and participative arrangements, the government in practice maintains an unqualified commitment to fragmented and hierarchical administrative structures and practices.

The third feature of the emergent British state is the increasing democratic deficit in relation to the organisation and operation of public services, despite significant constitutional developments in recent years. On the question of ownership, recent governments, including the New Labour government not only promote private ownership as the most desirable form of ownership for the public services, but also appear to be willing to go to almost any lengths to avoid any return to public ownership. In a series of examples where privatised public services have had major failures in service provision, such as rail transport or health service, successive governments have refused to countenance a return to public ownership, even when the public indicate support for such solutions (for detail, see Carter *et al.*, 2002: 45–48). Thus, there is an unwillingness to countenance any revision of the prevailing arguments about ownership.

However, one decisive step taken by the New Labour government has been to revise the constitutional settlement that underpins the British state, with the promotion of devolved forms of government since 1999 (Hazell, 2000). In theory the advent of devolved assemblies, such as the Scottish Parliament and the Welsh Assembly government, should allow these governments to address the deficiencies of current arrangements, to facilitate participative and involved forms of public service provision. Compared with previous arrangements, these bodies have the potential to enhance two dimensions of joined-up governance: vertically, giving a stronger and more legitimate voice to citizens when dealing with national government or the European Union as well as within the community; horizontally, providing for better policy integration, both in formulation and implementation. As well as new institutional structures the language of governance has changed – these governments have set a high premium on inclusivity and there is also a greater recognition that the policy-making process in these regions needs to be more iterative (with more bottom-up inputs for example).

However, while there is potential for change, albeit within specific regional contexts, there is little evidence of a revised assessment of the thrust of state sector restructuring, either nationally or regionally. Rather, the emphasis remains that of securing the continued private sector engagement and involvement in public service provision, via various forms of partnership and involvement, such as a recent advocacy of mutual forms of ownership (Mayo and Moore, 2001). What is no longer acceptable is the active involvement of public service employees on the one hand or the citizens on the other in public service policy formulation and provision. Rather, the thrust remains one of public service provision via a mix of private and public provision and the appointment of public bodies with little or no accountability to citizens and the workers who provide these services.

Public service workers and their unions

With the institutional and procedural reorganisation of the public services, there has been a re-making of state labour. Workers in this sector have faced a dramatic transformation in their work organisation and their employment relations. In the course of these developments, the prevailing forms of collective organisation, via trade unions, faced a series of challenges, which threatened to undermine the traditional approaches to union organisation and activity in this sector.

The re-making of state labour

The aim of successive governments has been to create a situation that ensured the 'free operation of product and labour markets' (Carter *et al.*, 2002: 48). During the 1980s and into the 1990s, managerial hierarchies were recomposed, performance measures were introduced, with consequences for the organisation of work in the public services, and workforces were employed on varied employment contracts (Power, 1997). Complementing this development, governments introduced legislation to restrict and curtail collective organisation and action for all workers, although against the backdrop of increasingly active public sector unionism (Fairbrother, 1989). These measures were maintained under New Labour governments, with a particularly strong defence of individualised employment relations.

The ready embrace of public choice arguments (noted above) by successive governments during the 1980s and 1990s has had important consequences for the work and employment configuration of the public services. Throughout the period there has been a steady erosion of the direct control and discretion exercised by professionals *qua* professionals, although there is an unevenness to this when areas such as health are compared with some of the other component areas of the public services (on nursing, see Adams *et al.*, 2000). The complement to this development has been the increased managerialism of the public services, and much sharper and visible delineation on the organisation of public service workers between managers and workers. In this process, local managements have assumed responsibility for designated budgetary matters, employee disposition and activity and the promotion of public services at this level; nonetheless, this devolution of responsibility was accompanied by a centralisation of strategic decision-making, financial disbursement and policy formulation, despite the apparent institutional and political devolution that marked the period.

Alongside the moves towards a more transparent managerial stratum in the public services, there has been a process of introducing a series of indirect controls over work-force performance. In a variety of ways public service performance is now counted, measured and catalogued. These measurements may take the form of performance tables in different public service areas of employment, with staff assessed in terms of waiting lists and operation rates (health service), literacy and numeracy assessments (education), passenger numbers (transport) and job placement (employment services). While in themselves such measures may be important in assessing the performance of an institution, the point is that such procedures are increasingly used to assess and evaluate work performance, either directly or indirectly. They become the yardstick for assessing productivity, competence and worth in the new public services.

Not surprisingly, against this backdrop, it can be argued that there has been a marked intensification of labour in the public services. The devolution of managerial responsibility and move towards performance measurement provide the ingredients for such a development. Increasingly workers find themselves in situations where they are directly and indirectly assessed in relation to their competencies and their performance. More broadly, public service workers, in the context of continued antipathy towards universal and standardised provision, face pressures to contain costs and improve productivity. Thus, work relations are defined in relation to a parcel of related developments: privatisation, out-sourcing, contracting-out, market-testing and PPPs. As part of this redefinition of work relations, there has been a major intensification of work, as indicated by hours worked, work and performance measurement and the recomposition of management hierarchies in these different areas of employment.

A further effect of the *reforms* during the 1980s and 1990s is that public service workers have experienced moves towards decentralised pay arrangements and flexible pay practices (White and Hatchett, 2001). More surprisingly, pay arrangements did not alter markedly during this period and the pattern of distribution was more or less in line with the past. Overall, there was a fall in comparative pay levels for these workers, with evidence of ongoing pay discrimination between male and female workers and problems in recruiting and retaining public service workers (White and Hatchett, 2001). It would appear that the election of the New Labour government in 1997 and the elaboration of the 'Modernising Government' programme had little or no impact on pay levels and outcomes.

Overall, the public service workforce has been recomposed and reconfigured during this period. It is a workforce that has undergone dramatic change, reflected most sharply in the recomposition of managerial hierarchies and the repositioning of public service workers. This is a workforce that faces an externally driven agenda of change, in the name of modernisation, and where work performance is measured and assessed in novel ways (for the public services). Central to this new form of public service provision is employment uncertainty and a tendency by governments to blame these workers for the apparent failures of the new institutions that are emerging, although such an accusation is denied at the most senior levels (Blair, 2001a,b). These are beleaguered workers facing an uncertain and clouded future, and in such circumstances it is not surprising that these same workers look to their collective organisations, their trade unions, for relief and support.

Unions in the public services

The reconfiguration of the state apparatus aimed, in part, to undermine the basis of collective organisation, thereby weakening trade union influence within the state. During the 1970s and the 1980s, public sector unions had emerged as potentially powerful and influential groupings, reflected in the patterning of major disputes that, almost without exception, occurred in the public rather than the private sector (Fairbrother, 1989). In view of this development, one of the prime objections of governments during this period was to undermine and marginalise unions in the state sector. One strand of policy was successive legislation during the 1980s and into the 1990s aimed at restricting the activity of unions as well as recasting the organisational basis of unions, via rules relating to union elections and other related arrangements. A second strand was to create public sector enterprises where managerial modes of work organisation prevailed and union influence was necessarily minimised. Thus in the context of the profound restructuring of the social relations of service and public sector provision, the conditions and circumstances of union organisation and practice also shifted.

Public service unions have retained relatively high levels of membership density; throughout the 1980s and 1990s membership remained high (Waddington, 1992). In the mid- to late 1990s, union membership density in the public sector was around 60 per cent, compared with private sector union membership density of around 20 per cent (Cully and Woodland, 1996: 220; Hicks, 2000: 334). While there has been an important degree of continuity in membership levels, it is also the case that there was a major shift in the balance of power between unions and employers during this period, to the advantage of employers on a number of issues. However, this has not been a straightforward process and unions have responded to the changed terrain of public service industrial relations in a number of ways.

Overall, there has been a decisive shift in the balance of power towards public service managements (Froud *et al.*, 1996). This shift has taken place in the context of profound changes in the managerial hierarchies in the public services (both public and private) with associated reformation of negotiating and bargaining relationships within these services. More specifically, it has been the case that public service managements have re-established negotiating and bargaining arrangements in the light of the changed relations between management and employers and in the context of the market relations that now prevail in the public services. The result is a reconfigured industrial relations world for the public services.

Nonetheless, the outcomes of these changed relations have been variable. On the one hand, as already noted, public service managements have been successful in introducing new forms of skill mix that reinforce the changes that have taken place in the reconfiguration of managerial hierarchies, as well as achieving an intensification of work across the public services (on the health services, see Adams *et al.*, 2000). On the other hand, public service workers, via their trade unions, have been successful in either opposing specific measures or ameliorating the harsher effects of policy, such as the ongoing resistance to the introduction of local or regionally based pay arrangements, particularly in the civil service and the NHS (Thornley, 1998; see also Bailey, 1994 and Beadle, 1995), the rejection or qualification of proposals for performance appraisal and the extension of team-based pay in areas of the civil service, and the complex struggles over 'best practice' initiatives in local government. These responses, and others, are part of the continued effectiveness in patterns of representation and collective organisation at local and national levels in many public service unions during this period (Fairbrother, 2000: 26–62).

Throughout this period of work and employment reorganisation, public service workers have responded in quite active ways, despite the range of legislative restrictions regulating strikes and related forms of action. Going back to the early 1970s, the trade unions that organised in the public services actively responded to government policies on work and employment conditions, as well as the early steps in public sector restructuring (Fairbrother, 1989). Throughout the 1980s and 1990s, these unions campaigned to defend themselves in a seemingly hostile work and employment environment. While this action was largely defensive in its focus, towards the end of the 1990s, there was evidence that these unions were beginning to rediscover a confidence and assertiveness in their activities that had not been evident previously. This growing confidence was apparent in two ways. First, in a range of disputes, workers undertook unofficial and official action in defence of their terms and conditions of employment, displaying a degree of co-ordination across workplaces within the same company or across companies that was relatively novel, in the post office and the railways respectively. Second, in a series of elections for senior union positions, left-wing and dissident leaders were elected, much to the chagrin of the New Labour government. The emergence of such leaderships sanctioned a more critical assessment of government policies and has been associated with a distancing that is beginning to appear between a number of these unions and the Labour Party. While this disquiet involves a broader range of policies and practices than those associated with the restructuring of the public services, it is the case that a core concern of trade unions is the attempt by New Labour to manage the public services at a distance.

The upshot is that trade unions remain key actors in the process of public service restructuring. The central point of these observations is that in the context of the profound restructuring of the social relations of public service provision, the conditions and circumstances of union organisation and practice also shifted. Against the backdrop of highly centralised forms of union organisation in the public services, and given the specificity of the restructuring of social relations, there was, as a consequence, the possibility of the emergence of distinctive and different forms of unionism. These are the prospects that will now be explored.

Unions repositioning themselves

With the restructuring of the public services, the prospects for unions went through some dramatic shifts. The first step in this process was a move within some unions to lay the foundation for more devolved and localised forms of representation and negotiation. Initially, the devolution of managerial responsibility to the office level opened up the prospect of wider bargaining opportunities at this level of organisation, providing the occasion for the active involvement of layers of union activists who previously would have played little active part in this area of activity. Such a refocusing of activity was most evident with unions that organised local authority and NHS staffs, but also with civil service staff (Fryer *et al.*, 1974; Drake *et al.*, 1980, 1982; Fairbrother, 1996). However, such refocusing was contested in some of these unions. In the highly centralised unions in the civil service, for example, where during the early 1980s the two main unions were under the control and influence of political machines, of the left in one and the right in the other, both leaderships remained committed to centralised forms of bargaining, in part as the condition for ensuring political control over the membership. As a result, the moves made to broaden the bargaining agenda at a local level were something that took place in the absence of national leadership involvement and, occasionally, in the face of outright hostility. It was thus often a detached process of reorganisation at the local level.

The importance of the first stage of union responses to state restructuring was that it produced a new generation of members who became used to a more direct involvement in union affairs at the local level. The model of the workplace steward was both encouraged and promoted, although often against a background of debate about how to best direct the activity of such representatives (Fairbrother, 1984: 88–95). Equally important, this was a period in which local bargaining and disputes became more common, accompanied by the emergence of more activist workplace stewards in greater numbers than previously (Fairbrother, 1994). The union density of almost all public sector unions was maintained during this period; workplace unions became part of the representative structures, with office negotiations becoming common, particularly on matters such as working conditions (Marsh, 1992; Fairbrother, 1994, 1996; Carter and Fairbrother, 1995).

The second step in the process of union reorganisation was merger and amalgamation, where, in part, unions sought to track the changes that were taking place in the restructuring of work and employment relations as well as prepare for ongoing change. The most notable merger in the early 1990s was that of the three principal unions representing workers in local government, the NHS and many of the privatised utilities, the National Union of Public Employees, the National and Local Government Association and the Confederation of Health Service Employees. The resulting union, Unison, established in 1993, became the largest in Britain, with nearly a million and a half members. Five years later, the then two largest civil service unions merged, although these two constituent unions were themselves the products of earlier mergers. Such developments were part of the reconstitution of union organisation in these sectors.

One important consequence of this recomposition is that during the 1980s and 1990s, the locus of union membership in the British trade union movement as a whole had shifted from the manufacturing and extractive industries to the public services. As part of this reconfiguration, the membership composition has changed, with an increasing proportion of female and black members in unions that recruit in the public services. A feature of these developments is that these unions are now dominant players in the union movement. By 1998, 7 of the 16 unions with 100,000 members or more organised predominantly in the public service areas, while a number of other unions had reasonably large clusters of members in these areas (for more details, see Fairbrother, 2002).

Thus, the pattern of union membership is changing in decisive ways, albeit slowly. While these changes and developments took place over a period of twenty years and did not comply with any straightforward sequencing or order of change, the outcome was a union movement that structurally was in a position to address the ongoing rigours of public service restructuring. The outcome is a tension within these unions between pressures for an older form of unionism, based on centralised and compliant approaches, and an emergent form where the emphasis is on local initiative, where members are able and encouraged to participate and where the balance between local and national leaderships is towards the former rather than the latter (for an elaboration of this argument, see Fairbrother, 1996, 2000). Although in practice the working-out of such tensions is partial, contradictory and subject to disputation and struggle within unions, it is also the case that there is a complex relationship between the process of public service restructuring and the forms of collective organisation and activity that are in the process of emerging (a complexity that industrial relations analyses fail to grasp, see McIlroy, 1997 and Kelly, 1996).

In effect, the complex process of depoliticisation, embodied in public sector restructuring and privatisation over the past twenty years, paradoxically provided the space for unions to review how they organise and operate. It is in this context that there have been marked debates about the direction of change and its significance, often around the question of whether there has been a renewal of unionism in this sector or not (Colling, 1995; Fairbrother, 1996, 2000; Kelly, 1996, 1998; McIlroy, 1997; Heery, 1998; Gall, 1998; Carter and Poynter, 1999). While there is an overall acknowledgement that the situation for unions organising in the public services has changed over the past twenty years, there is disputation about the nature and character of unionism that may or may not be emerging in this context. Nonetheless, there are a number of incontrovertible points to note. First, public service unions have maintained a significant presence both locally and nationally, throughout this period, in a way that their counterparts in the private sector have not managed (Fairbrother, 1989, 2000). Second, there has been a move within these unions to develop more localised and participative forms of representation, when compared with the past (e.g. Fairbrother *et al.*, 1996, 2000). Third, most of the major disputes in the 1980s and 1990s where union memberships have questioned the thrust and direction of employer strategies have involved public service workers and their unions. Fourth, such developments and experiences do not make for easy trade union-ism and these unions have been marked by often debilitating internal disputes as well as the emergence over the past few years of a new generation of left-leaning leaders. In this context, these unions have begun to question the ongoing relationship between unions and a Labour Party committed to furthering public service restruc-turing, albeit in less strident ways than under the previous Conservative regimes. On balance, it is reasonable to argue that these unions have undergone a complex process of renewal, so that these unions are structured and organised to enable debate and decision about their future direction and the policies they will pursue, a situation that did not apply in an earlier period.

Conclusion

The current phase of restructuring the British state has been in process for almost three decades. These shifts took place against a background where the public services had long been organised in centralised and hierarchical ways. In the context of increasing difficulties with private capital accumulation, growing trade union mili-tancy in the state sector and changes in government ideology, successive governments began to impose more stringent financial regimes on state services and to restructure the control of the work process. The outcome was a managerial and marketised state as the modern form of the capitalist state.

There were three inter-related elements to this restructuring process. First, there was a transformation of the bureaucratised relations of the past. This transformation involved a re-articulation of managerial and worker relations, in the direction of a recomposition of managerial hierarchies in the state sector, with a stratum of the public service defined as 'management' and the remainder as state workers. However, this was a complex process of change, involving the partial decomposition of managerial hierarchies and their recomposition in complex ways. As part of these developments, there has been a fragmentation of the previously relatively unified public services.

Second, the marketisation of work and employment relations was such that work and employment relations within the public sector were recast and the boundaries that defined the public sector were redrawn. As these *reforms* proceeded, the conventional understanding of the public services as owned and operated via the state was qualified and a public service sector partly under public ownership and partly under private own-ership and operation emerged; although of equal significance, the remaining public sector was increasingly characterised by market-type relations. The result was a per-meable relation between the public and private sectors in the provision of public services.

Third, work and employment relations in the public services have been trans-formed, from standardised and uniform work and employment relations to a much more variegated pattern of relations, marked by flexible practices, work intensification and work insecurity. These developments have been associated with not only emer-gence of a managerial stratum in the public services but also increased managerial dis-cretion. The outcome is a reconstituted state–labour process and a workforce that faces an intensification of work, involving all layers of employment, including professional workers. Thus, the relative anonymity of managerial staff, located and regulated within extended administratively controlled hierarchies, has ended. Under the NPM these staffs are highly visible and identifiable, involved less and less in a collective labour process and more and more in the control and supervision of the work of others.

The outcome was a paradoxical depoliticisation of the state apparatus. On the one hand, direct government engagement in management and labour relations in the state sector was minimised; on the other hand, the opaqueness of the traditional managerial relations in the state sector was stripped away as the reconfiguration of managerial hierarchies proceeded. This is a 'managerial' state where policies are presented in a 'depoliticised' way, as technical or non-political solutions, such as the provision of health care, the organisation of education, the provision of state benefits or the implementation of economic policies. Complementing this development, relations between management and labour have been recast away from the impersonal rule-bound management of the past and subjected to assessments in terms of market-type measures and assessments. As part of this feature of the new public services, work and employment relations have been individualised, with flexible forms of work and employment in the context of public service labour markets.

The restructuring of the public sector was driven by successive governments seeking to create what was seen as the basis for a modern capitalist state. These *reforms* were imposed in a top-down fashion, even after the constitutional re-settlement of the late 1990s. In this process the place of unions in the state sector polity changed dramatically. Those unions that organised public service workers found themselves marginalised from the early 1980s onwards and facing a hostile and unsympathetic employer, a situation that continued even after the New Labour government was elected in 1997. Nonetheless, this observation is not to suggest that unions were without influence. Despite the vicissitudes of the 1980s and 1990s, unions within the public services very much remained the voice of state workers and the uncertainties evident in the political struggles within some of these unions, between factions as well as between an emergent activist layer of local representatives and more cautious national leaderships, were a reflection of their continued presence and relevance. Thus whilst unions were excluded from any formal role in the process of reorganisation, and indeed attempted to oppose the thrust of the reforms, their continued presence remained a factor in the shaping of the emergent public services.

With the election of the Labour government in 1997, there was an expectation that the thrust of the reorganisation of the public services that had taken place would shift. Whilst it would be wrong to argue that there has been no change under New Labour, it also would be misleading to suggest that the broad brush of state restructuring, with the emphasis on managerialism and marketisation, has not continued. Indeed, in some ways there has been a decisive shift against trade unions under New Labour. For New Labour trade unions are a necessary interest group, along with business interests in all their guises, but increasingly one that should be secondary to the expressed concerns of business. Hence the embrace of the politics of partnership involves the espousal of a set of relationships where the parameters are defined in terms of the interests of capital rather than labour, whether such developments take the form of the PPP for public service provision or the partnership agreements between employers and trade unions over union recognition and representation. The point here is that unions remain marginalised and thus must look to themselves for solace and direction.

The key issue at stake in this complex history is that the modern state has been remoulded over the past two and a half decades, from a welfare state to a managerial state, where market relations prevail. The outcome is a decentred state, one where the ideal of institutional unity and universal provision has been replaced by institutional fragmentation, an uneven service and an individualised provision. But this has not been and is not a unilinear and irrevocable process; rather this process of change has been contradictory, contested and uneven. It is within this complex of developments that unions, as the voice of workers in the public services, may find their place as the defenders of a more involved and participative form of public service provision, involving the community and those who benefit from public services, in all their forms. In short, the tensions at the heart of the modern state provide the foundation for a popular mobilisation for publicly provided public services. It is this prospect that provides the continued rationale for and basis of collective organisation and action in and against the state.

References

Adams, A., Lugsden, E., Chase, J., Arber, S. and Bond, S. (2000) 'Skill-Mix Changes and Work Intensification in Nursing', *Work, Employment and Society*, 14(3): 541–556.

Bailey, R. (1994) 'Annual Review Article 1993: British Public Sector Industrial Relations', *British Journal of Industrial Relations*, 32(1): 113–136.

[Bains Report] (1972) Study Group on Local Authority Management Structure, *The New Local Authorities: Management and Structure*, London: HMSO.

Barber, M. (1992) *Education and the Teacher Unions*, London: Cassell.

Beadle, R. (1995) 'Opting Out of Pay Devolution? The Prospects for Local Pay Bargaining in UK Public Services: A Comment', *British Journal of Industrial Relations*, 33(1): 137–142.

Blair, T. (2001a) 'Blair: Trust Me on Public Services', *Guardian*, 11 September.

Blair, T. (2001b) 'Reform of Public Services', speech at Royal Free Hospital in London, 16 July.

Bonefeld, W., Brown, A. and Burnham, P. (1995) *A Major Crisis? The Politics of Economic Policy in Britain in the 1990s*, Aldershot: Dartmouth.

Burnham, P. (1999a) 'The Politics of Economic Manangement in the 1990s', *New Political Economy*, 4(1): 37–54.

Burnham, P. (1999b) 'The Recomposition of National States in the Global Economy: From Politicised to Depoliticised Forms of Labour Regulation', in P. Edwards and T. Elger (eds), *The Global Economy, National States and the Regulation of Labour*, London: Mansell, pp. 42–63.

Cabinet Office (1999) *Modernising Government*, Cm. 4310, London: The Stationery Office.

Cabinet Office (2001) *Civil Service Statistics 2000*, Norwich: HMSO.

Carter, B. and Fairbrother, P. (1995) 'The Remaking of the State Middle Class', in T. Cutler and M. Savage (eds), *The New Middle Class*, London: University College London Press, pp. 133–147.

Carter, B. and Fairbrother, P. (1999) 'The Transformation of British Public-Sector Industrial Relations: From "Model Employer" to Marketized Relations', *Historical Studies in Industrial Relations*, 7(Spring): 119–146.

Carter, B. and Poynter, G. (1999) 'Unions in a Changing Climate: MSF and Unison Experiences in the New Public Sector', *Industrial Relations Journal*, 30(5): 499–513.

Carter, B., Davies, S. and Fairbrother, P. (2002) 'The Rise and Rise of Market Relations in the British Public Sector: Implications for Industrial Relations', *Economic and Labour Relations Review*, 13(1): 36–59.

Certification Office for Trade Unions and Employers' Associations (2000) *Annual Report of the Certification Officer 1999–2000*, London: Brandon House.

Clarke, S. (1990) 'Crisis of Socialism or Crisis of the State', *Capital & Class*, 42: 19–29.

Colling, T. (1995) 'Renewal or Rigor Mortis? Union Responses to Contracting in Local Government', *Industrial Relations Journal*, 26(2): 134–145.

Crossland, C. A. R. (1956) *The Future of Socialism*, First edition, London: Jonothan Cape.

Cully, M. and Woodland, S. (1996) 'Trade Union Membership and Recognition: An Analysis of Data from the 1995 Labour Force Survey', *Labour Market Trends*, 104(5): 215–225.

Davies, S. (1991) *Agenda for the Future: The Civil Service Towards the Twenty First Century*, NUCPS, mimeo.

Drake, P., Fairbrother, P., Fryer, B. and Murphy, J. (1980) *Which Way Forward? An Interim Review of the Issues for the Society of Civil and Public Servants*, Coventry: Department of Sociology, University of Warwick.

Drake, P., Fairbrother, P., Fryer, B. and Stratford, G. (1982) *A Programme for Union Democracy: The Final Report for the Society of Civil and Public Servants*, Coventry: Department of Sociology, University of Warwick.

Fairbrother, P. (1984) *All Those in Favour: The Politics of Union Democracy*, London: Pluto Press.

Fairbrother, P. (1989) 'State Workers: Class Position and Collective Action', in G. Duncan (ed.), *Democracy and the Capitalist State*, Cambridge: Cambridge University Press, pp. 187–213.

Fairbrother, P. (1994) *Politics and the State as Employer*, London: Mansell.

Fairbrother, P. (1996) 'Workplace Trade Unionism in the State Sector', in P. Ackers, C. Smith and P. Smith (eds), *The New Workplace and Trade Unionism*, London: Routledge, pp. 110–148.

Fairbrother, P. (2000) *Trade Unions at the Crossroads*, London: Mansell.

Fairbrother, P. (2002) 'Trade Unions in Britain: Towards a New Unionism', in P. Fairbrother and G. Griffin (eds), *Changing Prospects for Trade Unionism: Comparisons Between Six Countries*, London: Continuum, pp. 56–92.

Fairbrother, P. and Poynter, G. (2001) 'State Restructuring: Managerialism, Marketisation and the Implications for Labour', *Competition and Change*, 5(3): 311–333.

Fairbrother, P., Moore, S. and Poynter, G. (1996) *UNISON Branch Organisation Case Study Reports*, presented to the Strategic Review Committee, UNISON, mimeo, p. 235.

Fairbrother, P., Paddon, M. and Teicher, J. (2002) 'Corporatisation and Privatisation in Australia', in P. Fairbrother, M. Paddon and J. Teicher (eds), *Privatisation, Globalisation and Labour: Studies from Australia*, Annandale, NSW: The Federation Press.

Farnham, D. and Horton, S. (eds) (1993) *Managing the New Public Services*, Basingstoke: Macmillan.

Foster, D. and Scott, P. (1998) 'Competitive Tendering of Public Services and Industrial Relations Policy: The Conservative Agenda under Thatcher and Major, 1979–97', *Historical Studies in Industrial Relations*, 6(Autumn): 101–132.

Froud, J., Haslam, C., Johal, S., Shaoul, J. and Williams, K. (1996) 'Stakeholder Economy? From Utility Privatization to New Labour', *Capital & Class*, 60: 119–134.

Fryer, R., Fairclough, A. and Manson, T. (1974) *Organisation and Change in the National Union of Public Employees*, Coventry: Department of Sociology, University of Warwick.

Gall, G. (1998) 'The Prospects for Workplace Unionism: Evaluating Fairbrother's Union Renewal Thesis', *Capital & Class*, 66: 149–157.

[Gershon Report] Gershon, P. (1999) *Review of Civil Procurement in Central Government*, HM Treasury.

[Griffiths Report] Griffiths, R. (1983) *NHS Management Inquiry*, London: DHSS.

Hazell, R. (ed.) (2000) *The State and the Nations: The First Year of Devolution in the UK*, London: Imprint Academic.

Heery, E. (1998) 'Campaigning for Part-Time Workers', *Work, Employment & Society*, 12(2): 351–366.

Hicks, S. (2000) 'Trade Union Membership 1988–99: An Analysis of Data from the Certification Officer and Labour Force Survey', *Labour Market Trends*, 108(7): 329–339.

House of Commons Public Administration Select Committee (2001) *Making Government Work: The Emerging Issues*, Report and Proceeding of the Committee, Seventh Report, House of Commons, London, HC 94.

[Ibbs Report] Jenkins, K., Caines, K. and Jackson, A. (1988) *Improving Management in Government: The Next Steps*, London: HMSO.

Kelly, J. (1996) 'Union Militancy and Social Partnership', in P. Ackers, C. Smith and P. Smith (eds), *The New Workplace and Trade Unionism*, London: Routledge, pp. 77–109.

Kelly, J. (1998) *Rethinking Industrial Relations*, London: Routledge.

Kerr, D. (1998) 'The PFI Miracle', *Capital & Class*, 64: 17–27.

McIlroy, J. (1997) 'Still under Siege: British Trade Unions at the Turn of the Century', *Historical Studies in Industrial Relations*, 3(March): 93–122.

Marsh, D. (1992) *The New Politics of British Trade Unionism: Union Power and the Thatcher Legacy*, Basingstoke: Macmillan.

[Maud Report] Committee on the Management of Local Government (1967) *Management of Local Government*, London: HMSO.

Mayo, E. and Moore, H. (2001) *The Mutual State: How Local Communities Can Run Public Services*, London: New Economics Foundation.

Mulgan, G. (2001) *Minutes of Evidence to the House of Commons Public Administration Select Committee for Wednesday 17 January 2001*, Minutes of Proceedings, Oral Evidence, House of Commons, London, HC 94-iii.

Pollitt, C. (1990) *Managerialism and the Public Services: The Anglo-American Experience*, Oxford: Blackwell.

Power, M. (1997) *The Audit Society*, Oxford: Oxford University Press.

Poynter, G. (2000) *Restructuring in the Service Industries, Management Reform and Workplace Relations in the UK Service Sector*, London: Mansell.

[Priestley Report] (1955) Report of the Royal Commission on the Civil Service 1953–1955, Cmd. 9613, 1955, London: HMSO.

Thornley, C. (1998) 'Contesting Local Pay: The Decentralization of Collective Bargaining in the NHS', *British Journal of Industrial Relations*, 36(3): 413–434.

Treasury (1984) *Economic Management*, Wellington: Government Printer.

Treasury (1987) *Government Management*, Wellington: Government Printer.

Treasury (1992) *Autumn Statement 1992*, London, November.

Treasury Select Committee Fourth Report (2000) *The Private Finance Initiative*, 23 March 2000.

Waddington, J. (1992) 'Trade Union Membership in Britain, 1980–1987: Unemployment and Restructuring', *British Journal of Industrial Relations*, 30(2): 287–328.

White, G. and Hatchett, A. (2001) *Public Sector Pay under Labour: Change and Continuity 1997–2001*, Paper presented at the 16th Annual Employment Research Unit Conference at Cardiff Business School, Cardiff University, 10–11 September, mimeo.

White Paper (1982) *Efficiency and Effectiveness in the Civil Service*, London: HMSO.

Whitfield, D. (2001) *Public Services or Corporate Welfare? Rethinking the Nation State in the Global Economy*, Sterling VA, London: Pluto Press.

Wilson, D. and Game, C. (1998) *Local Government in the United Kingdom*, Second edition, Basingstoke: Macmillan.

5 New public management in Denmark

The restructuring of employment relations in a welfare state labour market

Nikolaj Lubanski and Søren Kaj Andersen

The Danish public sector labour market is an integral part of the Danish welfare state. From this, it follows that the public sector labour market is more of a politically organized system of collective goods-production than a 'market' in the strict sense. Still, a process of public sector restructuring has taken place over the past two decades including new public management (NPM) initiatives. The trade unions have taken part in this development and the system of public sector industrial relations has moved into a position where pay issues are being woven into the fabric of central and local administrative policy goals, creating both opportunities and dilemmas for trade unions.

Introduction

Since the beginning of the 1980s, a modernization process has been going on in both state and local government sectors. The primary goal was to make the public sector more efficient in order to control public expenditure and to enhance the quality of public services. In the 1980s, the focus was mainly on making existing structures more efficient. New technology, simplification of rules and better financial management were the main focal points. In the second half of the 1980s, interest shifted towards creating organizations that were more flexible, developing management skills and introducing market mechanisms into the public sector.

The focus changed in the 1990s and heralded a move towards breaking public sector structures. The idea was to phase out the old bureaucratic and rule-oriented forms of government and replace them with a more decentralized system. Tasks and competencies were delegated to lower levels, for example, the regional/local authorities. The approach has been to change the bureaucratic form of government. Instead of setting up detailed central budgets, the form of government has shifted towards a more targeted mode of financial management. Furthermore, an increasing emphasis on organizational development and personnel policy has followed this change.

The 1990s were characterized by a further emphasis on human resources. To some extent, it can be said that the trend of human resource management (HRM) in the private sector came, with some delay, into the Danish public sector. But before the 1990s, the traditional structures hindered the possibilities for introducing HRM initiatives. Centralized financial structures and the seniority-based pay system gave institutions limited room to manoeuvre in attempting to introduce such initiatives.

However, after the structural changes of the 1980s, the focus gradually changed towards softer management issues, that is employee management. The importance of having motivated and responsible employees was to a greater degree acknowledged as a prerequisite for a successful modernization process in the public sector. This transformation process has been fuelled by employer interest in modernizing the public sector. In the wake of the financial crisis in the late 1970s and early 1980s, the growth in the public sector – and especially in public expenditure – was to be curbed. This factor – together with a profound change in the political climate – initiated the transformational processes that we are still witnessing at the beginning of the twenty-first century.

When looking at public sector restructuring in an international context, reference is often made to debates that are set within the framework of NPM (Pollitt, 1990; Hood, 1991; Osborne and Gaebler, 1992; cf. Ferlie *et al.*, 1996; Bach and Della Rocca, 1998). In the Danish context the scope of NPM analysis and debate has been limited (Klausen, 1996; Klausen and Ståhlberg, 1998).

Our aim is to analyse public sector restructuring within an NPM theoretical framework (on earlier work, see Due *et al.*, 1995, 1996; Andersen *et al.*, 1998, 1999). NPM is primarily a concept developed in an Anglo-Saxon context, and is therefore based – to some extent – on the particular empirical findings within this context. This makes it challenging to analyse whether it is as profitable to study the development of the Danish public sector from an NPM perspective. Therefore, the guiding question in this chapter is to what extent, and in which sense, have NPM-like initiatives has been introduced in the Danish public sector? The preliminary answer to this question raises a further issue: can the different empirical background in Denmark add some elements to the theoretical development of NPM analysis? Our main thesis is that initiatives that might be characterized as NPM have not caused a dismantling of existing labour–management relations in the public sector in Denmark. In accordance with this we will discuss to what extent NPM constitutes a useful analytical framework in understanding general processes of change in the Danish public sector and especially in focusing on relations between public sector employers and trade unions.

The chapter is structured as follows. In the first part, we argue that the Danish public sector labour market must be understood in 'welfare state' labour market terms. We then turn to NPM and discuss international debates on NPM from a specifically Danish perspective. Inspired by NPM analysis, the next section focuses on three dimensions of NPM initiatives: political-administrative reforms (the devolution of management), the introduction of competition and management-like experiments and the drive for efficiency. We then analyse the trade union response and stress the opportunities and dilemmas for the unions. In the final part we summarize the analytical aspects of the chapter.

The Danish welfare state labour market

Before discussing the process of restructuring and NPM-type initiatives in the Danish public services, we think it is important to outline some of the basic public sector labour market elements, which in many aspects are closely linked to the Danish welfare state. This is especially important when we look at the Danish public services in an international context.

It may be questioned whether it makes sense to refer to the Danish public sector labour market as a market in the strict meaning of the term. Since the 1980s, one dominant trend has been to consider marketization as the appropriate cure for the crisis in the public sector. Marketization is here understood as a variety of means to implement market-like conditions in the public sector, for example internal markets, contracting-out, privatization and so forth. However, this trend tends, to some extent, to rest on the assumption that we are dealing with a market comparable to a market in the private sector. There are good reasons to question this assumption.

Esping-Andersen (1990) has argued that welfare states can be analysed as representing different welfare state regimes or models. Esping-Andersen identifies three clusters of welfare state regimes: the 'liberal' welfare states (e.g. the United States and the United Kingdom); the 'corporatist' welfare states (e.g. Germany, Austria and France); and the 'social democratic' welfare states (e.g. Sweden and Denmark). This approach and especially the concept of de-commodification, which is the pivotal point of his analysis, have been widely criticized (Abrahamson and Borchorst, 1996; Jensen, 1998). We are not going to add anything to that debate, but we would like to emphasize that the so-called social democratic welfare state regime does pinpoint distinctive elements of the Danish public sector labour market.

Esping-Andersen argues that not only the public sector labour market but also the labour market as such is 'systematically and directly shaped by the (welfare) state' (Esping-Andersen, 1990: 144). In other words, (welfare) state policy and labour market policy melt into one specific welfare state regime. It is obvious that Denmark can be seen as part of the social democratic regime. Following Esping-Andersen's analysis, there are at least three dimensions that ought to be mentioned in order to give a rough picture of the specific conditions which surround both the labour market and public sector restructuring in Denmark.

First, many factors indicate that there exist no clear demarcation lines between the Danish welfare state and the labour market. The state not only caters for those incapable of work; the Danish welfare state is also the major agent for promoting full employment and the attempt to ensure the existence of a well-trained and flexible work force. This includes a wide range of programmes for education and training, job-creation, etc. The public sector plays a very visible role in these initiatives, for example by creating different kinds of temporary employment and training (Stokholm *et al.*, 1998). Welfare state initiatives also include retirement programmes and paid work absence (sickness, maternity, parenthood (for mother and father) or leave related) and further training. The importance of the active labour market policy (initiated by the welfare state) and the focus on problems related to entering and leaving the labour market has been analysed as the emergence of *the transitional labour market*

(Schmid, 1995; Due *et al.*, 1998a). Summing up, it seems that social policy in Denmark has become an integral part of labour market policy.

Second, since the 1960s the Danish welfare state has become a virtual employment machine (cf. Esping-Andersen, 1990: 149). In 1998, 34 per cent of the work force was employed in the public sector. If we include public companies (postal services, telecommunication, public transportation, etc.), 39 per cent of the work force can be found in the public services (Danmarks Statistik, 1998: 21). One outcome of this development is that for political decision-making, the views and attitudes of public service employees will always be considered important.

Third, the social partners in Denmark have played an important role in developing and adjusting the welfare state. This can be seen as the result of a centralized collective bargaining system, wherein close relations between the trade unions and the public employers were established over time (for details see Andersen *et al.*, 1999). A further element of importance is a long tradition of tripartite consultation and negotiation.

Following these arguments, it is our assumption that the Danish public sector labour market is an integral part of the Danish welfare state. As a consequence, the Danish public sector labour market must be seen more as a political organized system of collective goods production than a market in the strict sense. Using the words of Esping-Andersen the welfare state does not constitute itself as a '(perhaps odd) partner within the whole economy's labour market, the welfare state may, indeed, constitute a separate and distinct job market, or even ghetto' (Esping-Andersen, 1990: 160).

Characterizing the Danish public sector labour market like this, it becomes obvious that the political environment (cf. Beaumont, 1992) is of crucial importance in restructuring of the public sector and in developing relations between labour and management. Highlighting the importance of the political environment, it becomes an equally interesting task to analyse developmental trends in the political decision-making process. Focusing on the British context it has been argued that economic policy has become subject to constraints and forces that lie outside national control, a situation caused by the emergence of a global economy. At the same time severe economic problems have, since the 1970s, led national governments to try to disengage from political decision-making concerning economic issues (cf. Burnham in Chapter 2). The outcome has been a process of depolitization where 'political' problems such as inflationary pressure, budgetary deficit, exchange rate instability and other problems related to financial crises are put forward as 'technical' problems, which call for technical – not political – solutions.

Whether the same process of depolitization is taking place in Denmark may be questioned. Following Esping-Andersen's (1990) argument, the regulation of the labour market in the public sector is so inter-mingled in welfare state policies that the political actors will continue to seek and have influence on the overall patterns of regulation. This means that we have to have two issues in mind when analysing public sector restructuring. The first one is the characteristics of the labour market in the public sector, where we are dealing with a highly unionized sector, and a sector with a traditionally consensus-based relationship between the social partners (for details see Andersen *et al.*, 1999). Second, in our analysis of NPM in the Danish context, we should focus on the ways that the restructuring process has implications for the interface between the political and the managerial arena. Before going into the details of Danish public sector restructuring, an introduction to the applied NPM perspective will be given.

New public management and the Danish context

Over the past three decades, restructuring processes in the public sector have affected working conditions. The claim of the need to 'learn from the private sector' has not been absent from Denmark. Privatization, contracting-out, marketization and so forth have no doubt been part of the restructuring agenda (Due *et al.*, 1995).

NPM is a designation which has gained increased popularity – in spite of the fact that there exists little consensus in defining NPM (Ferlie *et al.*, 1996). NPM is a designation that covers a whole range of different ideas, visions and strategies in relation to public sector modernization. Although ill defined, its popularity probably comes from the fact that it is a convenient and trendy way to address a range of complicated developments. By adding the term 'new' to public management, it signifies a break with the past, and furthermore indicates that management is taken seriously in the public sector. It was an idea that fitted the political climate of the period nicely. However, the duality of NPM demands attention. On the one hand, NPM is used in criticizing the traditional character of the public sector, while on the other, NPM seems to be a normative idea which is often used as a means to state how the public sector *should* be arranged (e.g. OECD, 1995, 1997). This duality makes NPM an interesting framework to analyse the restructuring process in the Danish public sector.

When applied to a Danish context, the critique of public sector functioning centred around four main concerns (Klausen, 1996):

1   Random political decisions had left the public sector ill managed. It often lacked strategic and long-term management planning strategies because policies changed according to political whims.
2   The somewhat bureaucratic and rule-oriented governance structures along with the centralized public sector made it very difficult to adjust services to societal change. The necessary adaptations to demographic change, for instance, were often delayed due to these structures.
3   Public sector resource utilization was also criticized. The resource in-put/out-put relationship was very difficult to measure. This prompted questions concerning the productivity and efficiency of public organizations.
4   Public services were seen as lagging behind the private sector in matters of service. The 'customer' in other words had ceased to be the focus of public services. Public services were structured more by internal procedures than by the external needs of their clientele. The service management (or total quality management) trend in the private sector became the scaffolding of public service critique.

NPM is as mentioned more than just a critique; it is also a kind of ideology. It is an ideology of how public sector structures, management, tender and accounting systems ought to simulate equivalent private sector structures (Dunleavy and Hood, 1994). The idea of NPM often goes beyond reorganization (Klausen, 1996). Some of the traditional tasks carried out by the public sector, it has been suggested, could be transferred to private enterprises. Using the terminology of Osborne and Gaebler (1992), the public sector ought to be characterized by more 'steering' and less 'rowing'.

Following Ferlie and others (1996), it is possible to talk of four NPM models. These models were developed at different public sector restructuring stages and therefore also emphasize slightly different elements. The first NPM model, called the *efficiency drive*, was the earliest model to emerge. It represented an attempt to make the public sector more business-like through tighter financial control, audit extension and workload increase. The already mentioned idea of making the public sector more slim and efficient in ensuring money-value was included in this model. The second NPM model was characterized by *downsizing and decentralization*. It was here that a search for greater organizational flexibility came into focus. This approach involved a move towards increased decentralization of strategic and budgetary responsibility, contracting-out and a split between a small strategic core and a large operational periphery. The third NPM model, *in search of excellence*, abandoned the highly rationalistic approach of the two models mentioned above. Instead, it was inspired by the 'excellence' wave of the 1980s and emphasized how organizations managed change and innovation. The transformation process of public organizations was put to the forefront; the process in itself became equally important as the organizational out come. Radical decentralization along with result-oriented performance evaluation was seen as the groundbreaking means for inscribing organizational development into this model. The fourth NPM model, *public service orientation*, represents a fusion between private and public sector management ideas. In the view of Ferlie and colleagues (1996), this model is the least well developed and is still to reveal its full potential. Basically, it harvests ideas from the private sector and reinstates them into distinct public sector contexts. The main characteristics of this model are service quality concerns, consideration of the needs and values of users and, last but not least, a focus on managing the distinctive politics of collective provision.

This typology is reflected in Bach and Della Rocca's (1998) comparative analysis of public service management strategies in Western Europe. Bach and Della Rocca speak of three key dimensions underlying the apparently disparate set of management practices hidden within the NPM term. Moreover, this focal point is directed at labour–management relations. The first element is efficiency orientation and as such it is quite similar to Ferlie and colleagues' first model. However, the emphasis here is placed on the strong discretionary power given to managers. Tightening the control of staff is achieved by implementing more explicitly defined appraisal strategies and by firmly targeting performance goals. Such tightening strategies are sometimes linked to individual performance-related pay schemes. The second element concerns changes in organizational structures and devolution of management responsibility. This process creates more complicated public sector structures, because it facilitates a greater amount of fragmented and independent units holding responsibility in matters concerning budgetary and personnel practice. Nevertheless, some of these practices, especially in matters concerning pay determination, are still coupled to general industrial relations features. Finally, Bach and Della Rocca (1998) locate a third market-orientated element. This element stresses the shift from hierarchical management to contractual management schemes. Consequently, the boundaries of public services are redefined by making it possible for a smaller core of public staff to specify and buy services from a range of public and private sector agencies. Bach and Della Rocca (1998) thereby put less emphasis on the user element in NPM, in arguing that the concerns of this dominant efficiency and market orientation model are primarily about cost effectiveness. In their view, local managers are empowered to use resources more efficiently; hence devolution is pursued for the same reasons of cost effectiveness.

In our analysis of employment relations in the Danish public sector, these main elements of NPM are maintained. The usefulness of the NPM concept rests in its ability to capture changes such as *devolution of management practices, increasing market orientation* and *implementation of efficiency schemes*.

When analysing public sector restructuring in Denmark, the first issue on the agenda therefore is management devolution, since this process is a part of a general reform of the political-administrative structure. The stress is that local and regional managers should be given further responsibilities in order to fulfil their new role in public organizations. The second issue – market orientation – holds an equivalent importance because it is also an integral part of the process. Marketization of public services, that is the broader process of making the public service production more transparent, flexible, competition-based and more open to private enterprises, has been pursued in a number of ways in Denmark. This has also involved changes in employment conditions. A process of phasing-out of personnel employed as civil servants has taken place. Consequently, a vast amount of public staff are being employed on conditions that are apparently similar to those found in the private sector. The third issue – the efficiency drive – has been an overall target of public restructuring, due to the fact that the increase in public service workload had to be handled within the same – or even a reduced – financial framework. Therefore, an increasing emphasis has been put on ways to secure and enhance employee commitment. A range of new individual incentives has been introduced, including new pay schemes and new forms of labour–management co-operation.

Restructuring of public service production

As in most other Organisation for Economic Co-operation and Development (OECD) member states, the Danish public sector has been under economic pressure since the mid-1970s. Hence, the past three decades have been characterized by continual – although not dramatic – cuts in public sector spending. This has been a topic of major concern and interest, recently spawning unrest and lively debate in the hospital and public school sectors (Due *et al.*, 1998b). At the same time, economic pressure has not actually led to any dramatic downsizing attempts, nor has its presence triggered mass layoffs in the public sector. However, new public sector employment has ceased, thereby curbing the public sector employment growth rate.

Political-administrative reform – devolution of management

Instead of dramatic downsizing attempts, a restructuring process has taken place. One important path of development over the past three decades has been a reform of the political-administrative structure. Beyond doubt, the dominant drive to initiate restructuring was cost effectiveness (Bach and Della Rocca, 1998). Devolution of management has been pursued in order to use resources more efficiently.

The administrative modes which characterized the Danish public sector have steadily been changing ever since the expansion of the public sector started in the 1960s. Framework administrative schemes were introduced in this decade. The reason for this was that it relieved the elected politicians of their detail-laden administrative roles. However, the public sector was still characterized by a strong hierarchical administrative policy, a policy that was further confirmed by the expansion of 'planning schemes' in the 1970s. Here, the so-called plan perspectives for developing the public sector were constructed. Changes in the administrative philosophy gradually came about in the 1980s. These changes were due to the acknowledgement of the fact that both the hierarchical administrative systems and the designs of the planning schemes of the 1970s were tools that had had a limited effect. New types of administrative tools were therefore introduced in the 1980s. These tools were based on policy that, amongst other things, furthered economic incentives. Developments through the 1990s confirmed the move away from centralized administrative models, while shifting attention towards the wants and needs of public institutions and companies. These needs have focused on freedom of action, a freedom that has allowed them to prescribe the goals of their activities more precisely. The political contribution became that of determining the overall goals, framework and rules of the game.

Since the 1970s, three phases of devolution of responsibility have been implemented (Lægreid and Pedersen, 1994; Klausen and Ståhlberg, 1998: 32–34). The first phase can be characterized as being a *national structural phase*. An important and initial act in this phase was the 1970 municipal reform. Before the reform, Denmark was divided into 86 municipal boroughs and approximately 1,300 rural districts located within 25 counties. With the reform, these elements were consolidated to the present 275 municipalities and 14 counties. The aim of the municipal reform was partly to reform task assignment, meaning that municipalities were assigned a greater amount of administrative tasks. The idea in other words was to establish units (municipalities) that had a suitable population in relation to the tasks and services provided. Furthermore, consideration had to be given to whether the municipalities were big enough to bear the economic burden of having a professional administration. The municipal reform was also a reform of burdens. Before the reform, state authorities had in part financed municipal activities through reimbursements. After the reform, economic subsidy shifted towards an increase in generalizing the state subsidy schemes. Along with economic balancing and the implementation of municipal taxes, these initiatives were to finance municipal activities. The aim had been to strengthen the relationship between the competency and economic responsibility of municipalities. Examples of this decentralization were the 1976/1977 transference of central social services to the municipalities and the 'municipalization' of elementary schools in 1992 (teachers had until then belonged to the state bargaining sector; now they belong to the municipal bargaining sector). To sum up, it became the task of the Danish municipalities to spread the goods of the welfare state to the populace.

This development meant that the earlier known rural districts often metamorphosed into comprehensive bureaucratic entities. This leads us to the second phase – *a local administrative phase*. The characteristic contours of this phase became clear in the mid-1980s. Questions were asked as to whether the municipal bureaucracy functioned appropriately. Was there in fact substantial freedom in questions pertaining to municipal utilization of resources, and employee allocation etc., at the institutional level? In this period of development, the free municipal experiment was one among several components being tested. Another such component was that many municipalities joined their committees and administrations to one another. But perhaps the most important tendency was that the responsibilities were transferred from the counties and the municipalities to the institutional level.

The third and final phase is characterized as a *user phase*. Here the general idea is that the user of public services also plays an important part in securing the quality of these services. This quality control device is effective whenever the user is empowered to engage in direct dialogue with the management and employees of municipal administrations and institutions. The overall hope regarding public service is that participation will facilitate a greater notion of responsibility and satisfaction in the users and employees of these services (Finansministeriet, 1993: 100–103). This engagement of citizens has furthermore propitiated a range of legislation concerning user-boards. Such legislation is, for example, aimed at boards within the municipal elementary school (since 1990), and parental boards of municipal day care centres (since 1993). Legislation merely sets the overall framework such as member composition of the committee and its election rules; beyond this point it is up to the municipal committees to decide how great are the competencies allotted to the user-boards.

This process of devolution of management can be seen as an NPM initiative. The 'new' aspect is that the local/regional entities are given further tasks and competencies, and also that financial responsibility is delegated. The local/regional entities have become more independent of the central state-level regulation. They have been given the additional flexibility needed to solve tasks in ways that better fits the individual area in question.

An incentive for this devolution process was the 'user' orientation. A direct dialogue between the users and the institutions was seen as a way to ensure quality in public service production. Even though Bach and Della Rocca (1998) put little emphasis on this element, it must be seen as playing an important role in the changes that have come about in the Danish public sector. Therefore, the devolution of management was not necessarily a move away from political influence, rather politics had now become an issue at the lower regulatory levels.

Likewise, an important aspect was to give local and regional managers proper means with which to manage. In the traditional system, managers at lower levels of public organization had limited means for implementing strategic management strategies, simply following the rules that were handed down from the central administration. The managers were to some extent stuck with fixed budgets and regulations decided at central level, and often it was difficult to make decisions. Even decisions dealing with the number and the quality of employees were to be taken within narrow limits. So certainly, an aim of the devolution process was to 'free' managers by granting them the means to manage. Theoretically, this should lead to greater cost effectiveness, due to managers being responsible for their own budgets.

The introduction of competition and market-like experiments

Competition in and marketization of public service production has been introduced in a number of ways in the Danish public sector. An important NPM element has been to identify the parties which respectively plan public services, produce and finance them. The aim of separating these different roles has been to achieve a more direct focus on the factors of supply and demand (Andersen *et al.*, 1999), hereby reinforcing competitive incentives.

A fairly wide range of initiatives has been taken. The planning and production of public services have in some instances been transferred to private suppliers via licence, authorization or contracting-out. Likewise, other forms of financing are being tested, that is consumer-financed services. This however depends on the kind of activity and/or service provided. In spite of these initiatives, actual experience is relatively small in comparison to the political rhetoric concerning this issue (Madsen *et al.*, 1998). The status quo is that there has been a tremendous amount of talk, less action and – up to date – even less documented experience on the success and failure of introducing competition into public service production.

A process of privatization has taken place in the central state sector, although in most cases the state enters the new enterprise structure as a majority shareholder, so that the process is often referred to as *corporatization*, as it fails to meet the more stringent criteria for 'classical' privatization (e.g. a full transfer to private ownership). The Telecommunication Company, the postal services, Copenhagen Airports and a shipping line belonging to Danish State Railways (DSB) have so far been privatized. The DSB, is to become an independent limited liability company in 1999, cutting its formal ties with the state (for details see Andersen *et al.*, 1999).

Contracting-out is another strategy adopted when introducing market elements in the provision of public services, although in recent years we have only seen a limited development in this area. In 1994, the percentage of operational functions in the central state sector performed by outside suppliers was approximately 17 per cent, representing only a slight increase as compared with previous years. In 1993, the corresponding figure for Danish municipalities was about 9 per cent, matching the level of previous years (Ministry of Finance/Ministry of Internal Affairs, 1995). At the municipal level the main functions contracted out are technology-based, for example the environment, technical services, roads, etc., although in recent years tenders have been invited for some service functions, for example cleaning and transport, and more specialized functions related to information technology.

In individual municipalities, selected services – especially care of the elderly – have been contracted out on a trial basis. Such trials are likely to become more widespread and to be given a more permanent status. Compulsory competitive tendering has not been introduced in Denmark. A research project on contracting-out in municipalities shows that the scale of contracting-out cannot be explained by the political 'colour' of the single town council – other factors are decisive. In particular, the economic situation of the individual municipality has shown itself to be a decisive factor.

The pattern of public sector service development does not suggest an overall introductory move towards large-scale privatization, resulting in a shrinking of the sector. Rather, the tendency is towards a mix of privatized and public services, where the aim is to raise the level of efficiency by introducing market-like mechanisms.

There is a tendency to acknowledge the limitations as to how far it is possible to implement private sector elements in public services. The public sector has certain characteristics that differ from private sector logic. In a Danish context, it has been argued that the special 'political logic' does not disappear when public tasks are contracted out – this logic follows the tasks into the private sector. We never see marketization in the narrow sense of the word – politics do not leave the services – and thus private companies cannot control public services on strengthening market conditions (Åkerstrøm Andersen, 1996).

Market orientation has also been an important issue in employment relations. One of the main changes in the past decades has been in the employment conditions of the Danish public sector. Traditionally, employees in the sector were employed as civil servants. But in the past decade a process of phasing out civil servant status (tjenestemænd) – that is employees having certain rights (e.g. employment protection) and obligations – has taken place. In effect, there has been a shift from legislative control over contracts to collective agreements, a feature of other public sector employment. This change was a major prerequisite for the recent management devolution processes and hence also for the recent changes in the industrial relations system.

Slightly more than 20 per cent of public sector employees have civil servant status (1995), which means that their terms of employment are covered by legislation rather than by collective agreements. The most important differences between the employment terms for civil servants and others is that civil servants are not legally entitled to resort to industrial action (strikes). Furthermore, they are covered by a statutory pension scheme (in addition to the collective old-age pension) and are normally entitled to three years' pay if dismissed. The state sub-sector has by far the highest percentage of employees with civil servant status (almost 40 per cent), usually in senior positions, such as judges, police officers, the armed forces and certain groups in the DSB. In both sub-sectors – that is state and county/municipal – senior employees are usually granted the status of civil servant. This status is regarded to be a norm only in respect to areas which were originally looked upon as state sector core areas: police force, railways, postal services, primary and lower secondary school, the 'established' church.

The number of public sector employees with civil servant status suffered a considerable decline as a result of the transfer in 1992 of the teachers (primary and lower secondary school) to the municipal sector, meaning that all new teachers are now working under the terms of collective agreements. The transfer of some *état* services to the enterprise structure means that newly recruited employees will be agreement-covered – not civil servants (Due and Madsen, 1996).

As indicated in the previous paragraphs, this transformation of public sector employee status to agreements-covered schemes can be interpreted as a prerequisite in implementing new managerial reforms. When staff are employed on conditions similar to those in the private sector, managers are given further manoeuvrability. For instance, they are better equipped when wanting to recruit personnel, and the possibilities of dismissing those who do not fit in are likewise enhanced. The change in employment conditions is thus clearly a market-like initiative which paves the way for NPM forms. Such new forms are clearly converging towards forms which are already well known in the private sector (Madsen *et al.*, 1998)

To sum up, the process of corporatization in the central state sector is in fact redrawing the boundaries of the sector. While processes of contracting-out are being implemented, it nevertheless seems that they are not necessarily based on ideology; instead it is a matter of economics. If the politicians in a municipality decide to launch a process of contracting-out, this gives rise to the possibility of a democratic debate on costs, quality, etc. related to the specific services. When the services were delivered by public institutions alone, fewer people paid attention, although the opposite might also happen. This could be the case if contract information conducted with private suppliers is withheld from the public. Still, the overall result is a situation where 'politics' is moving into the private sector sphere.

The implemented changes concerning the employment status of public employees are a major break with the past. The process of phasing out civil servants during the 1990s has paved the way for implementing NPM initiatives to a larger extent than before the commencement of this process.

The efficiency drive

Changes in the political-administrative structure must be seen as a part of a general process of modernization in the public sector, a process that is aimed at enhancing flexibility and efficiency both in the organizational set-up and on the part of employees. The efficiency drive is a central element if we are to talk of NPM in the Danish context (Ferlie *et al.*, 1996; Klausen, 1996; Bach and Della Rocca, 1998). The number of public sector employees has remained static, but the workload is increasing. This is mainly a consequence of some significant demographic developments. In the near future there will be more elderly people and a growing number of children attending school. This means that more pressure is applied to balancing public sector budgets, since extra funding is out of the question; it likewise puts pressure on the efficiency of people employed in the public services. Thus, the need for enhancing flexibility and efficiency seems – especially from an employer's point of view – quite obvious (Ministry of Finance, 1995).

In many respects, the starting point of this process of enhancing efficiency was the 1983 reform initiative. The reform differed in several ways from previous initiatives. First, it was not the result of a commission, which means that the relevant actors (e.g. the social partners) were not included in the process. The government wanted to set their own agenda for the changes. They had lost confidence in the traditional procedure wherein the social partners played an important role in defining policies in relation to labour market issues. Second, the reform was adopted as a government initiative launched by a liberal/conservative government although the previous social democratic government had prepared the reform. Previously all reform initiatives had been internal administrative programmes. By using this strategy the government stressed the importance of the initiative. The reform mirrored a widely shared opinion, among both conservatives/liberals and social democrats, that the Danish welfare state was facing certain problems related to a growing bureaucracy, diminishing responsibility on behalf of the citizens and budgetary problems. Third, the modernization programme included an important theoretical perspective concerning democracy. During the 1980s, the Danish welfare state was criticized mainly because of the existing management and control mechanisms and the lack of citizen participation. New buzz-words which different institutions and political groups agreed upon as being especially important were decentralization, de-bureaucratization and self-governance.

The 1983 reform was followed by further reform initiatives during the 1980s and the 1990s, initiatives which mainly developed the initial idea of the 1983 reform. Whereas previous reforms to a large extent had been focused on restructuring of departments and directorates, a common trend which focused on public-personnel policies and working conditions emerged in the new reform initiatives.

Apart from changes in what can be termed macro level structures, it has been evident that public sector employers have been pushing changes at the micro level. Wage costs are huge in the public sector, which also seems to be the case for the future. The introduction of new technology can at best procure relatively small cost reductions in the public service sector. The dominant employer strategy in this situation has been to focus attention on HRM. The idea has been to increase employee motivation and efficiency through education and training (Ibsen, 1998). Recently reached agreements between public employers and trade unions can be seen as being part of such a scenario. Most importantly, the agreements concern a new pay-scheme system for public employees.

The outcome of the collective bargaining round completed in the spring of 1997 signalled a decision to go ahead with the long-mooted proposal to conduct a reform of Denmark's public sector pay system (Andersen *et al.*, 1999). The decision was reached primarily to meet employer demands for a more flexible pay system. The previous system was based on the principles adopted when passing the Act on Civil Servants in 1919 – a system which has also governed the agreement-covered public sector employees, even though they have gradually become the dominant group in the sector, and even though their working conditions are in some respects fundamentally different from those of the traditional civil servant group. The main goal of the new agreement was to devise a public sector pay system in which aggregate pay would consist of four separate pay components: (1) a basic wage fixed centrally; (2) a supplementary amount negotiated at decentralized and/or centralized level based on job function (special areas of work, responsibility, etc.); (3) a qualification allowance (education/further training, experience, etc.); and (4) a component based on results/performance (i.e. efficiency), to be agreed at decentralized levels (Andersen *et al.*, 1999).

Considered as a whole, the reform can be perceived as a showdown – as a determination to replace the automatic, seniority-based pay-increment system with a system in which pay more accurately reflects the actual qualifications and performance of the individual public-sector employee and of groups of employees. Since the introduction of the reform, several trade unions and public employers have made quite divergent statements concerning the percentage of the total wage sum that should be negotiated at the local level. Most parties say that their aim is to reach a point where 10–30 per cent of the total wage sum will be negotiated at the decentralized level while at the same time agreeing that this would take around 8–10 years to reach (Hoffman, 1998; Poulsen and Hedegaard, 1998).

Concluding, the 1999 round of collective bargaining in the public sector seems to confirm the success of the new pay system. By then around 95 per cent of local and regional government employees – and this includes large groups of employees like nurses and teachers – had been transferred to the new system. The pace in the state sub-sectors was a bit slower.

The efficiency drive has functioned as an essential incentive for public employers in the restructuring process. Changes in both the organizational set-up of the public sector and in the wage forms of public employees aim at enhancing flexibility and efficiency. Therefore, NPM in the Danish context clearly involves a tendency to emphasize efficiency, but attention should be paid to the fact that the changes concerning employment relations are mainly implemented through agreements between the social partners. In spite of the employers' outspoken interest in changing public wage forms, they have entered negotiations with the trade unions, knowing that it could take years before a real break with the seniority-based system appeared. It can – of course – be argued that the employers were left without alternatives, due to the very high rate of unionization among public-sector employees and the influential position of trade unions in general (Due *et al.*, 1996).

The overall picture shows that NPM-type initiatives implemented at the macro level were introduced through the system of public sector industrial relations. As a consequence, for example, a new pay system, which in the end probably will have widespread effects on personnel policies at the single workplace, cannot be introduced without the acceptance of the trade unions. This means that if we are to understand NPM in the Danish context we have to take the response of the trade unions into consideration. The characteristics of public restructuring in Denmark are very much shaped by the interests of the trade unions.

Trade union responses

The importance of restructuring the public sector during the 1980s and 1990s was mainly argued by employers. The Ministry of Finance, the National Association of Local Authorities (KL) and the Danish Federation of County Councils (ARF) set the agenda for discussions by producing numerous reports and analyses. During this period, the Danish public sector trade unions moved from a passive–reactive position to a more proactive involvement strategy in matters dealing with promotion and restructuring–modernization.

In earlier work, we have concentrated on public sector collective bargaining and trade union strategies in this respect (Due *et al.*, 1996); therefore, our main focus here will be on the ways the trade unions have tried to respond to the NPM-type initiatives taken by the public employers. Trade unions have in two areas implemented strategies with the aim of changing the agenda for NPM initiatives. One concerns the implementation of a more 'labour-friendly' version of HRM, referred to as 'the developing workplace' (Det Udviklende Arbejde – DUA). The other area concerns the endeavour to find new forms of employee representation structures. Both areas are central in the trade unions' attempt to formulate their version of NPM.

From a general perspective, and with a focus on the state sub-sectors, Pedersen (1996) lists three separate phases when summing up the response of the unions: (1) an ideological phase, in which the unions react passively or negatively; (2) a technical implementation phase, in which the debate is de-ideologized and various concrete projects (e.g. adaptation) are set in motion; and (3) an administrative-policy phase, in which pay issues are woven – at an increasing rate – into the fabric of central and local administrative-policy goals. Pay is no longer considered in isolation, but as part of a broader spectrum of workplace issues as described earlier.

The logic of this development has prompted the observation that the agenda for restructuring or modernizing Denmark's public sector is being drawn up – and defined in detail – with the active involvement of the labour-market parties, in this case elected politicians and trade union federations. This can be seen as a specific Danish aspect in the restructuring process. The reason for this Danish design in implementing NPM initiatives can be interpreted as the outcome of the shift in position adopted by the unions. Their fairly recent willingness to apply a broader socio-economic perspective when entering into a dialogue with the employers, that is the Ministry of Finance and the regional/municipal employer organizations, not just on pay issues but also on personnel and administrative-policy issues has secured them a position in the restructuring process (Pedersen, 1996; Ugebrevet Mandag Morgen, 1997).

The changes in the public sector have made it necessary for the trade unions to adjust their strategies (Pedersen, 1996). Already the shift in balance between the civil servant group and the group of agreement-covered employees had created a need for a reorientation of trade union strategies. When the employment status was changed, new ways of interest articulation were found. The need for this development was underlined by an increasing emphasis on developing human resources from the employer side. Therefore it became even clearer that there was a need for a trade union response to the new conditions.

An important response came in 1991 with the LO-congress (LO is the trade union confederation for blue-collar workers), where the so-called developing workplace (DUA) was launched as a new strategic orientation for the trade unions. With the launch of 'the developing workplace', the trade unions attempted to connect the development of the public institutions with the creation of more interesting jobs for the employees and the enhancement of their influence on the content and direction of this initiative. The aim was to prepare employees to take part in continuous organizational developments, and to use these changes as an opportunity to gain more influence on the managerial level. The decision of the trade unions to become involved in the process of change is closely related to: (1) the consequences of an opposition strategy (low wage increases, diminished or no influence on restructuring processes) and (2) their assessment of the potential benefits to be derived from the measures adopted in the public sector in order to promote 'the developing workplace'.

The DUA is a Danish or Nordic concept emphasizing that improvements in the efficiency and quality of public services are to be accompanied by improvements in working conditions, greater job satisfaction, development of competencies etc. for the individual worker. The term can be seen as a way the trade unions have tried to formulate a more acceptable and soft variant of NPM. Further, the term implies a tendency to move away from the traditional confrontational relationship between employers and unions. The emphasis is now on partnership, on common interests. Interestingly, even though the concept originally was launched as a trade union alternative to 'hard' forms of HRM, the public sector employers are increasingly using the term in publications and reports dealing with human resource policies (Ministry of Finance, 1994).

Nowadays, LO presents its vision of 'the developing workplace' as having three different aspects: (1) a job that offers opportunities for personal development in a working environment where the employees participate with a high degree of responsibility and competence; (2) products and services of high quality which are socially relevant and sustainable; and (3) companies that are sustainable in terms of the environment and socially responsible, among other ways by accepting shared responsibility for development and employment in the local community.

This vision goes beyond the general understanding of 'the developing workplace', where the concept is seen as more connected to the internal arrangements at the individual workplace. Such a conception is also reflected in LO's 'Toolbox: Training and Development', which was created with the aim of assisting the development at the individual workplace. The toolbox should be seen as an integrated proposal for the way the individual workplace can play a central role in the training of employees (Plant, 2001). LO's main focus is on the internal structures at the individual workplace.

The interest in both improving the efficiency and quality of public services and improving working conditions points towards a need for developing the co-operational relationship between management and employees at the workplace (Mathiesen *et al.*, 1998). From the employers' point of view a renewal of labour–management co-operation should secure the employees' active participation in the public sector modernization process. The employees' and the trade unions' main interest in such a renewal comes from the ambition of gaining more influence on both strategic and day-to-day decisions in the public institutions. Only in this way is it possible to carry out the intentions in 'the developing workplace'. Without influence on the managerial level, the employee side could be restricted to a passive (reactive) role in the changes.

This acknowledgement led the trade unions to press for changes in the participatory structures. In their view, traditional labour–management relations have given employees only limited influence. This pressure coincided with the employers' dissatisfaction with the existing system of employee representation. The public sector employer organizations have long been complaining about the employee representatives, who in their view reduce the flexibility of the workplaces (Due *et al.*, 1994). When an employee is elected either as shop steward or as health and safety representative, he/she gains greater security in employment, for example longer notice in case of dismissal, and the employer has to present further documentation, engage in consultation and so forth. The employers argued that close to every fifth employee was either a shop steward, member of a works council or part of the health and safety organization (Due *et al.*, 1994), an argument that must be seen in the light of the huge amount of relative small workplaces in the public sector. If a public institution employs ten persons in total and two of the employees are involved in one of these representation structures then the time used may seem a burden. In the employers' view, the amount of representatives was a problem when the public institutions were to be modernized (Due *et al.*, 1994).

At the same time there was discontent on both sides with the way the existing representation system worked. Generally, health and safety organization and works councils are two separate lines of representation, and in many workplaces both structures tend to be formalised, with only limited influence rather than the central focus of development of the workplace (Mathiesen *et al.*, 1998). This discontent made the social partners agree on commencing trials with new forms of representation both at the regional/local level and at the state level.

The process began in the regional/local sector with an agreement on commencing the so-called MAI project (MedArbejderIndflydelse) (Due *et al.*, 1994). The test period was between 1991 and 1993, where a number of municipalities and counties experimented with new forms of representative structures. The main element was the merging of the health and safety organization and works councils. Effectively, this meant a reduction in the number of employee representatives in exchange for further employee involvement. The MAI project concluded that the employee side gained more influence on the development of the institutions, communities and counties when the structures were changed (Due *et al.*, 1994). Due to the reduced number of representatives, they were able to build up a closer and more informal co-operation with management, which was taken to be a prerequisite for further employee involvement. This result however had a flip side for employees: the reduced amount of representatives made some groups feel that their interests were undervalued and generally a problem of communication arose due to fewer persons having information on the development of the workplace (Due *et al.*, 1994).

These trials in the regional/local sector were followed by a similar test period in the state sector from 1995 to 1998 (Mathiesen *et al.*, 1998). The social partners agreed upon the so-called MIO project (MedarbejderIndflydelsesOrgan) in the 1995-negotiation round. The purpose was to test new and different forms of labour–management co-operation, which would prepare the ground for future negotiations on changes in the representation system (Ministry of Finance, 1995). The MIO project was in many ways similar to the process in the regional/local sector, but with wider possibilities to create different solutions in the individual institution.

As was the case for the MAI project, the MIO project also demonstrated an increase in employees' influence on both day-to-day decisions and the more strategic considerations in the experimental organizations. The main difference between the existing system and the new test forms is the depth and the extent to which employees are involved (Mathiesen *et al.*, 1998). In the traditional works councils, information and consultation were the best the employees could hope for. In the test organizations within the frame of the MIO project, the employee side was to a much greater degree involved in the discussion, preparation and implementation of decisions which beforehand primarily were taken unilaterally by the management (Mathiesen *et al.*, 1998). It should be mentioned that these changes do not influence formal management prerogative; it is still the managers who hold the responsibility for decisions taken.

Generally, the experience of these trials has been positive. Labour–management co-operation was mostly developed in a direction that both parties approved of. As already mentioned, some new concerns arose mainly due to the limited number of representatives. With 'only' one system covering the tasks of both works councils and health and safety organizations, fewer representatives are involved. Consequently, the system can be more élitist, which may create problems of communication and problems of representing all the different groups at the workplace.

The MAI project concluded that the aggregate amount of time employee representatives used on their tasks was reduced, a result that added to the employers' interest in transforming the experiences from the trials into systems operating on a more permanent basis. It should be noted though that the MIO project did not confirm this result (Mathiesen *et al.*, 1998), which could explain why the employer-side in the state sub-sector was more reluctant to carry on in this direction.

The initiatives taken by the social partners show that the traditional consensus-based system is being developed into new forms of regulation rather than being abandoned. In spite of the fact that the new forms of labour–management co-operation started out as trials with a limited time-span, they are to be integrated into the IR system in the long run. After the MAI project the rules were changed so that it became possible for the individual county, municipality or institution to introduce labour–management relations similar to those tested in the project.

An important experience harvested from these test forms is that it is possible for both parties to gain from changing the existing structures. The main argument is that trade unions must be willing to give up some of their established rights in order to remain an integral part of public sector development. In the trials, they had to accept a reduction in the number of employee representatives (mainly in the MAI project), but gained further influence on the development of their workplaces in exchange.

These experiences do indicate the need for a proactive trade union strategy. As described, the employers are certainly inspired by the ideas in NPM and clearly want to create more flexible and efficient organizations within the public sector. If the easiest way to reach this target is through co-operation with the trade unions at the central level and the employee representatives at the local level, it seems like the employer side is able to see an advantages in pursuing this objective. But if they constantly run into difficulties in dealing with the collective bargaining system, employees certainly work for a more direct relation to the individual employee.

A recent survey of the approximately 12,000 public sector shop stewards within the LO area supports this assessment (Jensen *et al.*, 1999). Most shop stewards believe that the management at their workplace is interested in building up a more direct relation to the individual employee. The changes in pay structures and the decentralization process in general show that the managers are gaining the tools needed for realising such a strategy. Trade unions continuously need to formulate and reformulate strategies so that they are able to maintain their position in public sector restructuring.

Opportunities and dilemmas for labour

The initiatives taken to reform the public sector in Denmark already have had a range of implications for labour. Even though we argue that NPM is being pursued in a special Danish design where a more important role is given to the trade unions, it is clear that public employees are not and will not in the future be left untouched by the changes. The process of change creates both opportunities and dilemmas for labour.

Obviously, the situation outlined above poses a number of problems affecting the development of relations between the parties in Denmark's public sector labour market. The trade unions have become deeply involved in issues related to administrative policy – a development that has forced them to build professionalized secretariats capable of formulating the union position and conducting negotiations. This process can easily lead to a gulf between a union's officials (and professionals) and its members. Further, the various unions have not yet adopted a common position in support for the steps taken to renew the public sector – or its pay system. One possible outcome could be a rift in the trade union movement. The question is thus whether the system of collective agreements is capable of encompassing and solving the comprehensive and complex problems that now appear on the agenda for negotiations.

In spite of the fact that only a limited amount of data has been compiled on the results of implementing the new forms of joint influence and co-determination, (i.e. worker participation) in the Danish state and its county/municipal sub-sectors, at this stage both success and hardship have been reported. On the one hand, new worker participation forms are capable of developing into a more progressive and forward-looking co-operation, one that will include solutions to both present-day and long-term problems. This contrasts with activity in the traditional work councils where there is active passing of information and aiding consultation. On the other hand, evaluation has shown that the new schemes create situations in which employee representatives undertake a greater amount of work while simultaneously becoming more professional in their roles. There is, though a risk that the representatives may become more isolated from the colleagues whose interests they are supposed to represent (Due *et al.*, 1994; Mathiesen *et al.*, 1998).

Both the new framework agreement on worker participation in the local and regional government sectors and the agreement on the pay reform in both parts of the public sector bargaining system have put more emphasis on the role of the shop stewards (Jensen *et al.*, 1999). Recent developments in worker participation seem to indicate an ultimate merging of the existing structures, suggesting that the works council system and the health and safety system are to be reinforced, by linking them to the representative system applied to the collective agreements.

In this process of restructuring both social partners are interested in implementing changes through the existing – but renewed – system. The accumulated knowledge concerning the interests of the different groups of public employees points at the same overall trend. The tendency is that the existing system works as a guarantee against an extreme implementation of NPM initiatives, but it also gives the shop stewards a central role at the local level. They have to be able to negotiate the changes in their individual organization and participate in the restructuring process. This naturally requires a range of different skills. The afore-mentioned survey of shop stewards in the LO area shows that the employer side demands more skilled shop stewards if they are to play a central role in the changes (Lubanski *et al.*, 1999). If trade unions are not able to develop these skills then the employer side may be in a strong position to set its own agenda. This could create more dilemmas than opportunities for labour.

Analytical perspectives

We have asked the question: What is NPM in the Danish context? We have used this question in order to discuss to what extent, and in which sense, NPM-type initiatives have been introduced in the Danish public sector. By emphasizing three dimensions in the international debate on NPM – *the devolution of management practices, market orientation*, and *the efficiency drive* – we believe that it makes sense to characterize important parts of the restructuring process in the public sector in Denmark as NPM-type initiatives.

Having said that, it is quite clear that the restructuring process we have been witnessing in Denmark differs substantially from that of, for example, the United Kingdom. In other words, although the aims of restructuring the public services by and large seem to be identical across borders (cost reduction, efficiency and quality services), the actual implementation and the actual outcome of these processes differ from one country to another.

As we have shown the restructuring of the public sector in Denmark has included political-administrative reforms primarily aimed at devolving managerial responsibility to lower levels of authority, to counties and municipalities, and to single institutions or workplaces. It can be said that this process of restructuring has been followed by overall changes in employment relations – the phasing-out of the civil servant status, the introduction of the new pay system and a new structure for employee representation at the workplace level – among the most important elements. We have discussed these changes in an NPM perspective and stressed that the trade unions have taken part in this development. Agreements concluded at national level have paved the way for the introduction of these initiatives. In this sense the trade unions are taking part in both formulating and implementing these initiatives – and due to the fact that the agreements concluded at national level are framework agreements which have to be completed at the local level, this is at the same time a process taking place at the local level. If a public employer at the workplace level tries to introduce organizational changes which are not part of the above-mentioned agreements, this will normally be an issue for the works council or the new forum of employee representation. In this sense a dialogue on organizational changes will normally have to take place at the workplace level.

Consequently, NPM in the Danish format design ought to be able to include labour–management relations and involve the trade unions as part of both formulating and implementing NPM initiatives. This goes beyond the basic ideas of NPM, or alternatively the whole analytical set-up becomes so inclusive that it tends to disappear – meaning that if any initiative of restructuring can be included in this analytical framework it can become difficult to separate one strategy of restructuring from another. It should also be noted that identifying the aims of NPM (cost reduction, efficiency and quality in the services and so on) does not tell us much. It might be more interesting to study the ways in which these objectives are reached and thereby also what the consequences are for labour.

As a kind of framework for the discussion of NPM in the Danish public service, we introduced the notion of the public sector labour market as a 'welfare state' labour market in the beginning of this chapter. In addition, we questioned whether the restructuring of public services in Denmark reflects a process of depolitization. In attempting to answer this question we depart from the three features of the emergent 'managerial state' which Fairbrother (Chapter 4) emphasizes.

First, there is no doubt that the political decision-making process in Denmark has been influenced by more globally integrated financial markets, with the most prominent example today being the introduction of European Monetary Union (EMU). Even though Denmark is not an EMU participant, the tendency to picture economic problems such as trade imbalances, high wage costs, budgetary deficits and so forth as 'technical' problems is definitely evident. Still, some areas of welfare state services – for example hospitals and schools – seem to be politically 'high-profile' services in Denmark. This is manifest in the continual political debates on the quality of these services; however, the allocation of financial resources has also beckoned the attention of politicians and the general public.

Second, the three phases of decentralization or devolution of managerial responsibility could at first glance be identified as a reconfiguration of managerial hierarchies, and consequently as a sign of depolitization. But this is only partly true. Managerial responsibilities have been reconfigured, but responsibilities have been devolved to regional and local authorities, and thereby politicians at these levels have had an increasing amount of influence on the decision-making processes in relation to various welfare services. One could argue that by the phasing-out the civil servant status and the transfer of employees to the local and regional authorities (e.g. the teachers) the direct parliamentary control of labour relations has become a thing of the past (cf. Fairbrother, Chapter 4). However, negotiations on employment relations in the public sector in Denmark are part of a very centralized industrial relations system (for details see Andersen *et al.*, 1998, 1999). In these negotiations the government is represented by the Ministry of Finance, and the local and regional employers by their national peak associations. Strategies and initiatives are closely co-ordinated between these public employers. In spite of the devolution of management responsibilities, the Ministry of Finance is still a very important actor in the regulation of public sector labour relations.

Third, has the restructuring of the public sector in Denmark caused an individualization of work and employment relations? Once again the answer seems to be twofold. On the one hand there is a tendency towards individualization, and the introduction of the new pay system is definitely the most prominent example of this. The seniority-based system has been replaced by a system linking pay to qualifications, functions and performance. Basically, the way is paved for a pay system that in the end can become very individualized. On the other hand, this is yet to come. So far we have seen pay become differentiated among different groups of public sector employees due to qualifications and functions. This has all been part of agreements concluded at national and/or local levels. Performance-related pay is either absent or playing a very limited role.

Summing up, there is not a clear-cut answer to the question whether the concept of depoliticization enshrines the most important aspects of public sector restructuring in Denmark. The overall picture seems to reveal that not only processes of political decision making, but also the system of regulating industrial relations or employment relations has developed into still more complex processes. These processes are characterized by an interplay between actors at different levels of society (central state, local/regional and workplace levels) and at the same time different groups of actors taking part in these processes: politicians (at national and local/regional levels), trade union representatives (at national and local/regional levels), citizens (in the user-boards) and so on. We find it difficult to argue that 'politics' has turned to 'technical' solutions in general. Rather the process of political decision making has changed its character – the pattern of decision making and thereby also the pattern of power-relations have changed.

We have suggested that there is a specific form of interdependence between public-sector restructuring and the reforms of employment relations found in the public sector. This happens both because public sector restructuring (e.g. political-administrative reforms) creates a certain framework inside which public-sector employment relations might be changed, and because of the involvement of the trade unions in initiating such processes. As a consequence, we hold to our assumption that the Danish public-sector labour market is an integral part of the Danish welfare state, and that trade unions play an important role not only in relation to public-sector labour-market reform, but also in reshaping the Danish welfare state – a position which creates both opportunities and dilemmas for the trade unions.

Bibliography

Abrahamson, P. and Borchorstc, A. (1996) 'EU og Socialpolitik', in *Rådet for Europæisk Politiks Skrift* nr. 13.

Åkerstrøm Andersen, Niels (1996) *Udlicitering – Når det private bliver politisk*, København: Nyt fra Samfundsvidenskaberne.

Andersen, S. K., Lubanski, N. and Madsen, J. S. (1998) *At the Threshold of Multi-level Regulation – Public Sector Industrial Relations in Denmark*. Paper presented at the Public Sector Restructuring and Industrial Relations Conference, National Key Centre in Industrial Relations, Monash University, 10–11 December 1998, Melbourne, Australia.

Andersen, S. K., Due, J. and Madsen, J. S. (1999) 'Denmark', in S. Bach, L. Bordogna, G. Della Rocca and D. Winchester (eds), *Public Service Employment Relations in Europe: Transformation, Modernization or Inertia?* London: Routledge.

Bach, S. and Della Rocca, G. (1998) *The Management of Public Service Employers in Western Europe*. Paper presented at the 11th World Congress of IIRA, September 1998, Bologna, Italy.

Beaumont, P. B. (1992) *Public Sector Industrial Relations*, London: Routledge.

Bogason, P. (ed.) (1996) *New Modes of Local Organizing*, New York: Nova Science Publishers.

Bonefeld, W., Brown, A. and Burnham, P. (1995) *A Major Crisis? The Politics of Economic Policy in Britain in the 1990s*, Aldershot: Dartmouth.

Danmarks Statistik (1998) *Statistiske Efterretninger 1998*, København: Danmarks Statistik.

Due, J. and Madsen, J. S. (1996) *Forligsmagerne*, København: Jurist og Økonomforbundets Forlag.

Due, J., Madsen, J. S., Strøby Jensen, C. and Kjerulf Petersen, L. (1994) *The Survival of the Danish Model*, København: Jurist og Økonomforbundets Forlag.

Due, J., Madsen, J. S. and Vistisen, H. (1994) *Medarbejderindflydelse og decentralisering*, København: Kommunernes Landsforening.

Due, J., Madsen, J. S. and Vistisen, H. (1995) *The Impact of Inherent Features and Modernization Strategies on Industrial Relations in Denmark's Public Sector*. Paper presented on the 10th IIRA World Congress, Washington DC, 1995.

Due, J., Madsen, J. S. and Lubanski, N. (1996) *Koalitioner og kollektive aftalesystemer.* Politica 28. Årg. Nr. 2 1996. English version: *Coalitions and Collective Bargaining–the Fifth Sub Process?* Paper presented at the 10th IIRA World Congress, Washington DC, 1995.

Due, J., Madsen, J. S. and Mailand, M. (1998a) 'Arbejdsmarkedets parter, multiniveauregulering og transitionelle arbejdsmarkeder', in *Arbejdsmarkedspolitisk årbog 1997*, København: Arbejdsministeriet.

Due, J., Madsen, J. S., Petersen, K. F. V. and Strøby Jensen, C. (1998b) 'Denmark', in G. Fajartag (ed.), *Collective Bargaining in Western Europe 1997–1998*, Brussels: European Trade Union Institute.

Dunleavy, P. and Hood, C. (1994) 'From Old Public Administration to New Public Management', *Public Money and Management*, 14(3): 9–16.

Esping-Andersen, G. (1990) *The Three Worlds of Welfare Capitalism*, Cornwall: TJ Press Ltd.

Ferlie, E., Ashburner, L., Fitzgerald, L. and Pettigrew, A. (1996) *The New Public Management in Action*, Oxford: Oxford University Press.

Ferner, A. (1995) 'Public Sector Industrial Relations in Europe: Common Trends and the Persistance of National Variability', in *Industrielle Beziehungen*, 2(2): 111–127.

Finansministeriet (1993) *Nyt syn på den offentlige sektor*, København: Finansministeriet.

Finansministeriet (1994) *Medarbejder i staten*, København: Finansministeriet.

Hoffman, F. (1998) 'Løn som nyt styrings- og udviklingsinstrument', *Samfundsøkonomen*, no. 4/5, København: Dansk Jurist- og Økonomforbunds Forlag.

Hood, C. (1991) 'A Public Management for all Seasons', *Public Administration*, 69(1): 3–19.

Ibsen, F. (1998) 'Nye lønformer i den offentlige sektor – succes eller fiasko?', *Samfundsøkonomen*, no. 4/5, København: Dansk Jurist- og Økonomforbunds Forlag.

Jensen, P. H. (1998) 'Velfærdsstatens variationer, dynamikker og effekter', in *Den jyske historiker*, Århus: Historisk Institut.

Jensen, C. S., Navrbjerg, S. E. and Lubanski, N. (1999) 'Tillidsrepræsentant mod nye udfordringer', Præsentation af en tillidsrepræsentantundersøgelse, København: FAOS & LO.

Kickert, W. (1997) 'Public Management in the United States and Europe', in W. Kickert (ed.), *Public Management and Administrative Reform in Western Europe*, Cheltenham: Edward Elgar, pp. 15–42.

Klausen, K. K. (1996) *Offentlig Organisation, Strategi og Ledelse*, Gylling: Odense Universitetsforlag.

Klausen, K. K. and Ståhlberg, K. (1998) 'New Public Management', in K. K. Klausen and K. Ståhlberg (eds), *New Public Management i Norden. Nye organisations- og ledelsesformer i den decentrale velfærdsstat*, Odense: Odense Universitetsforlag, pp. 9–31.

Koimann, J. (1993) *Modern Governance*, London: Sage.

Lægreid, P. and Pedersen, O. K. (1994) *Forvaltningspolitik i Norden*, København: Jurist- og Økonomforbundets Forlag.

Lægreid, P. and Pedersen, O. K. (1999) *Fra opbygning til ombygning i staten – Organisationsforandringer i tre nordiske lande*, København: Jurist- og Økonomforbundets Forlag.

Lubanski, N., Jensen, C. S. and Navrbjerg, S. E. (1999) Tillidsrepræsentanten mellem arbejdsplads, fagforening og familie, Et kvalitativt studie af tillidsrepræsentantens arbejdsvilkår, København: FAOS & LO.

Madsen, J. S., Due, J. and Andersen, S. K. (1998) 'Historien om nye lønformer i den offentlige Sektor', in *Samfundsøkonomen*, no. 4/5, København: Dansk Jurist- og Økonomforbunds Forlag, pp. 29–39.

Mathiesen, K., Hvenegaard, H., Hasle, P., Hvid, H. and Keller, L. (1998) *Udvidet medarbejderindflydelse i staten (MIO)*, Copenhagen: Finansministeriet og Centralorganisationerne.

Ministry of Finance (1994) *Human Resource Development in Danish Central Government*, Copenhagen: Ministry of Finance.

Ministry of Finance (1995) *Welfare for Citizens – Effective Public Institutions*, Copenhagen: Ministry of Finance.

OECD (1995) *Governance in Transition. Public Management Reforms in OECD Countries*, Paris: OECD.

OECD (1997) *In Search of Results. Performance Management Practices*, Paris: OECD.

Osborne, D. and Gaebler, T. (1992) *Reinventing Government: How the Entrepreneurial Spirit Is Transforming the Public Sector*, Reading, MA: Addison-Wesley.

Pedersen, D. (1996) 'Personaleorganisationer og forvaltningspolitik i Danmark', in P. Lægreid and O. K. Pedersen (ed.), *Integration og decentralisering*, København: Jurist- og Økonomforbundets Forlag.

Plant, P. (2001) *Vocational Guidance for Low-paid Workers in Denmark*, http://www.gla.ac.uk/wg/danrep1e.htm (accessed 21 July 2005).

Pollitt, C. (1990) *Managerialism and the Public Services: The Anglo-American Experience*, Oxford: Blackwell.

Poulsen, J. S. and Hedegaard, F. (1998) 'Lønstyring og økonomisk råderum i kommunernes nye lønsystem', in *Samfundsøkonomen*, no. 4/5, København: Dansk Jurist- og Økonomforbunds Forlag, pp. 19–23.

Rhodes, R. A. W. (1997) *Understanding Governance. Policy Networks, Governance, Reflexivity and Accountability*, Buckingham: Open University Press.

Schmid, G. (1995) 'Is Full Employment Still Possible? Transitional Labour Markets as a New Strategy of Labour Market Policy', *Economic and Industrial Democracy*, 16(3): 429–456.

Stokholm, K., Due, J. and Andersen, S. K. (1998) *Social Dialogue in the Public Sector in Denmark*, Report compiled for CEEP, Copenhagen: FAOS.

Traxler, F. (1996) 'Collective Bargaining and Industrial Change: A Case of Disorganisation? A Comparative Analysis of Eighteen OECD Countries', *European Sociological Review*, 12(3): 271–287.

Ugebrevet Mandag Morgen/Strategisk Forum (1996) *Den udviklende personalepolitik. Et debatoplæg om kravene til fremtidens personalepolitik i kommuner og amter*, København: Mandag Morgen/Strategisk Forum.

Ugebrevet Mandag Morgen (1997) 'Overenskomstforhandlinger afgør velfærdsfornyelse', *Ugebrevet Mandag Morgen*, 3(January): 17–23.

6 Changing public sector industrial relations in the Australian Commonwealth

John O'Brien

Introduction

The context of this chapter is the relationship between the roles of government as an employer, as a prime generator of policy, as regulator and as financial controller. The overarching issue is the extent that it is possible to match the system regulating public sector industrial relations with the general policy directions of government, while the government maintains overall control of the nature and direction of state expenditure, particularly in a political environment that has encouraged the promotion and implementation of 'small government'. It will be argued that there are significant limits to the decentralisation of public sector industrial relations given the overall fiscal, policy, regulatory and employer responsibilities of government, even if there is a strong policy to decentralise industrial relations processes generally. The chapter will consider, in particular, how employees and their organisations have responded to the attempts by government to decentralise the regulation of labour–management relations, whilst retaining control over their employees. This chapter will concentrate on the Commonwealth sector, although the trends outlined below have their parallels, as well as divergences, in the States and Territories. The discussion will be largely confined to employees working within the core public service as distinct from those employed in statutory authorities.

The Australian federal state

Australia is a federal state. As a consequence there are separate industrial relations systems for each of the six States and the Commonwealth. With the exception of Victoria and Tasmania, where wages boards were developed, the predominant form of regulation has been compulsory conciliation and arbitration. At the Commonwealth level, the specific industrial relations power enshrined in the constitution was limited to the provision of conciliation and arbitration, although other powers, such as the corporations and external affairs, have been used more recently for industrial relations purposes. Both State and federal constitutions, however, give the various governments absolute control over the terms and conditions of their own employees, although power was often exercised through intermediary bodies. Nevertheless, governments were reluctant to give their own employees untrammelled access to the conciliation and arbitration system on the grounds that the determination of arbitral bodies might compromise the sovereignty of the crown over its 'servants' (Sawer, 1963: 36–37).

While governments are able to exercise power over their own employees that exceed that which can be exercised by private sector employers (Boston *et al.*, 1996; O'Brien and Hort, 1998), there was a strong disposition to place the responsibility for employment relationships on intermediate bodies (Caiden, 1965: 1–4; Caiden, 1967). In the Commonwealth and the States, the prime responsibility was given to Public Service Boards that generally played the role of employer of public service employees, but could also exercise influence over the employment conditions of employees of statutory corporations. The rationale for this arrangement was that public employees had a role in governance that was not dependent on changes in the political complexion of government (Caiden, 1967: 189). In the core public service, permanent employment was linked with the concept of public servants holding an 'office' in a manner similar to statutory office holders. The concept of 'office' is the basis of security of tenure in public employment and the notion of a 'career' public service (McLeod, 1994; Weeks, 1999).

Although ultimately subject to government, Public Service Boards became powerful instruments of governance both in the Commonwealth and the states. The *Sydney Morning Herald* suggested that it was not 'an oversimplification' to say that the New South Wales 'Government does anything the Board tells it to' (14 January 1956). Indeed the New South Wales Public Service Board saw itself as an executive arm of government with considerable operational autonomy from the government of the day in the organisation of the provision of state services (New South Wales Public Service Board, 1954: 5). In a real sense, the Board provided continuity of governance in the state (Alaba, 1994: 50). This was also the case in other states and the Commonwealth, although it is doubtful whether any of these bodies were quite as powerful as the New South Wales Public Service Board (Alaba, 1994: 42).

In the late 1970s, the relative autonomy of public employment authorities came into question as governments began to wrestle with the emerging fiscal crisis of the state. In the mid-1970s, the Royal Commission in Australian Government Administration argued for greater mainstreaming of employment arrangements as part of a general overhaul of the Commonwealth Public Service (Royal Commission, 1976). On election to office, however, the Fraser conservative government undertook a major restructuring of federal government functions to meet its commitment to 'smaller government'. This involved winding back federal government functions that had been extended during the period of the Whitlam Labor government. The principal form of labour flexibility within the Australian Public Service (APS) had been hitherto the 'temporary' public servant. The employment of temporary officers could deal with peaks and flows in labour demand; it was less useful for major restructuring purposes. This meant that the government needed the capacity to retrain and redeploy permanent officers and if necessary make them redundant as individuals, rather than abolish the offices they occupied. This objective was achieved through a number of measures: the Commonwealth Employees (Employment Provisions) Act 1977, the 'no work as directed – no pay' amendments to the

Public Service Act (1978) and the Commonwealth Employees (Redeployment and Retirement) Act 1979 (Simms, 1987: 28–30). These measures were widely regarded as an attack on the concept of permanent employment in the public service, as well as the industrial rights of public servants. It marked the beginning of the transformation of public service employee organisations from largely compliant staff associations to industrial unions prepared to use, albeit selectively, the full range of industrial tactics (Simms, 1987).

Four factors influenced the changes in the structure of public sector industrial relations in the late 1970s and the early 1980s. These were:

* the gradual decline of Public Service Boards as regulators of public service employment;
* the placing of public administration more explicitly under ministerial control;
* the rise of the 'new public management';
* the convergence between public sector industrial relations processes and private sector industrial regulation.

Restructuring the public sector workplace: an industrial negotiation model

Changes in personnel management tended to lag behind financial reforms and changes in general management and political coordination. By 1986, many of the personnel functions previously exercised by the Public Service Board were carried out by departmental secretaries. Staff establishments and industrial relations, however, remained under the control of the departments of Finance and Industrial Relations respectively. From 1983 to 1987, changes to personnel arrangements were largely legislatively based and encompassed alterations to personnel policies and practices. In that sense the changes were management-driven and were located within a wide-ranging recasting of the Commonwealth sector. From 1987 changes to employment relations took place in a more explicitly industrial context. In 1984, the Public Service Board embarked on a major review of the public service classification system. This process involved an extensive broad banding and simplification of the complicated classification systems that had developed in the Commonwealth sector (Priese, 1989; Dorrington, 1992; O'Brien, 1994b). The size of this task was beyond the capacity of any single agency. Such a process required the active involvement of public service unions. It suited the government and the unions to negotiate centrally, although the new arrangements could be subsequently implemented to meet the specific requirements of individual agencies. The managed decentralisation of the industrial relations system generally, after 1987, enabled the processes within the Commonwealth sector to be integrated into broader regulatory changes. The second tier and the structural efficiency wage principles required unions to negotiate with employers on issues of efficiency and productivity in exchange for access to arbitrated wage adjustments. By tying management-initiated organisational changes to the wages system, it was possible to incorporate unions into management agendas, while limiting the capacity of management to impose changes without negotiation.

The industrial democracy model of consultative management, employee participation and limited co-determination gave way to a more traditional industrial relations model of negotiated change.

Managed decentralism and productivity bargaining

The model of managed decentralism favoured by the Labor government was increasingly challenged by counter discourses of labour market reform. Sources of challenge included the employment contract model with its overt hostility to unions and conciliation and arbitration, as well as a more human resource management-oriented approach that advocated the primacy of 'employee relations' over 'industrial relations' (Nicholls, 1986; Hilmer *et al.*, 1989; O'Brien, 1994a). The Coalition parties developed an industrial relations policy that attempted to encompass both approaches by proposing the removal of unions' bargaining monopoly and the reduction of the power of the conciliation and arbitration system, within the framework of a system that encouraged more direct relationships between employers and employees (Liberal and National Parties, 1992). In addition, the Australian Council of Trade Unions (ACTU) demanded that the system of managed decentralism be replaced with a more comprehensive system of workplace-level award bargaining. The task for the federal Labor government was to develop an industrial relations model that accommodated the ACTU policy direction without adopting the more radical market-oriented agenda of the Opposition. The new regulatory model envisaged the encouragement of workplace bargaining within the industrial award framework with the Industrial Relations Commission retaining a diminished, but still significant, role in the regulation of industrial relations (Fox *et al.*, 1995: 531). Despite the initial rejection of the concept by the Industrial Relations Commission in April 1991, the Labor government/ACTU model of workplace bargaining was in place by the end of 1991.

The Labor government needed to demonstrate that its approach to workplace bargaining was a fairer and more effective system than the Coalition model. The obvious place to conduct such an experiment was in the APS. There was some doubt, however, that productivity-based bargaining could work effectively in a budget-funded environment. To overcome this perception the government established two groups to consider the implementation of workplace bargaining in the APS. The first group consisted of a number of departmental secretaries. They tackled the issue of productivity measurement by arguing that it could be related to 'performance management', which they said had been a central feature of the public service reforms in the 1980s. They argued that the focus on outputs and outcomes that had characterised the reform process meant that it was possible to identify productivity improvements even when 'their precise measurement was difficult to achieve' (Glenn, 1991: 6). They considered three models ranging from full devolution to partial devolution where agencies would share responsibility for funding wage rises with the government.

The work of the department secretaries was supplemented by three academic consultants: Professors John Niland, William Brown and Barry Hughes. They considered the utility of a number of methods used in the APS to measure productivity

(Niland *et al.*, 1991: 9–20). They opted for a system of productivity measurement that combined general performance indicators and quality-focused approaches to their development and application at the agency level. They were of the view, however, that 'measures of APS wide of productivity growth of an acceptable standard (were)...not available and (were)...unlikely to be so in the future'. Productivity could only be regarded as a 'sub-set' of performance. They proposed that a Public Agency Board be established to assess each agency's performance and its readiness for bargaining (Niland *et al.*, 1991: 61).

The creation of an additional central agency, however, would have interfered with the existing APS coordination arrangements, as well as adding an additional layer of centralised regulation when the government's overall policy objective was to promote workplace bargaining. The government requested the secretaries to revisit the issue in the light of the consultants' recommendations. They reaffirmed that the departments of Finance and Industrial Relations and the Public Service Commission would jointly supervise agency-level bargaining. A core of service-wide pay and conditions was to be maintained. Any additional productivity-based pay would be paid in the form of non-recurring bonuses that could be incorporated into pay structure at the conclusion of the agreement if productivity gains proved to be enduring. Agencies unable to bargain would have access to a proportion of funds returned to government provided that they implemented efficiencies and developed productivity improvement plans (Glenn, 1992: 2). This became known as the 'foldback' mechanism.

The dilemmas of a negotiated model of decentralised wage bargaining

The arguments about the productivity measurement in the APS were in part designed to convince the unions that there could be workable agency-level bargaining that would not compromise the regime of service-wide wages and conditions. Achieving the policy objective of introducing workplace bargaining for its own employees did not, however, sit comfortably with the desire of the unions to maintain a high degree of common conditions. Moreover, the secretaries and the consultants agreed on one issue: that it was difficult to measure productivity in non-market environments. This tentativeness did not make it easy for the government to convince the unions that agency bargaining would not have deleterious consequences for their members. The Public Sector Union conducted a survey of its members that revealed widespread concern about the loss of award conditions and job losses if agency bargaining proceeded. In September 1991, the union put three options to its members:

- reject bargaining altogether;
- negotiate bargaining on the union's terms; or
- withdraw from negotiations given the government's insistence that the wage claim made by the union could only be met through the adoption of agency bargaining.

Fourteen thousand nine hundred and sixty-nine members (of 17,753 who voted) opted for the second proposition, although it was not clear how this would be achieved.

In fact the union had no real choice but to accept some model of decentralised bargaining given both the government and the ACTU wanted a shift in that direction. Of more immediate concern was the impending federal election. The government (and the unions) needed to demonstrate that its model of decentralised industrial relations could work more effectively and equitably than that proposed by the Opposition parties. In December 1992, the government and 27 public service unions signed an agreement on the introduction of agency-level wage bargaining. This agreement provided for the development of 'more flexible' employment conditions at the agency level to be achieved in agency-specific agreements provided that there was 'no overall disadvantage to employees' (Department of Industrial Relations, 1992: 4). The agreement said that agency-level agreement should not achieve productivity gains through the application of a narrow 'costs offsets' approach or as a consequence of 'arbitrary job reductions'. This left the door open for productivity gains to be made through negotiated downsizing and voluntary redundancies. These agency level agreements would supplement a service-wide pay increase that was made in exchange for commitments to address a range of work organisation issues (Department of Industrial Relations, 1992: 13–21; O'Brien, 1997a).

Agency-level bargaining in the APS

The difficulty in finding a balance between the competing agendas of the government, the ACTU and the public sector unions is illustrated when the outcomes of these bargaining arrangements are examined. One of the first agreements made was in the Department of Defence, which was reached in the dying days of the 1990–1993 Labor government. With the re-election of the government, it became the template of subsequent agency bargaining. The department had undergone considerable downsizing since 1987. The civilian workforce had been reduced from 35,818 to 22,559 in that period, principally as a consequence of contracting out support functions such as maintenance (Wrigley, 1991). The agreement went to issues such as work organisation, employment conditions, work environment and training and skill formation. It was also agreed that a Defence Total Quality Management programme would be introduced (Department of Defence, 1994). There was not, however, any explicit explanation of how the wage adjustment would be paid. The Department of Finance required that agencies be explicit on this issue (Department of Finance, 1994). It seemed that the parties had agreed to little more than continuing the restructuring and downsizing processes that had been underway for some years. Indeed, this was revealed to be the case by the principal negotiator for the agency in a statement before the Senate Committee on Finance and Public Administration in 1994 (Gourlay, 1994: 167–168). Moreover, one of the union officials involved in the negotiations reported that there was an understanding between the secretary of the department and the unions that the programme of redundancies would continue within the agency (Heaney, 1998). Whatever rhetoric there was about avoiding negative cost cutting, this agreement would be paid for by both past and prospective job losses (O'Brien, 1994a, 1997a).

During 1993 and 1994, most APS agencies either managed to negotiate an agency-level agreement or gain access to the 'foldback' fund (O'Brien, 1997a).

Among the agencies that relied on this latter arrangement were the Department of Finance and the Treasury. This was a considerable source of angst amongst the agencies that had reached agreements (Halligan *et al.*, 1996: 46). The central agencies were accused of being 'free riders' on the efforts of other agencies. An evaluation of the system conducted by the Department of Finance and the Department of Industrial Relations confirmed this view, and also indicated that small agencies had found particular difficulty in identifying productivity savings (Department of Industrial Relations and Department of Finance, 1994). On the other hand, the system had been a continuing source of controversy within the Public Sector Union with the leadership proclaiming the gains that it had delivered to members, while dissident elements claimed that too many concessions had been made to achieve wage adjustments (O'Brien, 1997a: 184–185). It was no great surprise when the public sector unions agreed to return to a service-wide model of enterprise bargaining for the period 1995–1996. The only major concession made by the unions was to agree that they would not oppose the major overhaul of the Public Service Act and that appeals relating to the termination of employment would be dealt with under the Industrial Relations Act rather than APS-specific procedures (Community and Public Sector Union, 1994). The Secretary of the Department of Industrial Relations defended this reversal as merely mirroring 'standard practice in large private employers that operate in multiple workplaces' (Rosalky, 1995).

This episode of agency bargaining followed by a return to a more centralised mode of bargaining illustrates the conflicting objectives that governments need to meet when regulating their own employees. The government had a clear agenda to decentralise the wage bargaining system. The best way to do this was to demonstrate that it could work for its own employees. In the short term, there was an imperative to demonstrate its superiority over the more radical agenda of the Opposition. On the other hand, the government needed to maintain control over the costs of such a system. Thus the central agencies acted as the regulators on behalf of the government. In that sense the system was not wholly decentralised. The government also needed to wrestle with the practical problems of productivity measurement and the expectation from the unions that all employees would receive a similar wage outcome. The solution to these problems through the 'foldback' mechanism meant that some public service managers who had been able to bargain had to finance the non-bargaining 'free-riders'. Even for the bargaining agencies it was difficult to see how productivity gains could be made without either continuing job losses and/or work intensification for the remaining employees. Nevertheless, the process facilitated further the incorporation of public sector unions into a recasting of the APS.

The Commonwealth as 'ultimate employer': management agendas and union responses

When the Coalition parties were elected as the Commonwealth government in 1996, it was made clear that the APS would be a testing ground for the implementation of its industrial relations policy (MacDonald, 1998; O'Brien and O'Donnell, 1999). This policy was designed to reduce the role of 'outside bodies' such as industrial tribunals and unions in the regulation of workplace relationships (Reith, 1997a). The Workplace Relations Act 1996 established a regime of individual and collective agreements that supplemented the traditional award and agreement system with unions. While unions were not excluded from representing employees as bargaining agents, employers were given the opportunity of pursuing agreements with employees directly. This new regime presented some difficulties for public sector unions generally and the Community and Public Sector Union (CPSU) in particular. This section of the chapter will consider the response of the CPSU to this more contestable industrial environment.

The government was determined that all agencies would reach agreements and not be able to rely on a 'foldback' mechanism that some agencies had used during the Labor government's flirtation with agency-level bargaining (Reith, 1997a,b). Nevertheless, the government regarded itself as the 'ultimate employer' of public servants and therefore it was permissible for it to lay down parameters within which agency-level agreements would be made. The parameters included the following:

- that agreements were to be funded within agency appropriations;
- that agencies were to introduce a rationalised classification structure linked to service-wide benchmarks;
- that flexible remuneration arrangements were to be permitted;
- that all certified agreements were to provide for the making of Australian Workplace Agreements;
- be subject to coordination arrangements, including consultation with the Department of Workplace Relations and Small Business;
- be subject to ministerial clearance where significant policy issues are raised by agreement.

(Reith, 1997b)

On the face of it, the government was placing significant restrictions on the capacity of agency managements to negotiate specific arrangements with their own employees. The senior official responsible for coordinating agency agreement-making in the APS likened these arrangements to those that operated within large private corporations. While a corporation might allow its constituent enterprises considerable operational autonomy in employment arrangements, they are formulated within a framework of overall corporate policy (Yates, 1998a,b). If the government was to retain significant centralised control over its employees, this was not matched by the maintenance of service-wide arrangements that public sector unions had relied on in the past to maintain commonality of wages and conditions across the APS. The CPSU initially sought a service-wide framework agreement supplemented by agency-level arrangements, but eventually it was forced to accept that it had little option but to negotiate agency by agency.

This fragmented bargaining environment was complicated further by the government's determination to strengthen the notion of 'freedom of association', which it presented as the right to join or not to join a union, rather than the right to organise and to bargain collectively. The new legislative regime of agreements with employees effectively removed the bargaining monopoly from unions. They now had to compete with non-unionised employees as the representatives of employees in the agreement-making process. To test the strength of the unions the government required that all public servants reauthorise the deduction of their union subscriptions from their pay. The government claimed that direct deductions to the CPSU fell by 40 per cent (Yates, 1998b). Fearing that a Coalition government would remove deductions of union fees entirely, the CPSU had already embarked on an active campaign to persuade its members to pay their dues by alternative means (Stapleton, 1998).

Hitherto, public sector unions had been able to use either awards or service-wide agreements to maintain a high level of consistency in employment arrangements. These arrangements had been overlaid with formal consultation arrangements. These mechanisms were either no longer operative or were largely displaced by the new agreement-making arrangements. Thus the unions, and the CPSU in particular, faced an environment where their capacity to enforce service-wide arrangements was severely constrained, while the government as 'ultimate employer' could insist on the degree of uniformity consistent with its overall policy objectives. The difficulty for public service unions was that they were forced to operate in a decentralised environment where managements had greater authority to pursue the agendas set down by government as well as their own objectives. The new system was procedurally decentralised but in both a substantive and substantial sense still highly centralised. How did the CPSU fare in this contradictory environment?

The CPSU is somewhat reluctant to reveal overall union density in the APS, but it is clear that it is highly variable. In the large social benefit-providing agency Centrelink, it claimed a density level of about 75 per cent, although management claimed it was much lower. In the Department of Employment, Education, Training and Youth Affairs (DEETYA) and in the Australian Bureau of Statistics the density was in excess of 50 per cent. In central policy agencies such as the Department of Finance and Administration (DoFA), Prime Minister and Cabinet and the Audit Office, the density was around 35 per cent (interviews with union delegates, July/ August 1998; Colmer, 1998; Gepp, 1998; senior manager, Centrelink, 1999). These differing levels had a significant effect on the capacity of the union to influence bargaining processes and outcomes, without necessarily being the determining factor. Whatever the precise membership figures, by 1999 the union had decided that the public sector was not a growth area for members. It therefore, made a concerted effort to expand its membership in the private communication and television sector, building on its significant presence in the publicly owned Australian Broadcasting Corporation and in the partly privatised Telstra Corporation (Gepp, 1999).

In DEETYA, the secretary refused to meet with the union. Instead he organised an election of staff representatives to undertake negotiations with management. The CPSU ran a 'ticket' that included the national industrial officer for the agency in the staff ballot. It received 80 per cent of the primary votes and won all positions (Colmer, 1998). A similar attempt to marginalise the union failed in the second round of bargaining. In the Department of Social Security/Centrelink, the CPSU bargaining team refused to meet the management negotiators in the company of staff-elected representatives. In both cases the high level of union membership was instrumental in securing a union-negotiated agreement. In both these agencies the agreements largely conformed with the government's parameters, but the union believed it would be able to play a significant and continuing role in the restructuring of the classification system and in the operation of the performance management schemes that were to be undertaken as a result of the agreement (Colmer, 1998; Gepp, 1998). In Centrelink, the management, conscious of the strength of the union, did not press for the adoption of a performance-based classification system, but they saw the union commitment to discuss the issue as merely the first step in a comprehensive restructuring programme (interview with senior manager, Centrelink, 1998). The second agreement, however, provided for the introduction of such a system, with however considerable procedural protections for employees (Centrelink, 1999).

In contrast, in the DoFA, the union negotiators had to operate alongside non-union representatives in a process that was largely driven by management (Pollard, 1998). The DoFA management initially adopted a confrontationist approach. Union delegates believed that on matters of substance, the management was not really interested in negotiating either with union or staff representatives (interview with DoFA union delegates, 1998). Indeed the management was hostile to having a CPSU industrial officer as part of the staff team, although it eventually relented (Pollard, 1998). Management came to the negotiating table with its agenda firmly outlined; performance management was not negotiable. It was only willing to accept minor amendments to its proposals for broadbanding classifications; the issue of abolishing overtime altogether was non-negotiable. Union delegates perceived that management saw the role of staff representatives as one of convincing staff of the validity of the management's agenda, rather than being active negotiators on behalf of staff (interview with DoFA delegates, 21 July 1998).

When it came to voting on the agreement, the CPSU campaigned for its rejection. Union delegates, however, were under considerable pressure, both from management and staff, to support the agreement, particularly as staff faced the threat of losing the initial payment to be paid on certification. Moreover, a number of staff who had transferred from the former Department of Administrative Services when the two agencies had been amalgamated were facing redundancy. They were concerned to leave the service with the best possible final payout. Despite all that pressure only 63 per cent of the 70 per cent of the staff that voted supported the agreement (interview with DoFA delegates, 1998). Since the agreement was made, the management embarked on a concerted campaign to convince staff that they should accept individual contracts on the grounds that such arrangements fit better with the 'corporate culture' of the agency (O'Brien and O'Donnell, 2000). In the next round of agreement-making, DoFA management declined to offer any collective arrangements at all, insisting that any pay adjustments be made through individual contracts (Caird, 2000: 79).

Union influence

An indication of union influence can be gauged by the number of agencies that made agreements with unions compared with those whose agreements are with employees.

By mid-September 1998, about half of the agreements were with employees and the other half with unions. Nevertheless most of the large service agencies were relatively highly unionised and so the union agreements represented about 73 per cent of employees in the APS. The non-union agreements tend to be in small and policy-oriented agencies, although the Department of Health and Human Services has a non-union agreement (1998). On the other hand, the Workplace Relations Minister's own department, with the overall responsibility of coordinating agency agreement-making, has a union-negotiated agreement (O'Brien and O'Donnell, 1999). Indeed, it has been suggested by a consultant who was closely involved in the agreement-making processes that this development encouraged a number of agency managements to seek the relative convenience of an agreement with the CPSU rather than establish more complicated consultation and negotiation arrangements with staff generally (Heaney, 1998). In the second round of agreement-making during 1999–2000, the percentage of employees covered by union agreements seems to be increasing. By May 2000 some 92 per cent of APS employees were covered by agreements between agencies and unions rather than those directly between agencies and employees (Heaney Blaylock and Associates, 2000). The overall percentage of employees covered by union-negotiated agreements has continued to be around 73 per cent. Indeed, the CPSU complained to a parliamentary enquiry on public sector employment matters that it had played an important role in the negotiation processes in many non-union agreements, but that the final agreement with employees prevented the union having any formal status if disputes arise during the life of the agreement (Caird, 2000: 78–79). The union claimed that many non-union members wanted it to be involved in the negotiation processes, although there is no evidence that this was being translated into increased union membership. In fact the union seemed to be resigned to continual decline in membership in the APS. It was looking to the burgeoning private communications sector as a source of new members to bolster its substantial presence in the partly privatised Telstra (Gepp, 1999).

It seems that the CPSU adopted a 'hot shops' bargaining strategy. The union sought the best outcome within the government's parameters in agencies where it has effective organisation and membership density. It then relied on attempting to emulate the conditions and wage outcomes in agencies where it is not so strong. In this it is aided, to some extent, by agency managements who did not wish to have a wide disparity of outcomes across agencies that might occasion loss of staff to more favourable agencies. This was, for instance, the explicit intention of the management of the Aboriginal and Torres Strait Islands Commission (Ramsey, 1998). This coincidence of objectives between the union and managements did not, however, result in a uniformity of bargaining outcomes. This was dramatically illustrated after the 1998 federal election when there was a significant restructuring of government agencies. This had the effect of creating new agencies whose employees were working under different enterprise agreements. The government indicated that relocated public servants would have the same conditions but not the wages prevailing in their new agencies (Davis and Murphy, 1998). The CPSU argued that employees doing the same work in the new agencies should have the same wages and conditions (Caird, 1998). This was a particular problem in the newly created Department of Employment, Workplace Relations and Small Business. Former employees of the

DEETYA had differing pay and working conditions to those operating in the former Department of Workplace Relations and Small Business. As an interim measure, it was decided that former DEETYA staff would retain the pay arrangements of that agency but be subject to the working conditions operative within the Workplace Relations agreement (interview with union delegates, Department of Employment, Workplace Relations and Small Business, 5 November 1998). As a consequence individual agreements are now common in this agency, whereas there were no such arrangements outside the senior executive service in the former Department of Workplace Relations and Small Business. If nothing else, this indicated that there are significant limitations to devolved bargaining where the government is both the source of funds and the prime initiator of policy and administrative reorganisation.

The experience of agreement-making forced unions to reorient their work. When agency managements sought to negotiate with staff representatives and not solely with union representatives, CPSU delegates attempted to establish coalitions of union and staff delegates. Although it was not unusual for tensions to emerge, particularly over whether communications with staff would carry the union logo, a working relationship involving regular caucuses to establish a common position prior to negotiating with management and joint staff–union meetings took place in a number of agencies. This approach was viewed by delegates as portraying the union as willing to listen to and represent the views of all staff (interview with union delegates, Public Service and Merit Protection Commission, Audit Office, 16 July 1998). In the DoFA and the Department of Foreign Affairs and Trade (DFAT), however, CPSU opposition was insufficient to persuade staff to reject the agreement. Nevertheless, the loss of bargaining monopoly can present unions with an opportunity to incorporate non-union members into union strategies. It can also present recruiting opportunities if unions are seen as operating effectively, although there is no evidence, as yet, that this has resulted in membership increases (Colmer, 1998). On the other hand, it has been suggested that some staff representatives are former union members who had lost their confidence that the union would represent their interests effectively (Heaney, 1998). Moreover, the interests of lowly graded staff in large service agencies do not necessarily match those of middle management staff in policy agencies. In DEETYA, for instance, it was one of the union delegate's responsibilities to maintain close contact with middle level management staff (interview with DEETYA delegates, 23 July 1998). In Centrelink a group of middle level staff attempted to negotiate with the management separately, but without success. The union claimed that the management preferred the more 'realistic' stance taken by the union (Gepp, 1998). Nevertheless the more contestable and decentralised regulatory regime provided opportunities for managements to divide and rule their staff. The extent to which unions are able to resist this management strategy will continue to depend on the level of union density and extent of union organisation in any given agency. One of the emerging problems in the CPSU is delegate and officer exhaustion. The union continues to recruit inexperienced industrial officers while more experienced officials go elsewhere, and maintaining delegate enthusiasm is an ongoing problem. Inexperienced officials and delegates find themselves facing very experienced negotiators and consultants on the employer side.

Changing culture

While the CPSU and other public sector unions seemed to have maintained some role in the negotiation processes, they seemed less able to resist effectively employer strategies designed to strengthen managerial prerogative. Many agency managements saw the new agreement-making arrangements as an opportunity to facilitate 'cultural change' in the APS. The agreement between the Department of Finance and its employees speaks of the need to promote 'a working culture based on high performance, quality outcomes and modern management and work practices' (DoFA, 1997). The Public Service and Merit Protection Commission agreement claims that the success of the agency 'will depend on the creation of a workplace in which there is a bias for action and achievement' (Public Service and Merit Protection Commission, 1997–1999).

In the agencies where the unions were not well represented, agency managements were able to institute performance-based payment systems without much resistance from the union. In DoFA, where the unions played only a marginal role in the agreement-making process (Pollard, 1998), management was able to adopt an uncompromising approach to the promotion of a 'can do' culture which it said was 'action oriented' and where staff would be urged to be 'creative' and to 'get runs on the board', and would be rewarded for, being 'high performers'. Union delegates in the agency characterised the motivational exhortations of management as akin to that used by Amway, a pyramid-style marketing organisation (interview with union delegates, DoFA, 1998). These exhortations were matched by a concerted attempt to persuade employees that acceptance of an individual contract in the form of an Australian Workplace Agreement (AWA) was a clear manifestation that they had 'signed on' to the new culture. For those who relied on the 'safety' of the collective agreement, the payment system was clearly linked to performance (O'Brien and O'Donnell, 2000). The role of the union was reduced to assisting members who were the victims of the new culture. Some employees took redundancy packages, while others sought refuge in other agencies (Blackwell and Pollard, 1999). The success of the agency management in this case is indicated by the fact that it is resisting having any further collective arrangements with its employees. They have all been offered individual contracts as the only means of gaining wage increases (Caird, 2000: 79). Indeed the percentage of DoFA staff on individual contracts grew from 32 per cent in June 1999 to 52 per cent in June 2000 (Department of Finance and Administration, 2000). While the union has protested about this approach, it has been unable to resist it. Indeed there is active consideration being undertaken within the union about the desirability of offering a full range of industrial services to areas where it has only a minor presence. This was indicative of an implicit union strategy to concentrate its resources where it can make a real impact. Indeed the union has made significant internal structural changes that allow the centre to reallocate resources more easily to areas of strength or potential recruitment (Gepp, 1999).

Having said that, the CPSU has identified the issue of performance management as a key issue for its members and employees generally. It conducted a survey of its members in early 1999. While this survey had little quantitative value, its qualitative responses revealed a considerable discontent with the implementation of performance pay schemes in a number of agencies, including DFAT, DoFA and the Department of Heath and Aged Care, all agencies where the union had a minor role in the agreement-making process. Concerns were also expressed about performance-based pay processes in agencies where the union had played a considerable role in formulating agreements such as the Department of Employment, Workplace Relations and Small Business and in Centrelink, where the union has its largest concentration of members (O'Donnell and O'Brien, 2000).

In Centrelink, the agency that has the responsibility for administering and paying all pensions and benefits, the management adopted an aggressive rhetoric about running the organisation along business lines. All the keywords and concepts of the modern service delivery organisation were mobilised: 'customer service', 'strategic drivers', 'competitive business edge' through 'knowledge' 'quality', 'innovation', 'communication' and 'making a difference' through effective 'people management'. Total quality management is the key 'strategic driver' in this agency. The agreement between the CPSU and the agency pledges that both organisations are committed to delivering services 'to customers in a simple, efficient and accessible manner, Centrelink's key strategic business focus is on quality customer service' (Centrelink, 1997: 2). There is little challenge here from the union to the rhetorical shift from a welfare-oriented discourse to a business discourse. Having said that the CPSU was able to resist the management's desire to have a payment system linked more explicitly to performance, it did commit itself to the development of such a system during the life of the agreement (Centrelink, 1997: 38). In the subsequent agreement the union agreed to a performance-based classification and pay system, although it was able to use its industrial strength to insist that the criteria for advancement are explicit and that structured procedures are available for dissatisfied employees to pursue grievances (Centrelink, 1999: 40–67). The union was not able to resist the imposition of a performance-based classification system, claiming that its members were 'not afraid of performance assessment' and that in practice the new system did not amount to much more than a 'tick and flick' system of near automatic movement through pay points and increments (Gepp, 1999).

In DFAT, where the unions had about a 30 per cent presence, management adopted a performance management system designed to shift from a policy-oriented culture to one where the management of staff is given much greater emphasis (interview with senior manager, DFAT, 1999; O'Brien and O'Donnell, 2000). The implementation of the performance management system caused considerable angst within the agency. There was a view that the performance system was both divisive and driven by budget considerations. Union delegates claimed that after the first round of performance ratings were released in June 1999, there was notable decline in staff commitment and work effort in agency with a large number of 'type A' personalities who would do almost anything for superior ratings and overseas postings (interview with union delegates, DFAT, 1999). While there was support for a structured system of performance appraisal, there were considerable reservations about the fairness and efficacy of the performance-based system. The senior management, moreover, attempted to exclude the unions from the implementation committee, but eventually after discussions between the union and the secretary of the department, the unions were allowed access to the management–staff committee. In the lead-up to the negotiations leading to the next agreement, the CPSU identified employee disaffection with the performance pay scheme as the key issue in negotiations (Community and Public Sector Union, 2000). In the subsequent agreement it was able to negotiate a set of procedures that enabled staff to pursue grievances more effectively. This was not an inconsiderable achievement given the low union membership in the agency. But even in a highly unionised agency like Centrelink, the emphasis is on individual employee rights rather than the collective rights of unions. The union may represent an aggrieved member; it has no formal role in the implementation processes. The 'freedom of association' provisions of the legislation as incorporated in the government's parameters for agreement-making legitimises the capacity of management to reduce the union to supplicants rather than legitimate participants in managerial processes, which had been the case in many agencies through the formal joint council arrangements that had dated from the 1970s but had been effectively removed by the Workplace Relations Act.

The exclusion of public sector unions from mandated implementation and consultation procedures has meant in part that they have been forced to use external forms of regulation in order to have an impact on employment arrangements where they have members. This is particularly the case in areas of employment that are removed by government decision from the public sector.

The privatisation of public employees

It is useful, however, to consider the difficulties confronting public sector unions when government policy removes major functions from mainstream public employment and locates them in government-funded agencies that operate in a more explicitly market environment. As part of a wide-ranging programme of changes to labour market programmes, the federal government abolished the Commonwealth Employment Service (CES) and created a new government-owned company, Employment National (EN), that would compete with private employment agencies in the provision of employment services to the unemployed. In this more market-oriented environment the government insisted that employees of the company should operate with pay and conditions that were equivalent to those operating in the private employment services market. Many of the staff recruited to EN were former employees of the CES. The CPSU sought to ensure that EN employees carried their public service conditions with them to the new entity. The EN management insisted that the most appropriate form of regulation was an individual contract in the form of an AWA. Former employees of the CES were told that they would not be considered for employment within EN unless they accepted an individual contract. The AWAs, however, incorporated public service conditions at the time of the transfer of employees to EN. The CPSU took this issue to the Federal Court, arguing that former CES employees had been subject to unlawful duress in the making of AWAs (Ramsey, 1998; Stapleton, 1998). Subsequently the EN management sought to have an industrial award made in the Australian Industrial Relations Commission (AIRC) for EN employees. This was opposed by the union on the grounds that the Federal Court matter should be resolved before any further regulation was made for EN employees. This was rejected by the AIRC, which has said that it was prepared to hear the management's arguments in support of making an award (AIRC, 1999). Subsequently an award was made by the Commission that removed key public service conditions from employees of EN, including paid maternity leave (Baird, 1999). As this applied only to employees who had not been transferred from the APS, paid maternity leave was still a right enjoyed by former APS employees who had signed AWAs. In September 1999, the Federal Court ruled that the employees of EN had not been subjected to unlawful duress when employees were required to sign an AWA (1999 FCA [Federal Court of Australia] 1334). In a separate decision, however, the Court held that when employees are transferred from a public sector environment to a government-owned business, the employment conditions applying at the time of transfer must continue to apply until it is agreed otherwise by the relevant parties (2000 FCA 452). This limits the capacity of employers to unilaterally alter employment conditions when government agencies are privatised. For EN employees, however, this decision meant very little. EN had been unable to compete with private sector providers in successfully gaining contracts from the government to provide employment services. As a consequence, EN had little choice but to offer redundancy packages to a large proportion of its employees.

For the CPSU this episode was a mixed blessing. It had been able to use the Federal Court to limit the capacity of employers to unilaterally vary employment conditions of former public sector employees. On the other hand, it had been unable to resist the imposition of individual contracts on its members. Moreover, these various manoeuvres in both industrial tribunals and courts had absorbed a considerable proportion of resources in a union that was losing members as a result of public sector cutbacks. In addition, such activity is hardly likely to assist in the mobilisation of members to resist loss of conditions through the agreement-making processes or to fight reductions in the public sector generally. The CPSU had traditionally operated on the basis that it could negotiate in a direct and centralised way with government. The new legislation and the government's implementation of it for its own employees meant that the union was forced to operate in a decentralised way at the agency level, while using whatever opportunities presented themselves to resist broad structural changes affecting its members. It was more a matter of *ad hoc* scrambling rather than strategic adjustment to an environment that was procedurally decentralised but that enhanced managerial prerogative to pursue both substantial and substantive central agendas of government.

Conclusion

This overview of public sector industrial relations in the past 20 years has argued that it is difficult to match the rhetoric of devolved public sector management with the practices of government in controlling and managing its own employees. This difficulty arises from the fundamental tensions that arise from reconciling the responsibilities of government as financial controller, as policy generator and as employer. As financial controller, governments generally have sought to shift from a bureaucratic/administrative model of public governance to a more market-oriented managerialist model. This shift has involved placing more direct responsibility for financial and personnel management on its managerial agents within the overall framework of government control. This process has become more problematical when attempts have been made to match the policy objective of decentralised industrial relations with the necessity for the maintenance of financial control. It was argued that considerable centralised control of industrial relations was maintained to ensure that the policy objectives of the government were achieved for its own employees. There was also consideration of the problems presented to public sector unions in continuing to work effectively in an environment when many of the centralised institutions are rendered inoperative, while at the same time centralised control is maintained in a more unilateral way by government. There was, in addition, some consideration of the industrial fate of former public servants who had to operate within a marketised environment but still remained contractually bound to government as a provider of public services.

There is little doubt that there have been significant changes in the management of the public sector. There have been varying attempts to match industrial approaches to the 'new public management' model. The nature of the particular relationships between the industrial and the managerial have been contingent upon the extent to which it has been possible to match the process of decentralisation of industrial relations to managerial devolution, without compromising overall government control. In that sense the distancing of government from the provision of public services has been more apparent than real. The state has not 'withered away' (Fairbrother *et al.*, 1997), although it has reduced its role as a direct provider of public services. The control of the remaining functions may have undergone a process of apparent 'depoliticisation' (Fairbrother, 1998), but the reality of political control has not diminished. With governments having ultimate financial responsibility, control of the cost of public employees will need to be maintained, although the methods of achieving that objective will vary. Public sector industrial relations in Australia may have been decentralised in an operational sense, but this has not diminished the control of government over its employees. This situation is analogous to the experience of other countries. In New Zealand there has been little variation of non-wage core conditions across various departments despite the 300 collective contracts in the state sector (Walsh, 1998), although some diversity has emerged more recently (Walsh *et al.*, Chapter 7 in this volume). Centralised arrangements have largely survived in the education sector, although less so in the health sector (O'Brien, 1997b). In the United Kingdom the situation is less clear. In the education and health sector there is still a considerable degree of commonality of wage rates (Bach and Winchester, 1994). There seems, however, to be a greater diversity of arrangements in core government agencies (Corby, 1998). In Australia, the architecture of regulation may have changed but the reality of control has not diminished. The devolution of management responsibility inherent in 'new public management' tends to mystify the maintenance of central control. The procedural decentralisation of industrial relations processes masks the continuity of centralised control, albeit within a framework of enhanced managerial authority.

The outcomes from the various rounds of agreement-making in the APS also demonstrate the importance of strong workplace organisation in the maintenance of legitimacy for the CPSU and other public sector unions. Within agencies containing significant delegate structures and respectable membership levels, the CPSU had a likelihood of ensuring that agreement was with the union. Such outcomes reinforce the arguments of the proponents of delegate activism (Alexander *et al.*, 1998: 688) and their conclusion that 'union organisation and bargaining capacity, rather than management style, are decisive elements in maintaining (and extending) the union membership base' (Alexander *et al.*, 1998: 682). Similar findings were reported in the Australian Workplace Industrial Relations Survey 1995 that 'active' workplace organisation was important for maintaining employee satisfaction with their union (Morehead *et al.*, 1997: 142). Within the British public sector the existence of active delegate structures was far more significant in ensuring membership retention than were alternative strategies such as the provision of financial services (Waddington and Kerr, 1999: 164). The CPSU seems to have remained relevant to the agreement-making process in many agencies. It has had some successes in the legal arena. It seems to have less capacity to counter the ideological assault of management through 'cultural change' processes, although it is able to regulate it more effectively in agencies where it has significant presence and leverage. It has centralised its financial resources and reorganised its structures along agency lines. It is not clear as yet whether it can mobilise its members sufficiently to roll back the government objectives for the public service. It has survived, but it is not, so far, prospering. The re-election of the Conservative government in 2001 and 2004 will not make it any easier for public sector unions. Nevertheless, the process of transformation from an administrative to a more managerial model of the state has not been a smooth, uniform or uncontested process. Public sector unions, despite all the difficulties that they have faced, seem to have remained in the contest.

Bibliography

AIRC [Australian Industrial Relations Commission] (1999) CPSU, The Community and Public Sector Union and Employment National (case no. 357747) and Employment National (Administration) Pty Ltd and another and CPSU, the Community and Public Sector Union (case no. 34934 of 1988), *Decision*, 26 February.

Alaba, R. (1994) *Inside Bureaucratic Power: The Wilenski Review of New South Wales Government Administration*, Hale and Iremonger and Royal Institute of Public Administration, Australia (ACT Division), Sydney.

Alexander, M., Green, R. and Wilson, A. (1998) 'Delegate Structures and Strategic Unionism: Analysis of Factors in Union Resilience', *The Journal of Industrial Relations*, 40(4): 663–689.

Bach, S. and Winchester, D. (1994) 'Opting Out of Pay Devolution? The Prospects for Local Pay Bargaining in UK Public Services', *The British Journal of Industrial Relations*, 32(2): 263–282.

Baird, M. (1999) 'The Removal of Paid Maternity Leave', *AIRAANZ Review*, 1(1): 20–24.

Blackwell, R. and Pollard, C. (1999) Interview with Robyn Blackwell, Organiser, and Celia Pollard, National Industrial Officer, Community and Public Sector Union, 23 February.

Boston, J., Martin, J., Pallot, J. and Walsh, P. (1996) *Public Management: The New Zealand Model*, Auckland: Oxford University Press.

Caiden, G. E. (1965) *Career Service: An Introduction to the History of Personnel Administration in the Commonwealth Public Service 1901–1961*, Melbourne: Melbourne University Press.

Caiden, G. E. (1967) *The Commonwealth Bureaucracy*, Melbourne: Melbourne University Press.

Caird, W. (1998) 'Members Vote on Threat to Conditions', Commuity and Public Sector Union, *Bulletin, Department of Workplace Relations and Small Business*, 3 November.

Caird, W. (2000) Statement by Wendy Caird, National Secretary, Community and Public Sector Union, to the Senate Finance and Public Administration References Committee. Reference: Australian Public Service Employment Matters, *Senate Hansard*, 14 April: 78.

Centrelink Development Agreement 1997–1998 (1997) Centrelink, Canberra.

Centrelink Development Agreement 1999–2002 (1999) Centrelink, Canberra.

Colmer, V. (1998) Interview with Vivienne Colmer, National Industrial Officer, Community and Public Sector Union, by author, Melbourne, 12 July.

Community and Public Sector Union (1994) *Bulletin*, 20 July.

Community and Public Sector Union (2000) *Bulletin*, to DFAT members.

Corby, S. (1998) 'Industrial Relations in Civil Service Agencies: Transition or Transformation', *Industrial Relations Journal*, 29(3): 194–206.

Davis, I. and Murphy, K. (1998) 'Federal Bureaucrats Do Policy Shuffle', *The Australian Financial Review*, 22 October.

Department of Defence (1994), *Section 134C Industrial Relations Act 1998 Defence (Restructuring) Agreement*, Department of Defence, Canberra.

Department of Employment and Workplace Relations (2005) *Workplace Relations: Our Plan*, http:www.workplace.gov.au

Department of Finance and Administration (1997) *Certified Agreement*, Canberra.

Department of Finance and Administration (2000) *Annual Report 1999–2000*, Department of Finance, Canberra.

Department of Industrial Relations (1992) *Improving Jobs, Productivity, Pay in the Australian Public Service*, Department of Industrial Relations, Canberra.

Department of Industrial Relations and the Department of Finance (1994) *Interim Evaluation of Agency Bargaining in the Australian Public Service*, Department of Industrial Relations, Canberra.

Dorrington, J. (1992) 'The Nature and Measures of Industrial Relations Reform to Personnel Management in the Australian Public Service', in J. Halligan and R. Wettenhall (eds), *Hawke's Third Government: Australian Commonwealth Administration 1987–1990*, The University of Canberra and the Royal Australian Institute of Public Administration, ACT Division, Canberra.

Fairbrother, P. (1998) 'The Depoliticisation of the State and Implications for Trade Unionism: Recent Developments in the United Kingdom', Working Paper, no. 51, National Key Centre in Industrial Relations, Monash University.

Fairbrother, P., Svensen, S. and Teicher, J. (1997) 'The Withering of the Australian State: Privatisation and Its Implications for Labour', Working Paper, no. 54, National Key Centre in Industrial Relations, Monash University.

Federal Court of Australia (1999) Schanka v Employment National (Administration) Pty Ltd [1999] FCA 1334 (24 September 1999).

Federal Court of Australia (2000) Employment National Ltd v CPSU [2000] FCA 452 (11 April 2000).

Fox, C., Howard, W. and Pittard, M. (1995) *Industrial Relations in Australia: Development, Law and Operation*, Melbourne: Longman Australia.

Gepp, M. (1998) Interview with Mark Gepp, National Industrial Officer, Community and Public Sector Union, by author, Melbourne, 14 July.

Gepp, M. (1999) Interview with Mark Gepp, National Industrial Officer, Community and Public Sector Union, by Peter Fairbrother and author, 16 December.

Glenn, G. [Chair] (1991) *Improving Productivity: A Challenge for the Australian Public Service: A Discussion Paper Prepared by a Committee of Heads of Australian Public Service Agencies for the Minister for Industrial Relations*, Department of Industrial Relations, Canberra, September.

Glenn, G. [Chair] (1992) *An Approach to Workplace Bargaining in the Australian Public Service: A Paper Prepared by a Committee of Heads of Australian Public Service Agencies for the Minister for Industrial Relations*, Department of Industrial Relations, Canberra, April.

Gourlay, P. (1994) Statement to Conference, Senate Standing Committee on Finance and Public Administration, *Public Service Reform: Report of the Senate Committee on Finance and Public Administration*, The Parliament of the Commonwealth of Australia, Canberra, vol. 2, Conference Proceedings.

Halligan, J., MacKintosh, J. and Watson, H. (1996) *The Australian Public Service: The View from the Top*, Coopers and Lybrand and the Centre for Research in Public Sector Management, University of Canberra.

Heaney, D. (1998) Interview with Des Heaney, Workplace Relations Consultant, by author, Canberra, 2 July.

Heaney Blaylock and Associates (2000) *Information Service* [Re: wage bargaining outcomes in the APS], Canberra.

Hilmer, F., MacFarlane, D., Rose, J. and Mclaughlin, P. (1989) *Enterprise Based Bargaining Units: A Better Way of Working*, Report of the Business Council of Australia by the Industrial Relations Study Commission, Business Council of Australia, Melbourne: BCA.

Liberal and National Parties (1992) *Jobsback*, Canberra.

MacDonald, D. (1998) 'Public Sector Trade Unionism under the Howard Government', *Labour and Industry*, 9(2): 43–59.

McLeod, R. (1994) *Report of the Public Service Review Group*, Canberra: Australian Government Publishing Service.

Morehead, A., Steele, M., Alexander, M., Stephen, K. and Duffin, L. (1997) *Changes at Work: The Australian Workplace Industrial Relations Survey*, Melbourne: Longman.

New South Wales (1954) *Report of the Public Service Board for the Year Ended 30th June*, Sydney: NSW Government Printer.

Nicholls, H. R. (1986) *Arbitration in Contempt*, Melbourne: HR Nicholls Society.

Niland, J., Brown, W. and Hughes, B. (1991) *Breaking New Ground: Enterprise Bargaining and Agency Agreements for the Australian Public Service: A Report Prepared for the Australian Minister for Industrial Relations*, Department of Industrial Relations, Canberra, December.

O'Brien, J. (1994a) 'McKinsey, Hilmer and the BCA: The "New Management" Model of Labour Market Reform', *The Journal of Industrial Relations*, 36(4): 468–490.

O'Brien, J. (1994b) 'People Management and Industrial Relations: Rethinking the Employment Relationship in the Australian Public Service', *Public Service Reform: Report from the Senate Standing Committee on Finance and Public Administration*, The Parliament of the Commonwealth of Australia, vol. 1, Conference Papers, pp. 209–224.

O'Brien, J. (1997a) 'Employment Relations and Agency Bargaining in the Australian Public Service', in G. Singleton (ed.), *The Second Keating Government: Australian Commonwealth*

Administration 1993–1996, Centre for Research in Public Sector Management, University of Canberra, and the Institute of Public Administration Australia, Canberra, pp. 175–192.

O'Brien, J. (1997b) 'Occupational and Professional as an Industrial Strategy in the New Zealand State Sector', *The Journal of Industrial Relations*, 39(4): 499–517.

O'Brien, J. and Hort, L. (1998) 'The State of State Employment', *Australian Journal of Public Administration*, 57(2): 46–48.

O'Brien, J. and O'Donnell, M. (1999) 'Government, Management and Unions: The Public Service under the Workplace Relations Act', *The Journal of Industrial Relations*, 41(3): 446–467.

O'Brien, J. and O'Donnell, M. (2000) ' "Creating a New Moral Order": Cultural Change in the Australian Public Service', *Labour and Industry*, 10(3): 57–76.

O'Donnell, M. and O'Brien, J. (2000) 'Performance-based Pay in the Australian Public Service: Employee Perspectives', *Review of Public Personnel Administration*, 20(2): 20–34.

Pollard, C. (1998) Interview with Celia Pollard, National Industrial Officer, Community and Public Sector Union with author, Canberra, 1 July.

Priese, B. (1989) 'Productivity and Industrial Relations: Retrospect and Prospect', in C. Pirie and J. Power (eds), *Economic and Management Pressures on Australian Public Administration*, Canberra College of Advanced Education and the Victorian Division of the Royal Australian Institute of Public Administration, Canberra, pp. 129–142.

Ramsey, S. (1998) Interview with Steve Ramsey, National Industrial Officer, Community and Public Sector Union, by author, Canberra, 1 July.

Reith, P. (1997a) 'Agreement Making in the APS', *Press Release*, 5 May.

Reith, P. (1997b) 'Government Decision on Funding and APS Agreements', Press Release in *Department of Workplace Relations and Small Business 1998, Workplace Relations Advices 1997/22*, vol. 1, Canberra.

Rosalky, D. (1995) 'Starship Enterprise: The Next Generation', address given to the ACT Industrial Relations Society, Canberra, 10 August.

Royal Commission on Australian Government Administration (1976) [Chair: HC Coombs], *Report*, Canberra: Australian Government Publishing Service.

Sawer, G. (1963) *Australian Federal Politics and the Law, 1929–1959*, Melbourne: Melbourne University Press.

Simms, M. (1987) *Militant Public Servants: Politicisation, Feminisation and Public Service Unions*, Melbourne: Macmillan.

Stapleton, J. (1998) Interview with John Stapleton, National Industrial Officer, Community and Public Sector Union, by author, February.

Sydney Morning Herald, 14 January 1956.

Waddington, J. and Kerr, A. (1999) 'Membership Retention in the Public Sector', *Industrial Relations Journal*, 32(2): 151–165.

Walsh, P. (1998) 'From Uniformity to Diversity? Reinventing Public Sector Industrial Relations in New Zealand', *Australian Journal of Public Administration*, 57(2): 55–59.

Weeks, P. (1999) 'Reconstituting the Employment Relationship in the Australian Public Service', in S. Deery and R. Mitchell (eds), *Employment Relations: Individualisation and Union Exclusion*, Sydney: Federation Press, pp. 69–87.

Wrigley, A. [Chair] (1991) *Force Restriction Review: Report to the Minister for Defence*, Department of Defence, Canberra.

Yates, B. (1998a) Interview with Bernie Yates, First Assistant Secretary, Department of Workplace Relations and Small Business, 20 February.

Yates, B. (1998b) 'Workplace Relations and Agreement Making the Australian Public Service', *The Australian Journal of Public Administration*, 57(2): 82–90.

Interviews with community and public sector union delegates

The Australian Audit Office, The Public Service and Merit Protection Commission, Department of Prime Minister and Cabinet, 16 July 1998.

Centrelink (Department of Social Security), 22 July 1998.

Department of Employment, Education, Training and Youth Affairs, 23 July 1998.

Department of Employment, Workplace Relations and Small Business, 5 November 1998.

Department of Finance and Administration, 21 July 1998.

Department of Foreign Affairs and Trade, 12 August 1998.

Department of Workplace Relations and Small Business, 6 August 1998.

Interviews with agency management responsible for agreement making

The Australian Bureau of Statistics, 24 February 1999.

The Australian National Audit Office, 23 February 1999.

Centrelink, 16, 25 February 1999.

Department of Education, Training and Youth Affairs, 23 February 1999.

Department of Foreign Affairs and Trade, 25 February 1999.

Department of Workplace Relations and Small Business, 23 July 1998.

The Public Service and Merit Protection Commission, 17 February 1999.

7 Public sector restructuring, management strategy and trade union response

The New Zealand experience

Pat Walsh, Sarah Oxenbridge and Kurt Wetzel

Introduction

Since 1984, the New Zealand state and its role in the society and economy have been comprehensively restructured. Accompanying this has been a radical reshaping of the trajectory of economic and social policy. These changes have had fundamental implications for industrial relations in the public sector and for public sector unions and their members.

The restructuring programme has involved a substantial shift away from the strong social democratic ethos which had underpinned the role of the New Zealand state since the 1930s. A well-developed welfare state and a high level of state regulation of economic activity enjoyed strong public and political party support until the 1980s. Policy stability was facilitated by strong state structures. A unitarist state centralised power in the national government while constitutional and political structures enabled decisive action by the state. The most important of those structures were a unicameral legislature and the absence of a constraining constitution, allied to a strong two-party political system which ensured a majority party and conferred great power on it.

The Labour Party was elected to government in 1984 on a platform consistent with the social democratic tradition it had supported strongly for many decades. However, immediately following the election, the Labour government proceeded to implement policies quite at variance with those in its election manifesto but which it claimed were designed to build a more competitive and efficient economy (Bollard and Buckle, 1987; Easton, 1989). Tight monetary policies sent interest rates and unemployment soaring. The exchange rate was floated and rose quickly on the tide of record interest rates, thus diminishing the international competitiveness of New Zealand exports and giving a further boost to unemployment. Economic liberalisation exposed hitherto highly regulated and protected sectors of the economy to market forces by doing away with most subsidies and incentives, barriers to entry and other licensing requirements, and virtually all forms of price regulation. Tariffs and import quotas were reduced speedily, and several domestic industries, nurtured by traditional policies of import substitution, were threatened by international competition. The finance industry was deregulated. Exchange and interest rate controls were lifted; limits on foreign ownership of financial institutions and on the number of banks were eliminated. Labour shifted the tax burden to indirect taxes. It cut personal and company rates substantially and introduced a value-added tax on all goods and services. Other forms of indirect tax were also increased sharply. The National government, elected in 1990, embraced the new direction in economic policy but moved to extend it further into social policy. As Boston describes it, from 1991:

> National embarked upon a major transformation of most aspects of New Zealand's welfare state. These included large cuts in the value of most welfare benefits, a significant increase in the degree of targeting in education, health care and income maintenance, and major changes to the means by which social assistance is delivered, especially in health care and housing.
>
> (1999: 10)

The reforms of the 1980s and 1990s made New Zealand one of the most deregulated societies in the Organisation for Economic Co-operation and Development (OECD). The combined effect of the economic and social policies implemented by Labour and National was a radical repositioning of the New Zealand state and its withdrawal from areas of activity for which it had historically accepted responsibility (Kelsey, 1993; Sharp, 1994).

Intellectual origins of the New Zealand model

The radical repositioning of the New Zealand state was not accidental. It derived from a fundamental programme of state restructuring, implemented first by Labour and then by National governments, which has been remarkable for its scope, its speed and its theoretical consistency (Scott *et al.*, 1990; Boston *et al.*, 1996; Schick, 1996). This programme gained widespread international attention. In 1993, the World Competitiveness Report ranked New Zealand first internationally for quality of government (World Economic Forum, 1993). In the same year Osborne and Gaebler observed that in its public sector reforms, New Zealand 'has gone the furthest along the entrepreneurial path' (1993: 330). There have also been a number of major reports on public sector reform in New Zealand, including one by the International Monetary Fund (IMF), another by the British Treasury and Civil Service Committee and another by the Canadian Auditor-General (Treasury and Civil Service Committee, 1994; Office of the Auditor-General of Canada, 1995; Scott, 1995).

One reason for the degree of international interest in New Zealand is that its public sector reform programme has been unique for the degree to which it is grounded in and driven by an explicit theoretical framework. This framework has been articulated in many quarters but its clearest and most detailed statement is in the New Zealand Treasury's briefing papers to the incoming Labour government in 1984 and 1987 (Treasury, 1984, 1987). This theoretical framework drew from public choice and agency theories, transaction cost economics and the new public management (NPM).

Public choice, agency theory and transaction cost economics assume that individuals are rational self-interested utility maximisers and, second, that they will act opportunistically, where possible, to maximise their interests. Public choice theory rejects any notion of the public interest or altruistic behaviour by public officials (McLean, 1986). Instead, it focuses upon imperialistic behaviour by public officials who act to maximise the resources enjoyed by their agency and to advance their own power, reputation and careers. Agency theory focuses on the relationship between principals and agents who are engaged to do the formers' bidding (Moe, 1984). Its central objective is to ensure that principals are not exploited by the opportunistic behaviour of utility maximising agents. Analytically, its focus is on the design of optimal contracts. Agency costs are the costs of achieving optimal contracts. In contrast, transaction costs are the costs of ensuring the efficient production of goods and services. The analytical focus of transaction cost economics is the design of optimal structures for those transactions (Williamson, 1985). The key issue for transaction cost economics, and one which preoccupied New Zealand policy makers, is the question of which class of transactions are best suited to market provision and which to state provision. NPM theories have also been highly influential in New Zealand. Hood observes that:

> in the unique circumstances of New Zealand, the synthesis of public choice, transactions cost theory and principal-agent theory was predominant, producing an analytically driven NPM movement of unusual coherence. ... Indeed, the New Zealand Treasury's *Government Management* (1987) comes closest to a coherent NPM 'manifesto', given that much of the academic literature on the subject lacks either full-scale elaboration or enthusiastic commitment to NPM.
>
> (1991: 6)

These theories have shaped the restructuring of the New Zealand state. Their application in the New Zealand public sector has been as theoretical tools to design governance and managerial structures which minimise the capacity of individuals to act opportunistically.

State restructuring in New Zealand

The Treasury's briefing papers for the incoming government in 1984 offered a stern critique of the structure and activities of public sector organisations. According to Treasury (1984: 290), most government departments had neither clearly defined goals nor a management plan. They were concerned with input controls rather than output measurement. Treasury was critical of the limited discretion enjoyed by departmental managers, and their inability to adapt departmental operations to changing circumstances. For Treasury, it was vital to reorganise departmental structures and operations in a manner which would allow them to emulate the claimed efficiency of private sector firms: 'The aim of management should be the implementation of systems in the public service that can perform broadly the same role for the public service as the price system does in the private sector' (Treasury, 1984: 287).

Treasury argued that the remedy for the trading departments of the state was corporatisation (as it became known) – the commercialisation of state trading enterprises and the imposition upon them of a clear statutory objective of profit maximisation. This would eliminate the commercially distorting influence of political considerations upon micro-economic decision-making. The State-Owned Enterprises Act 1986 established state trading enterprises as autonomous commercial organisations called state-owned enterprises (SOEs). The SOEs were established as limited liability companies under the Companies Act (Scott *et al.*, 1990). Their boards were drawn mainly from the private sector, as were many senior management appointments. Their principal objective was now to be 'as profitable and efficient as comparable businesses that are not owned by the Crown'. All SOEs are required to provide ministers with an annual statement of corporate intent, specifying the organisation's objectives and activities. The ministers may require amendments to the statements and specify the amount of dividend payable by the corporation (Spicer *et al.*, 1996).

Privatisation was the next stage. Privatisation grew out of the process and the logic of corporatisation itself. It was argued that the SOEs lacked the discipline imposed upon private sector companies by shareholders and potential buyers, and, despite repeated assurances that the government would not bail out a failing SOE, it was widely believed that potential creditors would not subject the SOEs to the same intense scrutiny that they would a private sector company (Scott *et al.*, 1990). And, in addition, it was argued that the government was a poor shareholder, inasmuch as it would wish to maximise tax paid and dividend payouts, and would be suspicious of expansion and enhanced exposure (Scott *et al.*, 1990; Williams, 1990). In other words, continued public ownership was seen as incompatible with the new commercialised status of the SOEs. Fiscal concerns were also relevant. By 1987, gross public debt was 64 per cent of gross domestic product (GDP), with debt servicing swallowing 20 per cent of export income (Chew, 1989). Labour decided that large-scale privatisation was the solution. Accordingly, following the 1987 election, it instructed all SOEs to ready themselves for possible privatisation. Thirty-eight state assets were sold between March 1988 and December 1996, by both Labour and National Governments, for a net value of around $16 billion (Mascarenhas, 1991; Kelsey, 1995). The diverse range of businesses subject to privatisation may be roughly grouped within six industry sectors: petrochemicals, finance, infrastructure and transport, telecommunications, forestry and computerised information. Outside of these categories, other businesses sold were located in the radio, film, construction, steel manufacturing, printing and tourism sectors. Along with five large financial institutions, Telecom, the Tourist Hotel Corporation and New Zealand Rail were all sold to foreign interests. All banks operating in New Zealand, with the exception of one small regional bank, are now overseas owned. Domestic purchasers bought New Zealand Steel, the Development Finance Corporation, Petrocorp and the Government Print Office. Several airports in smaller cities were sold to local councils. Ownership of forestry cutting rights, mining licences and housing corporation mortgages was divided between overseas interests and New Zealand-based purchasers. Privatisation has slowed considerably in recent years. The New Zealand First–National Government coalition agreement of December 1996 included a prohibition on the privatisation of certain state assets. The Labour–Alliance government, elected in 1999, set itself firmly against privatisation.

In the second stage of its restructuring programme between 1987 and 1990, the Labour government turned its attention to the non-trading public sector. As with the first stage, the impetus for reform was articulated in Treasury's briefing papers to the incoming government. In *Government Management*, following the 1987 election, Treasury subjected non-trading public sector organisations to much the same criticisms made earlier of the trading sector and concluded that 'If the Government wishes to have a public sector capable of producing high quality advice, and managing its own affairs on a basis comparable with private sector efficiency, major changes in the nature of administration are essential' (Treasury, 1987: 49)

The State Sector Act 1988 and the Public Finance Act 1989 embody the principles articulated by the Treasury (Walsh, 1991a; Boston *et al.*, 1996). The private sector was held up as the model for the public sector to emulate. A key component of the NPM model was that managers should be given authority to manage and be held accountable for the efficient management of their resources. The New Zealand model adheres consistently to the separation of commercial and non-commercial functions, the separation of policy advice from service delivery and from regulatory, review and monitoring functions. Service delivery functions have in many cases been broken up into separate business units.

The State Sector Act replaced the position of permanent heads of government departments with that of chief executive, employed on a five-year renewable term. The Public Finance Act 1989 introduced an accrual accounting system and moved the budgetary focus from input controls – voting money for a department's programmes – to an output-based system – voting money for specific and agreed outputs (Pallot, 1991). Ministers and chief executives now negotiate a purchasing agreement in which chief executives contract with ministers to deliver agreed outputs and to report on results by way of a statement of service performance. Chief executives are responsible for ensuring the agreed outputs are in fact produced by their staff. This financial management system had major implications for employment relations. Most importantly, it meant that chief executives of government departments had to be made employers of their staff and responsible for their own employment relations policies if they were to be held accountable for what their staff did and produced. However, the State Sector Act did not cut departments loose entirely. The Act contains a number of provisions designed to guard against the discarding of traditional public service notions of merit and equity in employment policies and procedures. The State Sector Act also obliges chief executives to be 'good employers'. This requires them to provide good and safe working conditions, to appoint staff impartially and to provide opportunities for staff to develop their abilities. It also obliges chief executives to develop and implement an equal employment opportunity (EEO) programme and to have particular regard to the needs of women, Maori, ethnic minorities and workers with disabilities.

Public sector unions

This restructuring programme carried with it significant implications for public sector unions, which were organised around the traditional system of public sector industrial relations. The traditional system was highly centralised (Walsh, 1991b;

Boston *et al.*, 1996). Unions negotiated uniform and nationally applicable conditions of employment with central employing authorities. Negotiations were governed by a formal set of legislatively prescribed rules which required salaries and other conditions of employment to be 'fairly comparable' with those in the private sector. Deadlocked negotiations were referred to independent tribunals for binding arbitration. Subsequent disputes over the application or interpretation of employment conditions were quickly elevated to the centre and resolved there. It was a non-participatory system whose operation was remote from those whose fate was being decided. The mechanical application of established formulae to calculate pay rises meant that unions had only infrequent need to mobilise their members in support of pay claims. Union officials preferred to do deals with their employer counterparts. The system was highly politicised. In major disputes, unions tended to look either for an arbitrated solution or a political deal rather than to rely upon industrial militancy. Governments took an active interest in the outcome of industrial relations issues in the state sector, and for unions, an appeal to the electoral sensitivities of ministers was a frequently used option where other avenues had proved fruitless.

Public sector unions were large unions compared to their private sector counterparts. One major union tended to dominate among each occupational grouping. In the public service, the Public Services Association (PSA) represented all employees at all levels. In education, separate unions represented pre-school, primary, secondary, polytechnic and university teachers, while in the health sector unions represented nurses, doctors and other professional and non-professional workers. Public sector unions were centralised in structure, bureaucratic in their operation and cautious by inclination. Many originated as professional associations and retained this focus after developing as trade unions. Their role as professional associations contributed to high levels of membership despite membership being voluntary, unlike in the private sector.

Management strategy and union response

In the remainder of this chapter, we explore management strategy and union response in the public service, the commercialised state-owned enterprises and the public health sector. The three experiences are similar in many respects but also display important differences. The State Sector Act 1988 had a fundamental impact on management strategy and union response in the public service and continues to do so. Subsequent industrial relations legislation, the Employment Contracts Act (ECA) 1991 and the Employment Relations Act 2000, whilst not unimportant, did not reshape industrial relations in the public service to anywhere near the same degree. A similar process is evident in the SOE sector, where the major impact on industrial relations derived from the State-Owned Enterprises Act 1986. Subsequent legislation did not fundamentally alter the patterns established following the 1986 legislation. In contrast, the ECA 1991 had a significant impact on the public health sector and, although at the time of writing it was too early to be confident of the effects of the Employment Relations Act 2000, it was already evident that it was having an impact on health sector industrial relations.

The public service

The most important industrial relations changes made by the State Sector Act 1988 were the abolition of compulsory arbitration and the elimination of the obligation to maintain comparability with the private sector in pay and conditions. The most important operational change in the core public service (chiefly made up of government departments and ministries and a host of other agencies) was the shift to negotiations on a departmental or agency basis. This is called enterprise bargaining in New Zealand and was introduced into the public service in 1988, not by the State Sector Act itself but by agreement between the Labour government and the PSA prior to the Act. This was three years before the enactment of the ECA 1991, which had a radical impact on industrial relations in the private sector and on some areas of the wider public sector (Walsh and Brosnan, 1999). The 1991 Act prohibited compulsory union membership, greatly restricted union access to workplaces, introduced major obstacles to multi-employer bargaining and encouraged a shift to individual employment contracts in place of collective bargaining. The effect in the private sector was a rapid and large fall in both union membership and collective bargaining, and where collective bargaining did continue, multi-employer bargaining gave way to single employer enterprise bargaining. However, the effects of the 1991 Act were much less marked in the public service. The early and voluntary shift to enterprise bargaining, combined with the historical tradition of voluntary union membership in the public sector, meant that the impact on representation and bargaining in the public sector was less than in the private sector. The chief impact was on the opportunities the Act created for the formation of unions to rival established unions. This is explored in the following paragraph.

Since 1988, each government department or ministry in the public service has negotiated its own collective agreement (these were called collective contracts under ECA). In some departments more than one collective agreement is negotiated as management seeks to develop different sets of employment conditions for different groups. In addition, varying numbers of employees in each department are now employed on individual employment agreements. However, notwithstanding departmental negotiations, considerable central direction of the bargaining process has been maintained throughout this period (Boston *et al.*, 1996). Despite the decentralising intent of the State Sector Act, the Labour government assigned to its central agency, the State Services Commission (SSC), responsibility for negotiating employment conditions in all departments. This responsibility was to be exercised in consultation with chief executives but there was no doubt where the upper hand lay. The government was determined to ensure that negotiating outcomes were not inconsistent with its own policy and fiscal positions. The SSC reported to a cabinet sub-committee, which prescribed negotiating parameters. The SSC in turn imposed these parameters upon chief executives. From 1992, the SSC loosened its control inasmuch as it delegated negotiating authority to departmental chief executives. They now had hands-on responsibility for their own departmental negotiations in consultation with the SSC, thus reversing the earlier position. In reality, however, little had changed. The cabinet sub-committee still prescribed the negotiating parameters and the SSC laid these down in its letter of delegation to chief executives. The most important of these parameters was that any wage increases should be funded out of either down-sizing or elimination of particular services. Continued central influence over bargaining, combined with the fact that for a large proportion of employees departments recruit broadly similar skill sets from the same labour market, has meant that although there has been some variation across departments, similarities in bargaining outcomes have been more apparent.

Between 1988 and 1992, the SSC's approach to bargaining was developed in support of its wider managerialist strategy (Walsh, 1991a,b). The SSC placed a great deal of emphasis upon what came to be called its clawbacks campaign in which it sought to reverse negotiated gains made previously by public sector unions. This campaign had little success and in one sense was counter-productive in that it served to mobilise unions and their members in opposition. However, it did send very clear signals to managers, employees and unions that the comfortable ways of the past would not survive in the new environment and in that sense served its purpose. A second important managerialist objective was to shift managers from collective bargaining coverage onto individual employment contracts. It was argued that the new status of managers as responsible directly for their subordinates was incompatible with being employed under the same collective contract or agreement. This strategy had limited success until the passage of the ECA, which facilitated the negotiation of individual employment contracts.

The PSA as the dominant public service union found itself challenged by the growth of a number of small rival unions. The ECA removed the exclusive representation rights enjoyed by registered unions. This posed particular difficulties for the PSA, the largest union in the country, and one that increasingly operated as a federation of diverse groups. On the one hand, the PSA was vulnerable to defections both from members who were sceptical of the value of unionism at all and, on the other hand, from those who felt the PSA had not been militant enough in the new environment (Walsh *et al.*, 1998). A group of public health workers, angry with the PSA's opposition to a general strike in protest against the ECA, broke away in 1992 and established the National Union of Public Employees. Other workers in the Customs Department and in the Department of Social Welfare, as well as members in the utilities and local government, also split from the union. In 1994, a group of around 1,000 prison officers left the PSA to form the Penal Officers Association. TaxPro was set up in 1995 to recruit and represent non-union staff of the Inland Revenue Department, although the new union also attracted a large number of former PSA members dissatisfied with the outcomes of previous contract negotiations. The formation of these rival unions made the task of the PSA more difficult in a number of important negotiating situations. In the Inland Revenue department negotiations in 1996, the PSA's rolling strike strategy was undermined by TaxPro's acceptance of the department's offer. In contrast, at about the same time, the PSA settled a strike by prison officers which had involved the deployment of the military to staff the prisons while the breakaway union, the Penal Officers Association, continued the strike. However, the PSA, as with other public sector unions, has not been challenged by non-union bargaining agents as was envisaged by the National government in the enactment of the ECA.

After vigorous internal debate, the PSA's response to these and other challenges was to espouse a 'partnership' strategy in which public sector employers are invited to sign up to a partnership with the PSA in the management of their organisation. The adoption of this strategy was extremely controversial both inside the PSA and in the wider union movement. It is criticised both by those who see it as a betrayal of the principle of trade union independence and by others who see it as destined to failure through its expectation that employers will be willing to compromise on managerial prerogative to a degree not warranted by the present balance of industrial strength. The PSA, however, believes that the partnership strategy offers a way for the union to consolidate itself as a strong and effective presence in the workplace and that without it, union decline will continue to gather pace. The strategy has received a significant boost since the election of the Labour–Alliance coalition government in 1999, which has embraced it and has urged departmental chief executives to adopt it.

The State-Owned Enterprises

Public sector unions found life in the new commercialised SOEs very difficult. Their response was slow and, with few exceptions, ineffectual. They were taken by surprise by the speed and scope of the organisational changes, by the immediate introduction of entirely new bargaining arrangements and by a new managerial militancy imported from the private sector which they had not previously encountered (Walsh, 1988; Walsh and Wetzel, 1993). The SOEs inherited organisational structures which were inappropriate for commercially oriented enterprises. Decision-making in their parent government departments had been highly centralised, and politicised. All SOEs devolved decision-making authority to line managers, many of them recent imports from the private sector. New managers from the private sector were required in all SOEs, especially in accounting, financial, marketing and sales areas, which had not been priorities for government departments. Managers who had felt stifled in the public service were invigorated by the opportunity to initiate and be accountable. Those unwilling or unable to make the transition opted for redundancy and early retirement. Others were forced out. Downsizing was a continuing feature of the restructuring process. However, this was not accompanied by corresponding industrial protest, mainly due to substantial redundancy payments. This climate of severance prevented unions from acting as vehicles of protest and allowed the SOEs to introduce radical change without strong opposition from those facing job loss.

Three examples illustrate the process. The most radical restructuring occurred at the Forestry Corporation, which faced significant private sector competition and which was viewed from the outset as a clear candidate for privatisation. The corporation sold all assets related to logging operations except the forests and used contractors for planting maintenance and logging. (Forestry cutting rights were subsequently sold to the private sector.) The workforce fell almost immediately from 4,000 to 600 wage earners and from 3,300 to 620 salaried employees. Selected employees were given the opportunity to become contractors to the corporation, using their redundancy payments and the corporation's assistance in securing loans to purchase equipment. Their union, the PSA, was unable to negotiate an agreement for them and the remaining employees were placed on individual employment contracts. By shedding over 70 per cent of its employees and effectively deunionising, the Forestry Corporation virtually restructured industrial relations off its agenda.

The Electricity Corporation of New Zealand (ECNZ) offered a second approach to restructuring. It stopped thinking of itself as an integrated public utility and sought to create an internal market to provide a competitive edge within the organisation. It decomposed into a holding company with autonomous business units, each developing its own policies and conducting its own labour relations so that employment conditions could reflect not the corporation's overall situation but that of the separate units. To prevent cross-subsidisation, the business units deal with each other on a commercial basis and are free to contract with external organisations for services if dissatisfied with the performance of another unit. The management of each unit is given profit goals and freedom to pursue them and their compensation reflects their success in achieving those goals. Telecom took a similar approach. It enjoyed the unique luxury for a telecommunication company of a totally deregulated market with limited competition emerging only after several years. Telecom became a holding company for five (later four) autonomous regional operating companies and an international connecting company. Telecom's corporate headquarters staffs was slashed from 1,700 to 250. Only six of Telecom's 90 senior managers survived corporatisation. Twice in two years its senior managers divided subordinates according to competence and offered the bottom third redundancy. Telecom reduced its workforce from 24,000 to 8,700. As with Forestry Corporation, former Telecom workers have made use of their redundancy money to establish themselves as subcontractors for installation work. Subcontractors are used to gauge the relative productivity of employees and costs of any emergent competitor.

In all SOEs, management set out to reduce union strength and curb their influence over decisions, which in the private sector are normally considered to be managerial prerogative. Previously, unions had been routinely consulted on, indeed involved in important management decisions. SOE managers were determined to establish their authority and confine unions to a narrow role negotiating and interpreting collective agreements. Management's sense of urgency and empowerment together with demonstrable membership apathy or sense of powerlessness ensured they would be successful. In ECNZ and in Telecom, the creation of autonomous business units, the devolution of authority and the shift to bargaining on a business unit basis undermined the organisational base of the union. A counter-example was New Zealand Post, where the chief executive cited union cooperation as a key factor which contributed to its financial success (Parker, 1990: 8). However, there are few other examples of SOEs where unions mounted an effective response, and since the mid-1990s this has become largely a non-union sector of the economy.

The public health sector

The Labour government adapted the model established by the State Sector Act 1988 to the health sector. In legislation enacted in 1989, it established 14 Area Health

Boards, which negotiated a contractual agreement with the Minister of Health for the provision of health services for their region. Following this, the climate of industrial relations in the health sector became considerably more adversarial (Walsh and Fougere, 1989). However, until the enactment of the ECA 1991, there were no fundamental changes to bargaining structures or the provisions of collective agreements. The 1991 legislation, however, led to the break-up of the national awards in the health sector and their replacement by collective contracts for each Health Board. In addition, the scope of collective bargaining declined as individual employment contracts became much more common. Union membership fell among service and ancillary health workers but held up well among health professionals.

The National government elected in 1990 decided to extend the SOE model into the public health system. The Health and Disability Services Act 1993 introduced a competitive market based on 'managed competition' (Barnett and Barnett, 1996). The government established four regional funding authorities (later reduced to one national funding authority) charged with the purchase of health services from providers, whether public, private or voluntary. They were to source services competitively, with no preference for public over private providers. A set of commercialised provider units were established, organised around a major hospital or a group of hospitals. These were to be run like SOEs, on a 'business-like basis', and 'would make adequate provision in their pricing to make a return on assets' (Easton, 1997: 157). The National New Zealand First Coalition government, formed after the 1996 general election, moderated the corporatisation model by replacing the competitive profit focus with the obligation to operate in a business-like fashion.

Although employment relations in the health sector is formally decentralised to the provider units, the ministers of health and state services have annually issued directives to health sector managers which stress the need to negotiate enterprise and individual contracts, greater flexibility in working hours, reductions in, or the abolition of, penal rates and rollovers of existing conditions (Oxenbridge, 1994). Managers have become more aggressive. In negotiations with groups such as domestic staff and laboratory workers, managers have refused to renew or re-negotiate expired contracts, and have locked out and suspended workers. They have endeavoured to coerce junior doctors, house-surgeons and laboratory workers to accept individual employment contracts instead of collective contracts; they have transported strikebreakers from Australia during strikes by house-surgeons, nurses and laboratory workers; and they have used various mechanisms to prevent doctors and nurses from engaging in public or media comment regarding concerns over staffing levels and inadequate patient care.

In their efforts to reduce expenditure on labour costs they have contracted out the work performed by domestic and laboratory workers to private companies; in negotiations with technicians and nurses they have pursued 'cost-neutral' contract settlements (which effectively entail a reduction in real wages); they have settled contracts which have significantly reduced the take-home pay of nurses and domestic staff and they have cut the penal rates and allowances of workers across all occupational groups.

The fate of public sector unions in New Zealand

State restructuring in New Zealand has been probably the most radical in the OECD. It is uniquely based upon a clearly articulated theoretical framework grounded in public choice and agency theories, transaction cost economics and the NPM. The remarkable commitment of politicians and officials to this reform programme has ensured that it has maintained its momentum since it began more than a decade ago. The architecture of the New Zealand state has been transformed and the consequences have been profound.

The most significant consequence for the employees of the state and their unions has been the substantial downsizing of the state and corresponding job losses. The size of the state workforce has fallen both absolutely and as a proportion of the total workforce. By 1998, public sector employment had fallen by 26 per cent since 1983 and had declined from 35 to 22 per cent of the workforce. Public sector employment was 53 per cent of the private sector workforce in 1983; in 1998, this had fallen to 29 per cent. The reduction in the size of the state has been chiefly in the trading sector, where the twin effects of corporatisation and privatisation have seen employment fall by 77 per cent, and in central government departments and ministries, where the fall is 63 per cent. Employment levels in the public health sector have also fallen, but not by nearly as much, while employment in the education sectors have increased. One consequence of downsizing on this scale is that the activity of union officials has been directed much more than they would like at securing the best possible redundancy settlements for their members.

In response, unions have engaged in vigorous action to maintain or improve members' pay and conditions. This has been particularly marked in the health sector. Strikes have occurred on an annual basis in most major hospitals among most occupational groups. Nurses, junior doctors, domestics, and laboratory workers have been the most strike-prone groups, in terms of the frequency and extent of strike action. During 1992 and 1993 contract rounds, for example, nurses in nearly all regions engaged in three-day strikes and national days of action. In 1992, Southland region junior doctors engaged in a month-long strike. Wage rises have generally followed strike action, suggesting that strike action has proven to be successful. Other groups, such as domestic and laboratory workers, have placed bans on performing particular duties or working certain shifts. Nurses, house-surgeons and laboratory workers have all taken successful legal action to enable them to conduct strikes; to order employers not to approach workers directly to force them to sign individual employment contracts; or to penalise employers who have circumvented workers' chosen bargaining representative in an attempt to communicate directly with workers during bargaining. The senior doctors' and nurses' union, the Association of Salaried Medical Specialists (ASMS), and New Zealand Nurses Organisation (NZNO) have engaged in successful media publicity campaigns to highlight aggressive management tactics and declining staffing levels. Nurses, in particular, engender widespread public sympathy and are the most highly respected occupation in New Zealand. During negotiations, the ASMS and NZNO have bargained around issues relating to inadequate staffing levels and declining standards of patient care. Additionally, the ASMS has negotiated contract clauses which guarantee the right to adjudication or arbitration if contract negotiations stall.

Domestic and maintenance workers and their union, the Service Workers Union (SWU), have had to deal with the distinctive problems associated with the contracting out or competitive tendering of their jobs to private, mostly foreign-owned companies. Competitive tendering of non-core services began in the late 1980s and gathered pace in the mid-1990s. Contracting firms compete for tenders on the basis of the lowest operating costs, particularly labour costs. Thus redundancies, reduced hours and pay, and grandparenting contract conditions for existing staff while employing new staff on reduced conditions have become commonplace. Tendering processes have compelled the SWU to develop membership retention rather than recruitment strategies. The SWU has adopted a three-pronged strategy around contracting out: they have sought to prevent the process from occurring; officials have developed in-house tenders on behalf of those workers whose jobs are threatened; and they have fought to protect conditions for those workers employed by successful tendering companies.

The SWU uses grassroots 'organising model' strategies to build commitment among hospital workers. This involves identifying workplace leaders, recruitment by delegates and developing workplace committees (Oxenbridge, 1998). However, officials have encountered a level of resistance to the organising model among long-standing union delegates and have decided that it is somewhat easier to implement organising model strategies in greenfields in the private health sector. Public hospitals were traditionally the mainstay of membership in the SWU and its predecessor unions. However, membership in hospitals has declined significantly since the early 1990s. Consequently, officials are now beginning to target sectors of perceived recruitment potential in other areas of public health which have been contracted out to voluntary and private providers, particularly mental health and community trusts, aged care establishments and home care workers.

Public sector unions have had more success than their private sector counterparts in maintaining collective bargaining and collective representation. Although there was a pronounced shift to individual contracts after the ECA 1991, collective bargaining remains at much higher levels in the public sector than in the private sector. Similarly, trade union membership has held up much better in the public sector than in the private sector. Public sector union density is 65 per cent compared to 18 per cent in the private sector. The differences are even greater at a workplace level. Over 90 per cent of public sector workplaces are unionised compared to only 13 per cent of workplaces in the private sector. Moreover, average density at unionised workplaces is 74 per cent in the public sector and only 47 per cent in the private sector (Walsh and Brosnan, 1999). Unions survived relatively well in the public service and in the health sector as well as in the education sector, which has not been discussed here. Quite a different fate has befallen unions in the SOE and privatised sector, where they have been fatally weakened.

Associated with the higher levels of collective bargaining and representation in the public sector, and with restructuring and employer militancy in certain sectors, is a higher incidence of industrial action. During the period from 1986 to 1992, strikes and lockouts fell to historically very low levels in New Zealand. Such industrial activity as there was in the public sector in this period occurred mainly in the health and education sectors, where deeply embedded notions of professionalism were challenged by the new managerialist regime (Walsh and Fougere, 1989; Oxenbridge, 1994). From 1992, as the economy recovered somewhat, industrial activity rose. However, increasingly, industrial activity is concentrated in the public sector. Strike and lockout data were not recorded separately for the public sector until 1988. In 1990, 31 per cent of stoppages were in the public sector and 42 per cent of strikers were public sector employees. By 1995, public sector workers comprised 20 per cent of the labour force, but 43 per cent of stoppages and 79 per cent of strikers were public workers (Statistics New Zealand, 1997).

The advancement of pay and other employment conditions has been very difficult for public sector unions since 1988. A key reason for the enactment of the State Sector Act and in particular the abolition of compulsory arbitration was so that governments would no longer find their fiscal policy stance being undone by arbitrated wage settlements over which they had no control (Walsh, 1991a). Throughout this period, the government and its agent, the SSC, were determined to impose fiscal discipline upon public sector unions and employees. At first, the government strategy had limited success. Between 1986 and 1992, public sector wage increases were higher than those for the private sector. However, an important reason for this was that in the early part of this period, the public sector was catching up with the very large wage gains, which had been achieved in the private sector between 1982 and 1984, despite the imposition of a wage freeze in those years. From 1992 to 1995, however, the government's strategy had more success. Increases in labour costs in the non-trading central government sector lagged behind those in the private sector. Since 1995, wage increases have been broadly comparable in the public and private sectors. Unions in the public service and in education have had more success than their private sector counterparts in maintaining non-wage employment conditions. This has not been the case in the health sector, where management has gained the right to schedule work to coincide with peak demand and to increase the number of casual workers (Wetzel, 1998). While many of the settlements negotiated across all occupational groups have been of a cost-neutral nature – with penal rates traded off for minor increases in base wage rates – senior doctors have experienced significant wage increases of between 9 and 20 per cent each year.

At first public sector unions struggled in the new environment and managers, emboldened by managerialist ideology and favoured by new structures and ways of doing things, held the upper hand. In the early years, it seemed as though unions might be totally marginalised as the managerialist agenda carried all before it. In some organisations this did happen, even before the ECA brought its own set of problems for unions to cope with. Ten years on, however, the picture, whilst not a pleasant one for unions and their members, was by no means as bleak as might have been predicted. The commitment of many union members and officials, reflected in rising levels of industrial action, remained unbroken, although the future implications of a partnership model in the public service were difficult to foresee. The task facing public sector unions and their members is to retain and build upon the position established by the renewed activity of the recent past. The dilemma is that this activity has absorbed enormous energy and resources and the impact of a decade of continuous challenge has been profoundly demanding.

Public sector unions under the Employment Relations Act 2000

The Labour–Alliance government repealed the ECA in its first year in office and replaced it with the Employment Relations Act (Walsh and Harbridge, 2001). The Act does not return to the legislative regime of the pre-1991 period. In particular, it continues to prohibit compulsory union membership. However, it does restore a system of union registration and provides that only registered unions can negotiate collective agreements, which may apply only to union members. The Act does not mandate a return to the multi-employer award-bargaining of the past. However, it greatly improves union access provisions and sets as one of its key objectives the promotion of collective bargaining. It also introduces an obligation to conduct employment relations 'in good faith'. The jurisdiction of the good faith obligation is much wider than in other systems as it applies to all aspects of the employment relationship. It is too soon to say with any confidence what impact the Act will have. However, in its first year, union membership has had its first increase in over a decade and there has been a significant increase in multi-employer bargaining, particularly in the health sector. In the public service, however, where unions willingly embraced single employer bargaining over a decade ago, there has been little change to bargaining structures. It is not yet clear whether the new legislation is leading to more favourable bargaining outcomes for public sector unions. This will be of vital importance to the unions representing service and ancillary workers whose employment conditions were significantly undermined in some important respects during the 1990s. It seems likely that the most significant change for public sector unions, as for all unions, is the development of a policy climate which is supportive of and favourably inclined towards trade unionism. A policy setting in which the government gives its stamp of approval to trade unionism may send as clear a signal to chief executives and senior managers as did the reverse configuration during the past decade.

Bibliography

Barnett, P. and Barnett, R. (1996) 'Restructuring health: rhetoric and reality', in R. Le Heron and E. Pawson (eds), *Changing Places: New Zealand in the Nineties*, Auckland: Longman Paul, pp. 221–225.

Bollard, A. E. and Buckle, R. A. (eds) (1987) *Economic Liberalisation in New Zealand*, Wellington: Allen & Unwin.

Boston, J. (1999) 'New Zealand's Welfare State in Transition', in J. Boston, P. Dalziel and S. St John (eds), *Redesigning New Zealand's Welfare State*, Auckland: Oxford University Press, pp. 3–19.

Boston, J., Martin, J., Pallot, J. and Walsh, P. (eds) (1991) *Reshaping the State: New Zealand's Bureaucratic Revolution*, Auckland: Oxford University Press.

Boston, J., Martin, J., Pallot, J. and Walsh, P. (1996) *Public Management: The New Zealand Model*, Auckland: Oxford University Press.

Chew, S. K. (1989) *The Process of Privatisation in New Zealand: Implications for Ministerial Responsibility and the Continuing Role of the Government with Respect to State-Owned Enterprises*, Wellington: New Zealand Public Service Association.

Easton, B. (1989) 'The commercialisation of the New Zealand economy: from think big to privatisation', in B. Easton (ed.), *The Making of Rogernomics*, Auckland: Auckland University Press, pp. 114–131.

Easton, B. (1997) *The Commercialisation of New Zealand*, Auckland: Auckland University Press.

Hood, C. (1991) 'A public management for all seasons', *Public Administration*, 69: 3–19.

Kelsey, J. (1993) *Rolling Back the State*, Wellington: Bridget Williams Books.

Kelsey, J. (1995) *The New Zealand Experiment: A World Model for Structural Adjustment?* Auckland: Auckland University Press/Bridget Williams Books.

McLean, I. (1986) 'Review article: some recent work on public choice', *British Journal of Political Science*, 16: 377–394.

Mascerenhas, R. (1991) 'State-owned enterprises', in J. Boston, J. Martin, J. Pallot and P. Walsh (eds), *Reshaping the State: New Zealand's Bureaucratic Revolution*, Auckland: Oxford University Press, pp. 27–51.

Moe, Y. (1984) 'The new economics of organization', *American Journal of Political Science*, 28: 739–775.

Office of the Auditor-General of Canada (1995) *Towards Better Governance: Public Sector Reform in New Zealand (1984–94) and Its Relevance to Canada*, Ottawa.

Osborne, D. and Gaebler, T. (1993) *Reinventing Government: How the Entrepreneurial Spirit is Transforming the Public Sector*, New York: Penguin Plume Books.

Oxenbridge, S. (1994) 'Health sector collective bargaining and the Employment Contracts Act: a case study of nurses', *New Zealand Journal of Industrial Relations*, 19(1): 17–33.

Oxenbridge, S. (1998) *Running to Stand Still: New Zealand Service Sector Trade Union Responses to the Employment Contracts Act (1991)*, PhD Thesis, Industrial Relations Centre, Victoria: University of Wellington.

Pallot, J. (1991) 'Financial management reform', in J. Boston, J. Martin, J. Pallot and P. Walsh (eds), *Reshaping the State: New Zealand's Bureaucratic Revolution*, Auckland: Oxford University Press, pp. 166–197.

Parker, H. (1990) *The Company, Its Business Results and Directions*, presented at the conference 'Public Sector Personnel Policies: Next Steps', Melbourne, 16 February 1990.

Roth, H. (1992) 'Chronicle', *New Zealand Journal of Industrial Relations*, 17(3): 376–390.

Schick, A. (1996) *The Spirit of Reform: Managing the New Zealand State Sector in a Time of Change*, Wellington: State Services Commission.

Scott, G. (1995) *Government Reform in New Zealand*, Washington, DC: International Monetary Fund.

Scott, G., Bushnell, P. and Sallee, N. (1990) 'Reform of the core public sector: New Zealand experience', *Governance*, 3(2): 138–167.

Sharp, A.(ed) (1994) *Leap into the Dark*, Auckland: Auckland University Press.

Spicer, B., Emanuel, D. and Powell, M. (1996) *Transforming Government Enterprises*, Centre for Independent Studies.

Statistics New Zealand (1997) *Labour Market 96*, Wellington: Statistics New Zealand.

Treasury (1984) *Economic Management*, Wellington: Government Printer.

Treasury (1987) *Government Management*, vols 1, 2, Wellington: Government Printer.

Treasury and Civil Service Committee (1994) *The Role of the Civil Service*, vol. 1, London: HMSO.

Walsh, P. (1988) 'The struggle for power and control in the new corporations: the first year of industrial relations in the state-owned enterprises', *New Zealand Journal of Industrial Relations*, 13(2): 179–189.

Walsh, P. (1991a) 'The State Sector Act 1988', in J. Boston, J. Martin, J. Pallot and P. Walsh (eds), *Reshaping the State: New Zealand's Bureaucratic Revolution*, Auckland: Oxford University Press, pp. 52–80.

Walsh, P. (1991b) 'Industrial relations and personnel policies under the State Sector Act', in J. Boston, J. Martin, J. Pallot and P. Walsh (eds), *Reshaping the State: New Zealand's Bureaucratic Revolution*, Auckland: Oxford University Press, pp. 114–139.

Walsh, P. and Brosnan, P. (1999) 'Redesigning industrial relations: the Employment Contracts Act and its consequences', in J. Boston, P. Dalziel and S. St John (eds), *Redesigning the Welfare State in New Zealand*, Auckland: Oxford University Press, pp. 117–133.

Walsh, P. and Fougere, G. (1989) 'Fiscal policy, public sector management and the 1989 health sector strike', *New Zealand Journal of Industrial Relations*, 14(3): 219–229.

Walsh, P. and Harbridge, R. (2001) 'Re-regulation of bargaining in New Zealand: the Employment Relations Act 2000', *Australian Bulletin of Labour*, 27(1): 43–60.

Walsh, P. and Wetzel, K. (1993) 'Preparing for privatization: corporate strategy and industrial relations in New Zealand's state-owned enterprises', *British Journal of Industrial Relations*, 31(1): 57–74.

Walsh, P., Harbridge, R. and Crawford, A. (1998) *Restructuring Employment Relations in the New Zealand Public Sector*, World Congress of the International Industrial Relations Association, Bologna, 21–24, September 1998.

Wetzel, K. (1998) *The Labour Relations of New Zealand's Health Reforms*, Unpublished Mimeograph, College of Commerce, University of Saskatchewan.

Williams, M. (1990) 'The political economy of privatisation', in M. Holland and J. Boston (eds), *The Fourth Labour Government: Politics and Policy in New Zealand*, Auckland: Oxford University Press, pp. 140–164.

Williamson, O. (1985) *The Economic Institutions of Capitalism: Firms, Markets, Relational Contracting Out*, New York: The Free Press.

World Economic Forum (1993) *World Competitiveness Report*, Lausanne: International Institute for Management Development.

8   The restructuring of national states in the global economy

Bob Carter

The idea of globalisation has seemingly swept away everything in front of it. Politicians and a legion of writers and commentators testify to the idea that the national state has been fatally weakened by the growth of transnational companies, international trade, financial liquidity and rapid, unregulated communications (Ohmae, 1990). Attempts by national governments to control economic activities within their national borders are portrayed in the dominant model as ill judged and fated to failure. Moreover, this verdict comes from the left as well as those celebrating the triumph of the market. Hardt and Negri, for instance, state:

> The primary factors of production and exchange – money, technology, people and goods – move with increasing ease across national boundaries; hence the nation state has less and less power to regulate these flows and impose its authority over the economy.
>
> (2000: xi)

There are, of course, opponents of these perspectives (Boyer and Drache, 1996; Hirst and Thompson, 1996; Rainnie, 1997; Weiss, 1998), and contributions to this volume are similarly sceptical and continue a critical tradition that contests this consignment of the state to a simple irrelevancy. In doing so, they once again assert the importance of the state in general, but also as an employer of labour in its own right, a focus much neglected even in an earlier period when the state was subject to much more attention (Carter, 1997a). Within these areas there are a number of particular concerns. Burnham's contribution examines the state in relationship to both the globalisation process and class strategies, concentrating on depoliticisation, and this concept is effectively interrogated by a series of national studies detailing not only the nature of state restructuring but also the consequences of state strategies and restructuring on the fortunes and prospects of state-based trade unions. These levels of analysis and the tensions between them are the basis of this concluding chapter.

Globalisation and the state

Burnham's characterisation of the role of the capitalist state and its current strategy of depoliticisation should be evaluated against what is, in effect, the mainstream view. Sociological perspectives and political economy see a diminished role for the state. This is well represented by Strange's contention that 'Where states were once the masters of markets, now it is markets which, on many crucial issues, are the masters over the governments of states' (Strange, 1996: 4). The specific ways in which markets apparently dictate to governments are specified by Hardt and Negri, who maintain that:

> Government and politics have become completely integrated into the system of transnational command. Controls are articulated through a series of international bodies and functions.
>
> (2000: 307)

There are, of course, perspectives opposing these claims and maintaining that the relationship between state and market is more complex than one of simple opposition, where the state weakens in the face of external forces. Weiss, for instance, provides authoritative support for the continued relevance of the state, using the term state denial to refer to:

> the proliferation of theses which portend the diminution or displacement of states as power actors in the domestic and international arenas. These range from the collapse of the welfare state and the death of industrial policy to the end of national diversity and the demise of the nation state.
>
> (1998: 3)

What the various different versions have in common is, according to Weiss, that they remain blind to the *variety* of state responses to international pressure, and to the *sources* and *consequences* of that variety for national prosperity (1998: 3). In contrast to the denial thesis, Weiss advances the notion that some states have transformative capacity: that is the ability to adapt to external shocks and pressures by generating ever-new means of governing the process of industrial change and augmenting a society's investible surplus.

While giving general support to the notion that states are not being overwhelmed by external market forces, but rather are in part the actors and in part the medium through which changes occur, there is no emphasis here on class relations. It might be possible to detect a proxy for class struggle in the form of domestic economic crisis, deficit finance, competition and world recession. But Weiss's main emphasis, however, is on variation by denying that there is a single, dominant tendency that can be detected in the strategies of advanced capitalist countries. A central feature of Weiss's perspective is that states have developed unevenly and that their histories continue to have consequences. In short, states do not behave uniformly just because they might face similar environmental conditions (1998: 10).

Burnham's view is simultaneously more abstract and more specific, dealing with core features of the capitalist state and current strategic orientations. Approaching the subject of globalisation through writings on international relations and political economy, he takes issue with the dominant view of globalisation, arguing four points.

First, there has been an inadequate theorisation of globalisation, which presents state and market as an external relationship of opposition. Second:

> governing strategies since the 1990s are characterised by a technocratic embrace of the 'end of ideology' in the 'age of globalisation'. Behind such rhetoric lies a concerted attempt to restructure relations between labour, capital and the state to both enhance accumulation and reduce excessive claims (or 'overload') on the political executive.
>
> (Burnham, Chapter 2: 15)

Third, current state policies are usefully understood in terms of the *politics of depoliticisation*, which involves a shift from discretion-based to rules-based economic policy, a reassertion of the boundaries separating legitimate political, economic and industrial activity and a fragmentation/devolution of decision-making in numerous arenas (Chapter 2: 12–13). Finally, and, given the focus of the book, more specifically, he argues that, as an integral part of the process of depoliticising labour–management relations in the public sector, we are witnessing 'the creation of "managerial states" ' (Chapter 2: 22). The contention here is that the first two claims are defensible, with the first, in particular, being a fundamental contribution to the emerging debate. The third and fourth contentions are not proved and, at best, are in need of qualification, especially when considering labour within the state.

Drawing on a largely British Marxist tradition, Burnham places class at the centre of analysis of the state, contending that rather than viewing the relationship between states and markets as 'external and contingent' it should be seen as 'internal and necessary', while at the same time recognising that 'the institutional form of this relationship varies given the historical character of the class struggle' (1997: 153). This point is further reiterated within the context of a world economy in which governments must participate in international summits to maintain the global flow of capital whilst limiting any negative impact of increased openness on their governing strategies (Chapter 2: 14). This implies, although it does not make explicit, antagonisms between nations, and hence could incorporate an evaluation of the particular and hegemonic position of the US in the nexus of international relations, a current absence noted by Rainnie and Fairbrother (Chapter 3).

This framework allows Burnham to counterpoise the past and present economic strategies adopted by states: 'governments across the world in advanced capitalist states have attempted to control inflation by adopting "rules based" rather than "discretion based" economic strategies' (Chapter 2: 20). Through this formulation he is thus able to offer a more concrete claim that:

> In the last 25 years, the strategies adopted by advanced capitalist states to manage labour and money look remarkably different from the received models of post-war regulation. In many cases overtly politicised forms of labour management and inflation control involving voluntary restraint, incomes policies and the machinery of tripartism, have now given way to depoliticised forms of management.
>
> (Burnham, 1997: 153)

These developments, it is noted, are not altogether new but they do enable the shoring up of demands for low inflation that entails a primary focus on capping wage settlements. For this reason, it is simplistic to view these developments as giving power to markets over states. Rather, it is possible to see the re-regulation of financial markets 'as providing the strongest possible public justification governments can muster for maintaining downward pressure on wages to combat inflation and thereby achieve price stability' (Chapter 2: 20). The mechanisms which governments have utilised in order to control inflation have consequently become 'rules based' rather than 'discretion based', with government responsibility off loaded in two ways: to an international regime (such as the Exchange Rate Mechanism (ERM)) and to a national body given a statutory and independent role (such as an independent central bank).

This analysis is developed through the example of the ultimate failure of British post-war economic policy, government intervention and tripartism. Burnham maintains the progressive turn to a rules-based system since the 1980s has seen both above mechanisms used, enabling the government of the day to establish:

> credible rules for economic management, thereby altering expectations concerning wage claims, in addition to 'externalising' the imposition of financial discipline. The stronger (and more distant) the set of 'rules', the greater manoeuvrability the state could achieve increasing the likelihood of attaining objectives.
>
> (Chapter 2: 19)

The decision to join the ERM in 1990 played exactly this role. While this membership ultimately failed to hold, and Britain was forced to leave the ERM, the policy was replaced by the increasingly independent role of the Bank of England, culminating in the formation of the Monetary Policy Committee and the Bank's formal independence – one of the early acts of the incoming New Labour Chancellor. In this respect it followed both France and New Zealand.

Class and the state

The class relations represented by the state and emphasised in Chapters 2, 3 and 4 are important for understanding the context and dynamics of the introduction of what has widely been termed new public management (NPM). Without an appreciation of these class relations, changes at the level of individual states appear as organisational ones to be evaluated on their own terms, as more efficient, effective, economical, and ideologically neutral. This approach is reflected by McKevitt, who states:

> The central theme of this movement [NPM] is the notion of removing organizational differences between the public and the private sector so to reduce public sector inefficiency by the method of a sharp focus on getting results through hands-on management.
>
> (1998: 14)

Viewed through the prism of class relations, this movement is part of the expansion of the capitalist mode of production through the commodification of social relations that had hitherto escaped the direct experience of the extraction of surplus value. This expansion of these social relations is two-fold, both national and international, as transnational service corporations take up roles previously performed by state organisations. The pressure to continue these policies is unrelenting and recent General Agreement on Trades and Services (GATS) discussions increase it further. US negotiators, for instance, made health care a special target in the 2000 round of talks: 'The United States is of the view that commercial opportunities exist along the entire spectrum of health and social care facilities, including hospitals, outpatient facilities, clinics, nursing homes, assisted living arrangements and services provided in the home' (Kuttner, 1999). Rainnie and Fairbrother highlight the essentially political nature of this process and the opposition to which it has given rise. However, the labour opposition they detail includes many countries that are weak within the hierarchy of capitalist nations (Chapter 3: 35). As the focus of the book is on those changes in state form in countries within the metropolitan heartland of capitalism, this raises the question of the nature and extent of resistance to these processes and how they are reflected in the individual accounts.

There is a common focus on state restructuring in all the chapters, but it is not at all clear that common assumptions about its class nature, or the concepts used, bind the various chapters together to provide a coherent account of the significance of changes in state forms. The nature of the state is regarded in some as relatively unproblematic. The designation of the state as capitalist in nature (Rainnie and Fairbrother, Chapter 3; Burnham, Chapter 2) is abstract but does highlight the need to examine both the partial nature of its practices and the potential conflict between it and labour as a social force. More particularly, it encompasses the role of the state as employer and the potential for class conflicts within the state. Struggles within the state cannot be constricted within a framework that regards them as simply and routinely economic, as is the case in much of the industrial relations literature. Such an emphasis on conflict and class interests might also help to explain the relationship of the state's changing form to its functions.

There is little doubt that the restructuring of state provision and work organisation has impacted on class relations, although only Fairbrother addresses these relations directly. It is not clear whether contributions that simply work with notions of the social democratic state (Walsh *et al.*, Chapter 7; Lubanski and Andersen, Chapter 5) are underwriting a tradition that saw the state as neutral and relations within it as unproblematic or simply reiterating that the world used to be a more agreeable place. In response to these positions, it is possible to both insist that relations within the state always constituted class relations and to discern a tendency within state employment to create clearer managerial strata that for a number of practical and theoretical reasons should be considered as new middle class (Carchedi, 1977; Carter and Fairbrother, 1995; Carter, 1997a). However, this latter tendency towards polarisation is not fully realised and in places has been negated. In schools in Britain, for instance, it is possible to see the strengthening of the head as a manager less involved in a labour process, and, conversely, it is also the case that other managerial functions have not coalesced into particular tasks performed exclusively by managers. There has been a growing complexity in the social relations inside schools, as managerial hierarchies have been constructed, extending the managerial tasks across a wider group (Carter, 1997b). Similarly, as mentioned earlier, general management in hospitals failed as doctors used their knowledge to frustrate and panic non-clinical managers into acceding to their demands in the face of claims that not to do so would cause them to be responsible for patient deaths. The response has been to incorporate doctors in clinical governances (Harrison and Pollitt, 1994).

There are other conceptualisations of the state that blur rather than clarify class relations within it. The claim, for instance, that the form of the British state has been decentred, as indicated in Chapter 4 in a somewhat ironic title, can be misleading and contrary to indications in the text itself. As is noted by Fairbrother (Chapter 4), and is evident in New Zealand and Australia (Walsh *et al.*, Chapter 7; O'Brien, Chapter 6), decentralisation has progressed simultaneously with a centralisation of decision-making. Those responsibilities that are devolved are only those that are thought possible to monitor effectively, and hence the simultaneous introduction of performance targets, making local managers accountable (see also Hoggett, 1994). The continued centralisation, in part reflected in Britain by the desire for joined-up government, is both reinforced and limited by a culture of administrative centralism (House of Commons Public Administration Select Committee, cited in Fairbrother, Chapter 4: 59). The traditional, bureaucratic nature of the central British state has indeed undergone changes towards managerialism. Such a description, however, refers to a mode of operation, rather than the purposes of that operation and thereby masks class interests. Equally, to describe transitions from a welfare state to a managerial state (Fairbrother, Chapter 4: 69; Walsh *et al.*, Chapter 7) gives the impression of an earlier, more benign organisation than is warranted by the evidence: it would be just as one-sided to characterise the state of the earlier period, especially in Britain, as a welfare state. Moreover, welfare policies were intimately tied to class interests and strategies (Clarke, 1993). It is simply insufficient to argue that 'the distinctive organising principles of the public domain are based upon public discourse leading to collective choice based on public consent' (Ranson and Stewart, 1994: xii). The state carries out complex and contradictory functions that impact upon the class relations of society in general and its employees in particular (Carter, 1997a), but recognition of the complexity does not imply neutrality of the state, let alone that the state is the repository of community values (Gowan *et al.*, 2001).

Depoliticisation: specific or general tendency?

Ranged against a particular version of conformity – the weakening of the state – Burnham comes close to substituting another uniform tendency, positing that advanced capitalist states will respond through depoliticising not only their macro-economic management, but also state functions and services. The first part of this movement, as noted earlier, is stated unequivocally and can be successfully defended, not only in the British case, but in other countries as well. Reference to the case of Germany offers support to the thesis, in that it has both an independent central bank, long charged (for historic reasons) with keeping down inflation, and is a member of the single European currency. The external rules-bound mechanisms are therefore firmly in place. Moreover, one could add that the role of the Bundesbank had until recently significance outside its national boundary:

> the Bundesbank became the de facto European central bank, not just because of the size of the German economy, but because its independence from the German government and its insulation from political pressure made it uniquely capable of behaving in conformity with the pressures of internationalized capital markets.
>
> (Streeck, 1996: 307)

Elsewhere, there are examples of other countries in which the government has been able to use outside pressure as the justification for changes:

> When the French government decided in 1983 to support European integration, it justified its decision to follow a policy of deflationary competitiveness as one of the constraints imposed by Brussels. Similarly, the Maastricht Treaty puts severe constraints on public deficit and debt during the intermediate phase towards adopting a single currency: the Italian political crisis is the direct outcome of such a supranational constraint. Finally, when the Swedish government decided to adhere to European union, the argument did not relate only to the issue of the access of Swedish firms to the large European market. Rather, it was also convenient to present the unprecedented surge in unemployment and the drastic reform of welfare, the tax system and industrial relations as the inescapable consequences of adherence to Europe.
>
> (Boyer and Drache, 1996: 20)

The establishment of the European Central Bank gives further support to the argument that depoliticisation is taking place. Streeck indicated the role it would play, claiming that it:

> would operate like an independent regulatory agency, reflecting and responding to objective market forces rather than a political will to correct or, for that matter, distort markets; protecting the common currency from being put at the service of political purposes like full employment; and accommodating, not political pressure, but an international capital market that has long outgrown national borders and national control.
>
> (Streeck, 1996: 307)

The second claim, that states are depoliticising their functions and services, is presented as follows:

> we are witnessing the creation of 'managerial *states*' as part of a process of depoliticising labour-management relations in the public sector, as responsibility for the

operational activity of state bodies shifts from central government and is placed in the hands of managers who represent a more distant and disembodied form of regulation via financial control and restriction.

(Burnham, Chapter 2: 22, emphasis added)

In effect, this position ends up close to denying the earlier emphasis on class struggle as a determinant of the specific institutional form of the state. Rainnie and Fairbrother note that Burnham overlooks the way in which state relations are emergent as the site for labour struggle, both within and against the state (Chapter 3: 45), but an equally telling criticism is that, for historical and contemporary reasons of class relations, it cannot be assumed that tendencies will manifest themselves in the same form in different societal formations. Moreover, there is little evidence in the chapter to indicate that the thesis is based on much more than the British experience. References are made to other countries but these do not form part of a developed argument.

While there is, therefore, evidence that the institutions and mechanisms of external regulation are being established, there is no evidence presented within the chapter that, outside Britain, they have the necessary consequence of depoliticising the wage relationship, nor of restructuring relations within the state in a manner that supports the depoliticisation thesis. Indeed, elsewhere there is evidence that for various historical and political reasons, there is a far from unproblematic development in Germany, Italy, Spain and France (Bach *et al.*, 1999). Nor within other chapters is the concept of depoliticisation universally supported, with the authors of chapters on Denmark, Australia and New Zealand finding little attraction to it, despite the fact that the latter country in particular has seen the most concerted attempt to change the policy direction and the nature of policy implementation.

It may be therefore that a credible case for the idea of depoliticisation can be made for the macro-economic management of Britain, with implications for industrial relations. In particular, governments have retreated from intervention in private sector industrial disputes. However, this has proved a relatively easy option given the record, historically low levels of industrial disputes in this area (Fairbrother, 2000). This direction in policy may therefore prove to have had specific origins and features that are not necessarily replicated through time or elsewhere. Even if the more limited claim, restricting depoliticisation to Britain, is accepted, it does not follow that the government can be as successful in distancing itself from its own employees, in the manner claimed by Burnham, and further elaborated by Fairbrother. Some limitations to the effectiveness of the strategy are noted by Burnham. These include tendencies to reduce the ability of the state to control the effects of policy through a reduction in the significance of state managers and regulator capture; the tendency for the state to be re-engaged with decision-making because of its necessary involvement in the accumulation process; finally, the political character of decision-making is likely to be highlighted by government actions that undermine the language of stability, prudence and external constraint.

The initial impression that depoliticisation is both coherent and successful as a strategy is clearly questioned by these qualifications. However, the qualifications aside, it continues to concentrate on only one side of the relationship of depoliticisation, that of government intention and its effectiveness, and ignores the political reaction of labour. Depoliticisation can only be considered a success in its own terms if labour accepts its premises. Here evidence suggests that, at least as far as policies to restructure the state through privatisation and marketisation, this has been far from the case.

State, employment and depoliticisation

Part of the argument in defence of the state and against the idea of its erosion is the contention that there are areas and activities for which the state cannot be replaced. Hence Boyer and Drache contend that social policy – including welfare, health and education entitlements as well as employment security – is an exclusively national (as well as regional) responsibility, not a supra-national one (Boyer and Drache, 1996: 7). Even if this is accepted, however, there are various ways in which the state can discharge its responsibilities and in the past two decades the organisation of state provision in the countries studied has undergone a radical transformation through the processes of privatisation, the establishment of Agencies, compulsory competitive tendering, market testing and the separation of purchasers from providers of services. Collectively these practices are considered as comprising evidence of the general tendencies towards depoliticisation. Alongside the disengagement of the state from the key aspects of economic policy formulation and implementation, there is claimed to be a parallel and related process creating modern, managerialised public sectors.

In place of political determination of detailed policies, responsibilities are decentralised onto managers, who have discretion and are focused on outputs as opposed to issues of equity guaranteed through standardised processes. It is not the intention here to discount these tendencies *in toto*. However, the case can be made that the depoliticisation process is far from uniform, as are the consequences for class relations, and that one of the responses, that of trade unions in the direction of renewal, is less pronounced than is claimed. This is true both within countries and between them.

The strength of the argument for depoliticisation, particularly within the British context but also in Denmark, mirrors the more general one in Burnham, and remains at the level of macro-economic control. It is less successful in its claim that part of the process also entails depoliticising labour–management relations in the state sector, taking responsibility for state bodies away from direct government involvement and placing it in the hands of state managers. This is not to say that these latter movements have not taken place, although the idea that the state previously had direct and unmediated control over enterprises is unsustainable given the difficulties that successive governments have had with, for instance, civil service reform (Fry, 1993; Fairbrother, 1994), the relative autonomy of public employment authorities (O'Brien, Chapter 6: 97) and the opaque relations within the workplace mentioned by Fairbrother (Chapter 4: 68); rather, the argument here is that despite the changes and developments much of the state sector, and many relations within it, remain politicised.

The argument for continued politicised relations is not a technical one about the precise nature of the reformed modes of control but one related to levels of political and social consciousness. This is implicit in Ferlie and others' observation that:

> The failure to depoliticise core public service functions is evident as there continues to be intense public dislike, media coverage and political action around, for example, attempts to develop explicit rationing in the NHS.
>
> (1996: 227)

If depoliticisation is an ideology claiming that governments do not have responsibility for policy and structures, then it can only be considered successful if large sections of the population and different interest groups believe it. Reforms are insufficiently advanced in Denmark to warrant this conclusion and Lubanski and Andersen maintain that politics has become 'an issue at the lower regulatory levels' (Chapter 5: 80). Similarly, O'Brien claims that in Australia 'the reality of political control has not diminished' (Chapter 6: 112).

The results of any depoliticisation strategy in Britain have at best been uneven, reflecting the distinction between macro-economic measures and aspects of social policy and organisation. When the Bank of England raised interest rates in January 2000, for the third time in five months, neither news nor editorial coverage in the *Guardian* and the *Financial Times* even mentioned the government, suggesting that the distancing of government from the decision was successfully achieved. Conversely, the simultaneously maturing crisis in the National Health Service (NHS), highlighted by flu cases that amounted to much less than an epidemic, brought forth a torrent of criticism of the government, including from Labour-supporting medical staff. So charged was the political atmosphere that the government was being held accountable for the most local and specific of difficulties, causing the prime minister himself to adopt a high profile position and to announce major new resources. What is true for the NHS in Britain is also true of education. A government that declared its priorities were 'education, education, education' is not one that will escape responsibilities when results are thought to be poor. A number of initiatives have been taken that could be construed as depoliticisation, such as the establishment of Education Action Zones (Hatcher, 1998) and the proposals for city colleges outside of local education authority (LEA) control, but the vast majority of students are still directly affected by government and LEA decisions and education policy remains highly politicised.

There is indeed an emergent managerial state that has reconfigured relations of service delivery, but its effects are far from uniform. Privatisation, competitive tendering and marketisation to an extent take the state out of the frame, although in some areas, such as rail transport, its role in determining the nature of regulation does not protect it from political scrutiny. Where the state does remain as the service provider, decentralisation may not exclude ministers issuing detailed directives on a range of issues (Walsh *et al.*, Chapter 7: 127). Nor is it possible in all situations to determine a clear move from impersonal rule-bound management of the past to one in which managers have a clearer line management authority (Fairbrother, Chapter 4: 68).

In many areas of the state where professionals were employed, authority previously lay with professional expertise, much to the frustration of the formal controllers of the service. Control of day-to-day medical services, for instance, was in the hands of consultants and general practitioners and the move to wrest control through the implementation of general management advocated by the Griffiths Report (1983) is widely recognised as having failed. This is not to say, however, that financial controls and structural changes have not been further tightened, putting pressure on local Trusts to manage their resources more closely (Carter and Poynter, 1999), but the government's role is highly visible, compounded by its intervention down to the level of determining which drugs may be prescribed. Although no doubt exaggerated, this feeling that the public services were producer controlled does highlight that the level of state control was less than unqualified.

The step back from intervention in private sector industrial relations and from some day-to-day economic decisions does not require, or make necessarily possible, the achievement of the same position in the public sector. There is a danger in short of mirroring the tendencies among government ministers noted by Kelsey, namely those ministers:

> confused the *managerial* functions of chief executives, for which they were responsible to the minister, with the minister's *political* accountability to the electorate. The public could not get at the chief executive; but it expected the minister to answer in Parliament, and to the media, not only for policy but also for individual cases.
>
> (1995: 145, emphasis in original)

Many of the changes to which the depoliticisation thesis draws attention are important and deserve attention. The structural reorganisation, the decentralisation of decision-making, individualisation of work and employment relations, flexibility etc. and the recruitment and construction of personnel prepared or forced to take more proactive stances have greatly altered the experiences of working for the state. However, in some ways the increased managerialism runs counter to the principles of depoliticisation outlined by Burnham. Instead of a movement from discretion to rules-based management, Fairbrother, for instance, claims a movement in the opposite direction: from impersonal rules-bound management of the past to variegated patterns of relations and increased managerial discretion, albeit subordinated to assessments in terms of market-type measures (Chapter 4: 68).

Towards union renewal?

The changes outlined certainly threatened the traditional organisation of trade unions, but whether these have pushed unions towards renewal in any fundamental sense has still yet to be demonstrated. Decentralisation of bargaining may have stimulated some examples of more engaged local organisation of unions, but equally there is evidence that it has undermined traditional forms of representation, without the generation of effective alternatives. Evidence from both New Zealand and Australia is mixed, with examples of unions that have adopted the organising model, unions that have atrophied and others that have been incorporated and/or have adopted the partnership approach (O'Brien, Chapter 6: 105–110; Walsh *et al.*, Chapter 7: 124–126, 128–129). Studies of local government members in Britain (Colling, 1995), NHS members (Carter and Poynter, 1999) and Unison organisation in the NHS and across a number of sectors respectively (Fairbrother *et al.*, 1996; Poynter, 1998) show little evidence of a new generation of members who became used to a more direct involvement in union affairs at local level (Fairbrother, Chapter 4: 65).

What is evident across almost all countries is the higher level of union density in the public sector, compared to the private sector. However, evidence of union renewal that appeals to this continued high density is in danger of ignoring that continued formal membership masks the hollowing out of union organisation (Poynter, 1997). Similarly, union mergers may increase the importance of particular public sector unions within the Trades Union Congress (TUC) (Fairbrother, Chapter 4), and are indeed a response to changes in employer organisation, but they equally demonstrate defensive tactics in the face of an inability to counter employer initiatives. In some senses, they do not directly track changes that were taking place in the organisation of work and employment relations (Chapter 4: 65); this logic could equally have led to further fragmentation. Within the most important of the British mergers, Unison, the competing traditions of the constituent unions have arguably led to a greater centralisation through the attempts to control branches in a way that was quite alien to one of them (Carter, 2001), making innovation and militancy more, not less, difficult. Finally, increased membership does not necessarily indicate the nature of unionism that is being maintained or strengthened. Walsh and others signal the importance of the 'development of a policy climate which is supportive of and favourably inclined towards trade unionism' (Chapter 7: 131), but it was exactly this kind of climate that heavily influenced the forms of unionism within the public sector that have made them vulnerable to policy changes (McIlroy, 2000).

Conclusion

By taking the state seriously, all the chapters either explicitly or implicitly reject the notion associated with many accounts of globalisation that the state is being marginalised. This argument is most clearly developed in Burnham's account, which stresses the classical Marxist relationship between the mode of production and the nature of the capitalist state. It does more than this, however, in that it also poses a current political response to problems of legitimacy and accumulation in the form of depoliticisation. Evidence is produced that effectively demonstrates this strategy's implementation of macro-economic management, and the claim is extended to encompass the form and nature of the management of public services, not only in Britain but also more universally in leading capitalist nations.

This latter claim is given further weight by Fairbrother's examination of the restructuring of the British state, which has undergone a combined process of recentralisation and decentralisation through the mechanisms of regulation, civil service agencies, compulsory competitive tendering, marketisation and so on. While these changes have been gathered together under the banner of NPM, the emphasis of Burnham, Rainnie and Fairbrother's chapter, and Fairbrother's chapter is on the class nature of the strategy. In other words, none of the processes claimed as integral to NPM can simply be evaluated in their own terms, as being primarily concerned with efficiency, effectiveness and economy. There are various ways of reducing the burden on capital, expanding market opportunities and direct capitalist relations, removing the political visibility of the capitalist state and weakening the power of organised labour following a period of public sector militancy.

While all of these motives might explain the strategy of the state, they are not necessarily coherent, successful or universal. One principal objection is that the concept concentrates only on one side of the relationship of capital to labour and thereby effectively is insensitive to conjectural issues of class struggle. Moreover, the state performs many complex tasks. Insistence that it is a capitalist state should coexist with an appreciation that it still oversees and coordinates the production of use values that would be necessary in any large society, such as the acquiring of language and writing skills. In places, these aspects are unsatisfactorily categorised under the concept of welfare state. It is the complex relationship of this role with the reproduction of capitalist social relations that makes class a difficult and fluid concept in the state sector (Carchedi, 1977; Carter, 1997a). Writers have a tendency thereby to vacillate between a characterisation of the state as capitalist and its employees as workers without an examination of the necessary tension between the two.

Trade union strategy is a mediation between the levels of analysis. The very resistance that trade unions represent means that the structure of class relations cannot be formally read off from occupational classifications and formal job descriptions. Moreover, the unevenness of trade union organisation and consciousness and the different labour processes within the state sector should caution against the belief that a common state strategy will have a uniform outcome. What is true of variation within a state is equally the case across states, as evidence from the national studies above demonstrates. The societies may all be capitalist, but actual class relations and levels of organisation differ for historical and economic reasons.

This caution should also be extended to the responses of unions. The argument that there is a necessary correspondence between depoliticisation and union renewal should be avoided. Centralised bargaining and bureaucratic unionism have long been features of state sector unionism. Government moves towards decentralised bargaining have generated no automatic response from union leaders for union organisation to mirror the changes. The logic for union renewal – the need for unionism based on democratic, participatory and locally based forms of organisation – is persuasive. As the locus of managerial decision-making becomes lodged at local level it seems appropriate that unions respond by building up local organisation to challenge new-found managerial prerogatives. While it is possible to find relatively isolated examples of this movement in Britain and other examples in New Zealand and Australia, the logic appears to be being defied. A number of factors have influenced the relative conservatism of union organisational forms. National officials are not anxious to devolve power and, in the absence of a membership crisis, they are not being forced on the pain of survival to innovate. While it is therefore possible, for instance, to point to growing national trade union leadership opposition to government policies in Britain (and one that reflects genuine membership disillusionment with New Labour), it is not necessarily the case that such opposition will be accompanied by a restructuring of internal union relations.

If change from above is problematic, it is equally far from automatic from below. Fragmentation of bargaining and the creation of business units have undermined the power of local branch organisation without satisfactory alternatives emerging. In Australia and New Zealand there are examples of the influence of the organising model (for an overview of the model, see Bronfenbrenner *et al.*, 1998), but its impact in the British public sector is minimal. The level of commitment that the model requires is made more difficult by the growing intensification of labour in the public sector and a concomitant restriction of time allowed for trade union duties. Transformation, if it is to come, will therefore depend on wider movements for change, linking political ideas and social movements outside the workplace to demands and changes within it. All the contributions here question the role of the state in theory: wider movements and ideas would inevitably challenge the state more practically, causing its partial nature to be more visible.

Bibliography

Bach, S., Bordogna, L., Rocca, G. and Winchester, D. (1999) *Public Service Employment Relations in Europe: Transformation, Modernization or Inertia?* London: Routledge.

Boyer, R. and Drache, D. (1996) *States Against Markets: The Limits of Globalization*, London: Routledge.

Bronfenbrenner, K., Friedman, S., Hurd, R., Oswald, R. and Seeber, R. (eds) (1998) *Organizing to Win: New Research on Union Strategies*, Ithaca, NY: ILR Press.

Burnham, P. (1997) 'Globalisation: States, Markets and Class Relations', *Historical Materialism*, 1: 150–160.

Butler, T. and Savage, M. (eds) (1995) *Social Change and the Middle Classes*, London: UCL Press.

Carchedi, G. (1977) *On the Economic Identification of Social Classes*, London: Routledge.

Carter, B. (1997a) 'Restructuring State Employment: Labour and Non Labour in the Capitalist State', *Capital and Class*, 63: 65–84.

Carter, B. (1997b) 'The Restructuring of Teaching and the Restructuring of Class', *British Journal of Sociology of Education*, 18(2): 201–215.

Carter, B. (2000) 'Adoption of the Organising Model in British Trade Unions: Some Evidence from Manufacturing, Science and Finance (MSF)', *Work, Employment and Society*, 14(1): 117–136.

Carter, B. (2001) 'Redefining Public Sector Unionism: Unison and the Future of Trade Unions', review of M. Terry (ed.), *Capital and Class (Head and Hand Supplement)*, pp. 64–68.

Carter, B. and Fairbrother, P. (1995) 'The Re-making of the State Middle Class', in M. Savage and T. Butler (eds), *Social Change and the Middle Classes*, London: UCL Press, pp. 133–147.

Carter, B. and Poynter, G. (1999) 'Unions in a Changing Climate: MSF and Unison Experiences in the New Public Sector', *Industrial Relations Journal*, 30(5): 499–513.

Clarke, J. (1993) 'The Comfort of Strangers: Social Work in Context', in J. Clarke (ed.), *A Crisis in Care? Challenges to Social Work*, London: Sage.

Colling, T. (1995) 'Renewal or Rigor Mortis? Union Responses to Contracting in Local Government', *Industrial Relations Journal*, 26(2): 134–145.

Fairbrother, P. (1994) *Politics and the State as Employer*, London: Mansell.

Fairbrother, P. (2000) 'British Trade Unions Facing the Future', *Capital and Class*, 71: 47–78.

Fairbrother, P., Moore, S. and Poynter, G. (1996) *UNISON Branch Organisation: Case Studies, Summary Reports and Recommendations*, mimeo.

Ferlie, E., Pettigrew, A., Ashburner, L. and Fitzgerald, L. (1996) *The New Public Management in Action*, Oxford: Oxford University Press.

Fry, G. (1993) *Reforming the Civil Service*, Edinburgh: Edinburgh University Press.

Gowan, P., Panitch, L. and Shaw, M. (2001) 'The State, Globalisation and the New Imperialism: A Roundtable Discussion', *Historical Materialism*, 9(1): 3–38.

[Griffiths Report] Griffiths, R. (1983) *NHS Management Inquiry*, London: DHSS.

Hardt, M. and Negri, A. (2000) *Empire*, Cambridge, MA: Harvard University Press.

Harrison, S. and Pollitt, C. (1994) *Controlling Health Professionals*, Buckingham: Open University Press.

Hatcher, R. (1998) 'Profiting from Schools: Business and Education Action Zones', *Education and Social Justice*, 1: 19–16.

Hirst, P. and Thompson, G. (1996) *Globalization in Question*, Cambridge: Polity Press.

Hoggett, P. (1994) 'The Politics of the Modernisation of the UK Welfare State', in R. Burrows and B. Loader (eds), *Towards a Post-Fordist Welfare State?* London: Routledge, pp. 38–48.

Kelsey, J. (1995) *The New Zealand Experiment: A World Model for Structural Adjustment*, Auckland: Auckland University Press/Bridget Williams Books.

Kuttner, R. (1999) 'The American Health Care System: Wall Street and Health Care', *New England Journal of Medicine*, 340: 664–668.

McIlroy, J. (2000) 'New Labour, New Unions, New Left', *Capital and Class*, 71: 11–45.

McKevitt, D. (1998) *Managing Core Public Services*, Oxford: Blackwell.

Ohmae, K. (1990) *The Borderless World: Power and Strategy in the Interlinked Economy*, London: Collins.

Poynter, G. (1997) 'Trade Unions and New Labour', *Soundings*, Autumn, 111–124.

Poynter, G. (1998) 'The New Workplace Relations in National Health Service Trusts', *Centre for Comparative Labour Studies*, University of Warwick, Working Papers, 18.

Rainnie, A. (1997) 'Globalization and Utopian Dreams', *Contemporary Politics*, 3(3): 277–285.

Ranson, S. and Stewart, J. (1994) *Management for the Public Domain*, Basingstoke: Macmillan.

Strange, S. (1996) *The Retreat of the State: the Diffusion of Power in the World Economy*, Cambridge: Cambridge University Press.

Streeck, W. (1996) 'Power Beyond the Nation-State: the Case of the European Community', in R. Boyer and D. Drache (eds), *States Against Markets: The Limits of Globalization*, London: Routledge, pp. 299–315.

Weiss, L. (1998) *The Myth of the Powerless State*, Ithaca, NY: Cornell University Press.

Weiss, L. (1999) 'Managed Openness: Beyond Neoliberal Globalism', *New Left Review*, 238: 126–140.

Index

eBooks – at www.eBookstore.tandf.co.uk

A library at your fingertips!

eBooks are electronic versions of printed books. You can store them on your PC/laptop or browse them online.

They have advantages for anyone needing rapid access to a wide variety of published, copyright information.

eBooks can help your research by enabling you to bookmark chapters, annotate text and use instant searches to find specific words or phrases. Several eBook files would fit on even a small laptop or PDA.

NEW: Save money by eSubscribing: cheap, online access to any eBook for as long as you need it.

Annual subscription packages

We now offer special low-cost bulk subscriptions to packages of eBooks in certain subject areas. These are available to libraries or to individuals.

For more information please contact webmaster.ebooks@tandf.co.uk

We're continually developing the eBook concept, so keep up to date by visiting the website.

www.eBookstore.tandf.co.uk